A PICTORIAL HISTORY OF LOVE

A PICTORIAL HISTORY OF
LOVE

PAUL TABORI

SPRING BOOKS · LONDON

Picture research by Dora Beitsch

PUBLISHED BY
SPRING BOOKS
HAMLYN HOUSE · THE CENTRE · FELTHAM · MIDDLESEX
© COPYRIGHT 1966 PAUL TABORI
REPRINTED 1968
Printed in Czechoslovakia by Polygrafia, Prague

CONTENTS

LOVE AMONG THE PRIMITIVES

PSYCHOLOGISTS and mythologists tell us that with prehistoric man promiscuity predated monogamy by millions of years. Although the theory is quite incapable of proof, we have a reasonably close image of the ages before recorded history in the still surviving primitive tribes of Africa, Asia, Polynesia, Melanesia and Australia. Their numbers are constantly shrinking, and those that have managed to escape the usually deadly effects of the white man's coming have largely lost their ancient customs and traditions, but an amazing amount survives. As we learn more and more to appreciate the values they represent, systematic efforts are being made to record and preserve them in every possible way. Sir John Lubbock was among the first who pointed out that the so-called 'savages' held the key to many of the psychological, social and sexual riddles of the modern world.

It seems to be true that while the sexual relations of prehistoric men varied in duration, intensity and regularity, there must have been a basic element which transcended the purely physical. Love does not require a highly developed culture in which to exist.

Lubbock quoted the example of the Veddas, a savage tribe in the interior of Ceylon. Small in stature, and incredibly filthy, 'it was difficult to imagine more barbarous representatives of the human race'. According to Davy they did not even have personal names and left their dead to rot on the ground 'yet indeed possessed one striking quality, to do them justice: they were kind-hearted, affectionate and faithful to their wives; they abhorred polygamy and it was recognised among them that only death could separate the spouses. In this respect, they differed completely from their more civilized neighbours'. Bailey had visited them, accompanied by a chief from Candy who was outraged by the backwardness of the Veddas, and scandalized at their being content with a single woman, living with her for the whole span of their lives. 'This is only fitting for a monkey,' he said.

The Australian aborigines, when the white man first encountered them, were polygamous, though they considered the man who took more than two wives to be selfish. When a married man died, his brother inherited his wife. This tradition indicated their very highly developed sense of family loyalty. Not that there was much tenderness between the sexes—at least, not in public. Edward John Eyre described how he saw natives returning to their tribe after a long absence, hardly giving their wives a glance. Though there were long and involved courtship ceremonies, there was

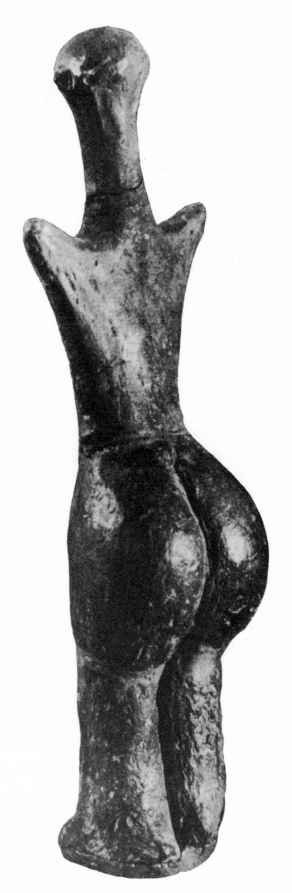

Prehistoric female figures; compare with the finely detailed but still primitive work of the 17th Century Nigerian youth (right)

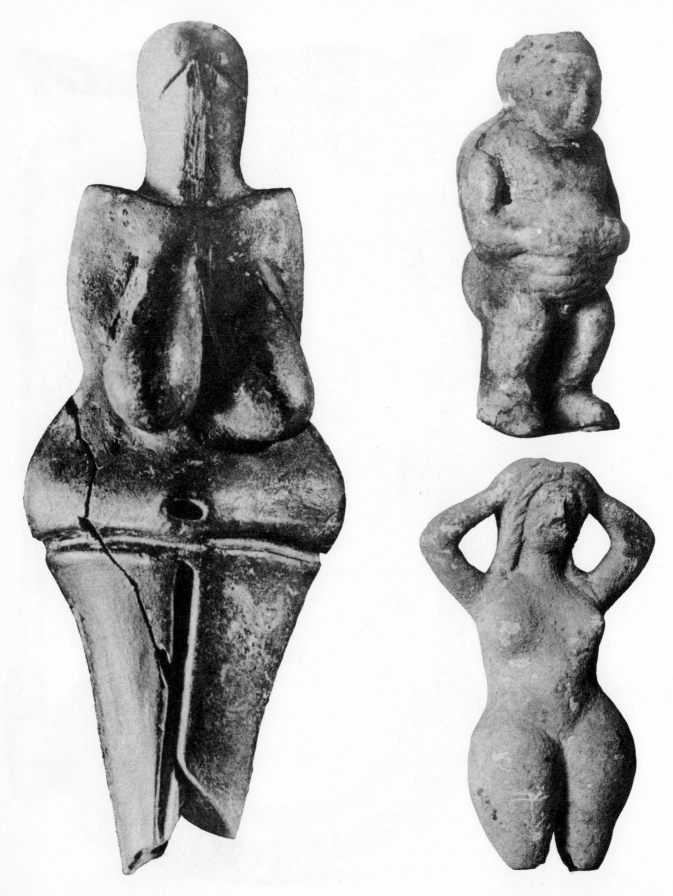

Three stages of courtship in New Guinea
Below: The village chief at a courtship ceremony
Right, above: The bridegroom makes his offer—feathers, shells and three pigs—to his in-laws
Right, below: The marriage is preceded by several days of dancing and festivities

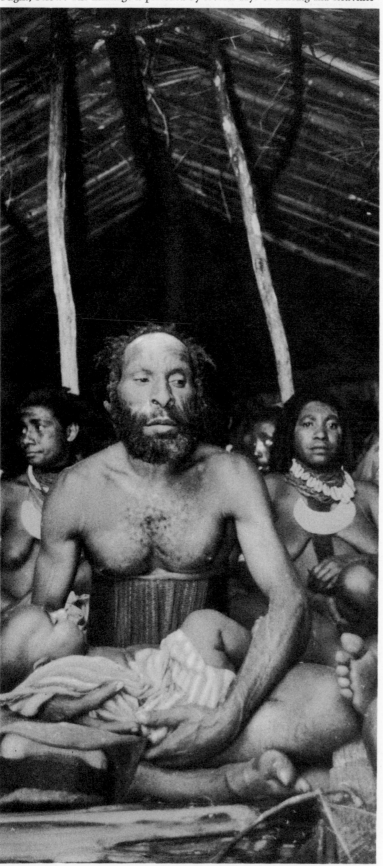

no marriage ceremony. They cared little for chastity before marriage, and a woman was more highly valued for her work potential than her beauty.

Yet there were a number of complex rules about mating. Tribes were divided into several sub-orders, or clans, according to the animal or plant with which they felt a special religious relationship, and members of these clans could not inter-marry, even if they were not of the same family or tribe and came from the other end of the continent. A man would acquire extra wives as he grew older, often by inheritance, giving him a younger mate when his first wife was too old to work and carry. This left the young men rather short of marriageable girls. So, although at first sight the polygamous system suggests a general licence, in fact it worked in the opposite way. The twin factors of clan relationship and dearth of young women often left a man only one or two possible choices within his tribe.

In recent years, anthropologists have discovered a very complex tribal system among the aborigines of Australia, and a far more sophisticated attitude to marriage, sex and love than the 19th century explorers could suspect. They did not of course possess the psychological and analytical knowledge to evaluate their observations, nor did they live close enough to their subjects.

The Fijians, according to early visitors, kept their women in a purely subordinate condition. They were often whipped or kept tied up; they could be sold and bought, and for many years the set price of a woman was a flintlock musket. Though in some things their morality was fairly elastic, in others they went to the opposite extreme. On some islands it was considered improper if husband and wife spent a single night under the same roof. When a chief died, some of his servants and several of his wives would be killed to 'keep him company'.

THE ORIGIN OF THE KISS
When Elliott translated the Bible in 1661 into Algonquin, he had to make up a word for 'love' as it did not exist in the language. There are (or were) quite a few primitive peoples which had no expressions for affection, tenderness, or any of the nonphysical aspects of sexual relationships. The outward signs of love have a considerable variety.

Innumerable theories have been evolved as to the origin of kissing. Look at the pigeons, billing and cooing, said Herbert Spencer. 'It is obvious that their real intention is to taste one another. That's why dogs jump up at their masters or snap at their hands—to get a taste of the subject of their

A marriage in New Guinea
Left: The bride and groom don their finery
Right: Dancing before the ceremony

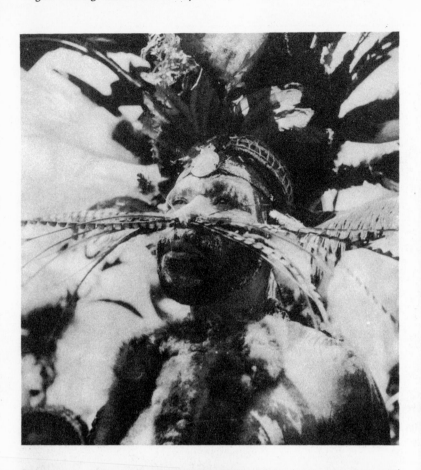

Three rather idealized 18th century pictures of New World marriages: Red Indian (below); Mexican (right, above); Panamanian (right, below)

As in many primitive societies the New Guinea natives kiss by rubbing noses

loyalty and love. Maternal love causes cows to lick the heads of their calves. Human kisses must have developed from the instinct tied to the sense of taste.'

Not so, say the partisans of the sense of touch, following in the footsteps of Charles Darwin. Pigeons prove nothing. In any case, no bird can taste with its beak; hens swallow corn and pebbles without discrimination. As far as the cow is concerned, the Spencerian deduction is one-sided. The calf returns the maternal caress and the cow likes it—although she tastes nothing, only feels a titillating touch.

The psychoanalysts smile at these theories. Kissing, they say, is a survival of infantile complexes. No human being can rid himself of these early experiences and we all use kisses to invoke and relive the time we spent at our mother's breast. This is Havelock Ellis's theory; among other things, it explains why pipe-smoking or even the sucking of cigars are such popular male pleasures.

Lombroso, the great Italian physiologist, tried to discover the first traces of the kiss as an essential part of love or affection. He claimed that he found it among primitive tribes of Tierra del Fuego. Maternal love, Lombroso said, was expressed since prehistoric times by the aboriginal mothers of this inhospitable land in the same way—kissing their child's face. Lombroso explained the origin of this maternal kiss. These tribes had no drinking vessels, no gourds, cups or glasses. When they drank, they sucked water through a straw or lapped it up. Mothers with children too young to lap would fill their mouths with water and press it to the child's. This led in time to the kiss, which in Lombroso's opinion is nothing but atavism.

Few anthropologists have accepted this theory based on a single observation, and the mothers of Tierra del Fuego are not the only primitives who learned to kiss.

There are two conclusions to be drawn from the various theories. By and large, three senses are involved in every kiss—touch, smell and taste, of which, at least among the white races, the first is the most important. Secondly, non-sexual kisses have the same origin as sexual ones—the eternal human quest for sensory pleasure.

PRIMITIVE MARRIAGE

Long before the Bounty mutineers arrived, the Tahitian girls had a reputation for being generous lovers. Captain Cook described how the aristocracy of the islands formed a society called *arioi*; all men and women belonging to it considered themselves married to each other. If any of the female

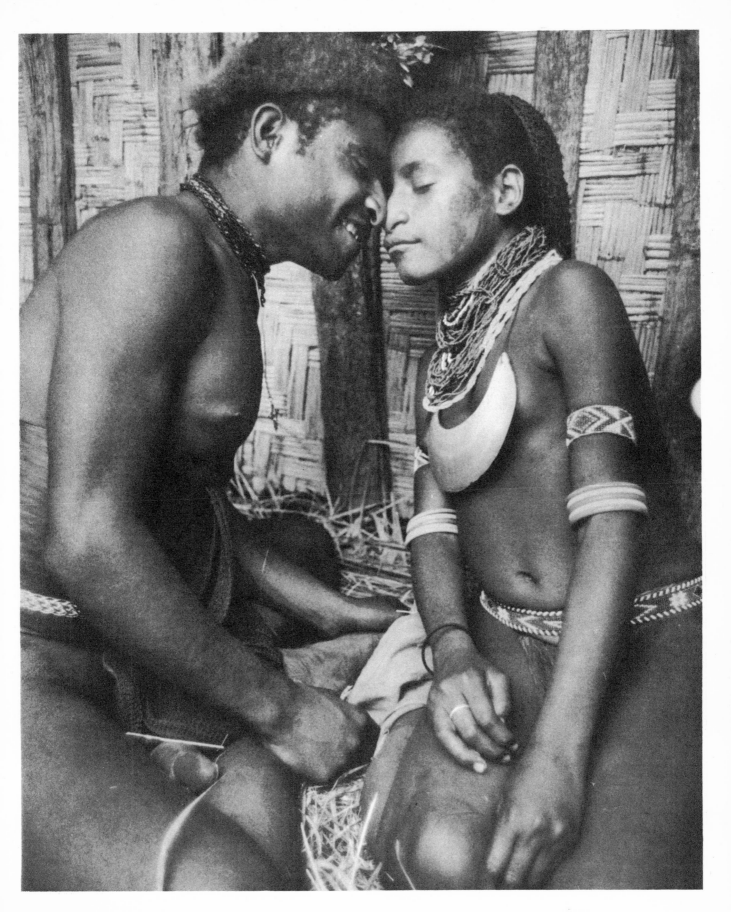

members bore a child it was usually killed, but if the baby was allowed to live its parents were considered to be seeking a permanent relationship. They were excluded from the society and the woman was called a 'child-bearer', an extremely pejorative term. However, Cook remarked, married women were faithful to their husbands and extremely modest. Perhaps they followed the same principle as the Maoris, among whom girls had considerable sexual licence before marriage, but once they chose a partner, they clung to him with loyal affection.

Psychologists and anthropologists still argue whether primitive man was strictly monogamous or whether he lived in the Tahitian form of group-marriage. Polygamy and polyandry (long practised in Tibet) also have their partisans. The truth, as usual, is probably a combination of all these theories. The family is the oldest human unit and nothing better has been invented though there have been some remarkable attempts to replace it with something more flexible. Women have resisted these attempts firmly and successfully; it is their shield and haven, and though man might wander, he is pulled back again and again to this ancient institution.

As prehistoric man gradually turned from a nomadic hunting existence to a more settled one, women became much more valuable, for they were better at home-making than wielding a spear. Every tribe tried to increase its stock of women and eugenics was an early practical discovery. Incest carried no moral stigma, but it weakened the constitution of the tribe, and so exogamy, marriage outside the family, became advisable. In the vernal mating season young men sallied forth and carried off the maidens from the neighbouring tribes. The tradition of acquiring a bride by force survives in many a colourful ceremony to this day.

The Eskimos believed that to remain unmarried after puberty was a denial of Nature which amounted almost to immorality. He was supposed to be master in his house, but this did not infer the wife's complete submission. If he wanted a second or third wife, he had to ask the first one's permission. Usually she agreed without any hesitation; a barren woman would very often ask her husband to bring another woman into the igloo. It happened only very occasionally that there was any jealousy, especially if all wives were treated with equal affection.

Eskimos were polygamous and polyandrous; if a

The Eskimos considered that to remain unmarried for long after puberty was immoral

tribe had more men than women, the women had the right to keep a second husband, provided the first agreed. If a married woman fell in love with a bachelor, she did not have to leave her husband. It was very rarely that the husband (provided he found his rival worthy of it) would deny his wife the right to live for a while with the other man. If this other man was married, quite often the two husbands simply exchanged wives for a while.

It was also usual for a husband to take an unmarried male relative into his home as his wife's second spouse. Peter Freuchen described the case of a young man married to a middle-aged woman, who was irked that an elderly neighbour had a beautiful young wife. So he suggested an exchange, to which the old man agreed for a limited period. When the time was up he demanded the return of his wife. The young man asked for a prolongation, because the woman was expecting a child. 'You're too old, anyhow, to become a father, and my wife is too old to bear a child,' he argued. Again the old man agreed; but when, after the child was born, he claimed back his original spouse, the young husband refused—and this time finally. 'The child is mine and its mother's,' he explained. I'm not willing to part with it—neither is she. So we have no choice but to continue living together...'

Which is just as good an excuse as any other for love.

CHOOSING A MATE
It is generally accepted that the family was the basic unit of the earliest communities, and even in its most primitive form woman played the major part in the creation and maintenance of this unit. There are some Malayan tribes where even today the family consists solely of the mother and her children; strictly speaking the father does not belong to it, and is linked by far stronger ties to his brothers and sisters than to his wife and children.

Among the cannibal tribes of New Britain, it was part of the duty of the chief to make sure that no warrior married unless he could keep his wife in the way to which she was accustomed. The Koyukums believed firmly that no husband would ever beget children unless he killed a stag before his marriage, proving thereby his skill and strength. Some tribes of the Zambesi demanded that the suitor should bag a rhinoceros before the wedding.

Certainly love was often subjected to a rigorous test, both physical and financial, before the suitor earned his reward. And it is characteristic that no primitive tribe ever demands of a woman any similar proof of her 'true passion'.

This difference between the demands made on

Courtship involves much innocent rough and tumble
wrestling among the Latuko people of the Sudan

the sexes, the conditions to be fulfilled before love could achieve its goal, is even more marked among the tribes where men had literally to fight for their brides. In Kamchatka, when two suitors had chosen the same girl, they fought with cudgels until one of them collapsed. Among the Maoris of New Zealand, both would-be husbands took hold of one arm of the girl and started to jerk and pull at her, using her as a sort of living rope in a tug-of-war, and whichever of the two managed to break her away from his rival and finally and firmly clasp her in his arms was declared worthy of her. This could not have been a very pleasent wooing for the girl involved.

Among the Dongolowiks, it was the other way round—the woman inflicted the pain, and the rivals had to suffer. She tied a sharp knife to each elbow and leaned forward with the knife-points resting on the legs of the two suitors. The prize was given to the one who best endured this torment.

Among many different tribes, where girls were traded in marriage, a daughter was considered a valuable piece of property. It was only logical that where she represented such high value, she could not dispose of herself; that her love and her body were not hers to give, at least not in any form that would deprive her family of the price she would fetch. The most northern tribes of Eskimos preserve the tradition that as soon as a girl is born, the father betrothes her to a male child. The Australian aborigines betrothed children before either of them were born.

On Tonga, among the Aroraes, there used to be an especially charming way of choosing a husband. The girl would sit on the ground floor of a house while the suitors (whom she had not seen before) would dangle leaves of the cocoa palm from the attic above. She pulled at a leaf and asked to whom it belonged. If the voice that answered did not please her, she reached for another—and so on, until she found the voice she fancied. Having made their choice by the palmleaf, they stuck to it, and resigned themselves even to polygamy. 'The custom of having only one wife,' a Tongan girl once remarked, 'is a very good one, provided the husband loves her; if not, it is a very bad one, because he would tyrannize over her the more; while if his attention was divided between five or six and he did not treat them very kindly, it would be easy to deceive him!'

Generally, bachelorhood was a rare condition among the primitive peoples. Even today, the average Hindu believes that until he has found a wife, a man is only half a man. Among the Yahgans of Tierra del Fuego, only the idiots and the dumb do not marry. In Korea the bachelor was called a *yatow*, and even a married boy of thirteen or fourteen could freely abuse and beat up a yatow—not to mention giving him orders which the yatow had to obey, though twice his age. To possess a woman, to live with her, has always represented in the savages' view, merit, male glory and an advantage which is worth a great deal of trouble.

Once married, the women's position must have differed widely in prehistoric times, as it does today, according to geography. In Eastern Greenland and Tierra del Fuego, for instance, no marriage was fully valid until the first child was born. In the Abipono and Sawanese tribes, after her first child is conceived, a woman remains in her father's house until it is born. The Ainus of Yeddo lived with the wife's parents until the arrival of a child. With the Cherkesses, the young people lived apart as long as they were childless. In the Baele and other tribes when the wife remains barren the marriage is annulled. In Siam, where the husband has to pay for his wife, this payment is contingent on her becoming a mother.

There are very few primitive tribes who do not know the institution of marriage, though until fairly recently, some of the smaller Bushmen Tribes of South Africa ignored it; there was a haphazard and frequent exchange of partners, with no attempt to establish the parentage of children.

But almost everywhere, the mother's role was highly respected. There are still many tribes, like the Namagquas of Africa, where the boys bear the father's and the girls the mother's name. Among the tribes of East Central Africa, all children bear the name of the mother's tribe; according to them the child inherits the spirit and invisible parts of his father, but the body and visible parts of his mother, therefore it is better if he bears her name. The strange custom of the *couvade* (in which the father takes to bed when a child is born) can best be explained by the husband wanting to establish firmly his share in the offspring—even to the extent of pretending birth pangs and groaning with pain.

There are, of course, many primitive communities in which women are despised and kept in servitude, used as beasts of burden, forced to walk behind the husband who may ride in state. Yet the fact that wives have to be purchased in the great majority of tribes shows their economic importance. The simplest way is to exchange a female relative for a wife; this used to be the custom in Australia. Elsewhere the suitor might follow Jacob's example, and earn his wife by servitude. This is expected in certain tribes, even if cash is paid also. There are societies where a husband must

join the wife's tribe for the rest of his life.

The purchase price can vary enormously. Obviously a pretty, healthy, hard-working girl fetches far more than an old and ugly one; a high-born girl is valued higher than the common run. And of course, with world-wide inflationary tendencies, the good old days, when half a string of dentalium shells bought a bride for the Caribs (though if she was of noble blood, skilled in weaving baskets and baking bread, she fetched up to two strings), have long passed. There was a time when the Vancouver Indians purchased a wife for £20; when a wealthy brave of the New Mexico Navajos could expect a veritable Venus for a dozen horses. It is still possible to obtain a Kaffir beauty for ten to twenty cows (according to her charms) and the poor Damurs sell their daughters for a single one. In Uganda, prices have risen since the thirties, when three or four oxen, a few sewing needles and some gunpowder, totalled an acceptable offer. The rich Bashkirs were prepared to spend three thousand gold roubles while the poor of the same Asiatic tribe were content with a cartload of wood or hay. Values have always varied—in some areas of India, two baskets of rice were considered sufficient; in the Fiji Islands, whale-teeth or maybe

a musket satisfied the future father-in-law. In Anyoro hire purchase was an accepted system—the poor bridegroom could pay in instalments, but any children born to the couple were the property of the father-in-law, and had to be redeemed with a cow or ox for each.

IDEAS OF BEAUTY

It is obvious that the ideals of beauty differ both historically and geographically. We can still trace these variations all over the world. Australian aborigines are amused by the sharp noses of the white people, sneering at the 'axe-shape' and considering their own flat noses perfect. Tahitian women used to say 'What a pity that white mothers keep on pulling at their babies' noses—that's why they grow so long'. In some parts of Indo-China, women still paint their teeth black—and when one of them was asked how she liked the beautiful young wife of the British envoy, she replied contemptuously, 'her teeth are white like a dog's'.

Women of the primitive tribes, usually spent less time and care on personal adornment than the men. The reason was simple: women had to be courted; for a man to remain unmarried was shameful and humiliating, therefore it was the men

On Tonga, on the other hand, the girl did all the choosing. In this picture are all the traditional requirements for courting—music, palm trees, and moonlight. Only the guitar is new

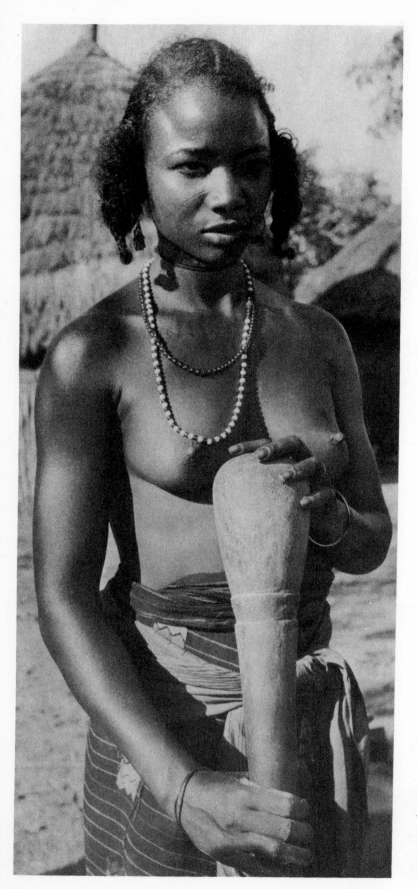

who had to make themselves pleasing and exciting to women. Most anthropologists found that men of the savage and semi-civilized peoples were always vainer than the women. (Some sociologists maintain that this applies to the civilized nations as well).

Among most of the primitive peoples, women age much sooner than in the temperate climes. A European lady of fifty appears much younger and far more vital than a thirty-year-old in Indonesia. In India or Arabia, their prime is past by the late twenties, and there has been considerable argument as to the cause of this. The climate, the early start of sexual life, too strenuous physical exercise and work, have all been blamed. Probably it is a combination of all these things.

JEALOUSY

Jealousy, another basic element of love, sometimes takes peculiar forms within the primitive communities. Among the natives of the Palau Islands, it is forbidden to discuss the wife of any man—or even mention her name. Koriak women deliberately neglect their appearance, walking about unkempt and ragged lest they should find any admirers—in which case their husbands would stab them to death. Among the Kurds of Northern Persia, it was considered both immoral and obscene if a European physician enquired about the health of a Moslem's wife or daughter. In Japan, when a girl married, they used to shave her eyebrows—as a fine, thick eyebrow was considered the supreme allure of a woman.

Nor was jealousy confined to the men. Hooper saw two young Indian girls near St James's Bay who fought wildly until one of them collapsed half dead. They were both in love with the same man. In China, it happened not infrequently that a girl committed suicide rather than marry the man she loved—because she was jealous in advance of any future attachment he might form.

DIVORCE

There were, until recently, several tribes where separation or divorce were completely unknown—as in the Andamans, among the Papuans of New Guinea or the Singhalese. But these were mostly at an extremely low level of civilization. The Dyaks of Borneo seldom have less than three or four wives during their lifetime and by the age of eighteen women often have had three husbands. In the Sudan a traveller met a forty-five year old Bedouin who had 'consumed' more than fifty wives. Among the primitive tribes, divorce usually depends purely on the husband's will. The Aleuts, for instance,

simply exchange a woman of whom they become tired for food or a piece of clothing. Among some Central African tribes, it was a cause for divorce if the husband was too lazy to sew his wife's clothes, but among many tribes where the woman is little more than a beast of burden, she can be discarded if she proves unfit for work.

Yet there are many communities in which divorce is restricted. Among the Kukis of Assam, the marriage cannot be dissolved once the wife has borne a son. The Senegals and Tipperahs require the permission of the husband's tribal brothers and the village Council of Elders for a separation. Among the primitive Moslem tribes, it is still possible for the husband to get rid of his wife by repeating three times: 'I divorce thee'. In Madagascar, the wife also has the right to terminate a union unilaterally. In Burma, if one of the partners refused to terminate the marriage, the other could depart—but had to leave all possessions behind.

DEATH AND MOURNING

The belief in some sort of survival after death is one of the most general among the primitive tribes. In the Congo, until not long ago, wives were killed and buried with their husbands; even his servants

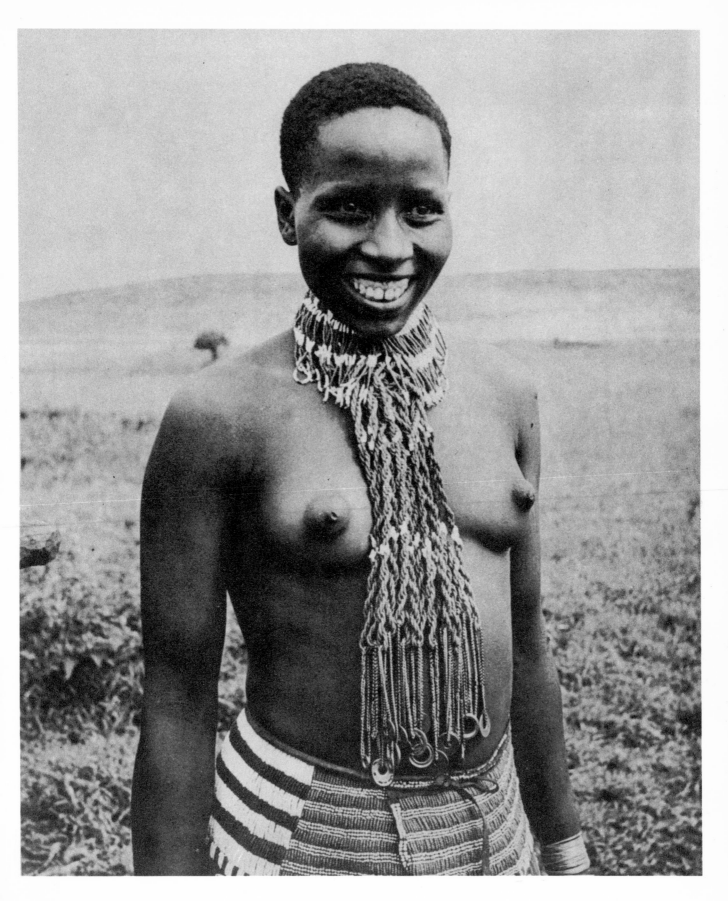

were sacrificed so that he should have love and service in the Other World. In Polynesia and Melanesia many tribes followed the same custom; in Fiji, wives were buried alive with their dead husbands. Those reluctant to follow him into the grave were considered adulteresses. The Tacullies forced a widow to lie on the funeral pyre of her husband until the heat became unbearable. In the Marquesas, or among the Tartar tribes of Asia, no widow could re-marry. In pre-Revolutionary China, marriage of widows was considered indecent and high-born ladies had to suffer eighty bamboo strokes for such a transgression.

Elsewhere there was a prescribed period of mourning. In some tribes the widow's head was shaved and she was allowed to re-marry only when her hair grew to its original length. Again, in other communities, the widow divested herself of all her ornaments, cut her hair short, and blackened her face. She had to pretend to be ugly even if she was beautiful; she was not even allowed to wash.

A Greenland folktale, speaking of a faithful widow, says: 'She mourns so deeply you cannot even recognize her under the dirt...'

Can love ask for more?

A proud and well-dressed beauty of Central Province

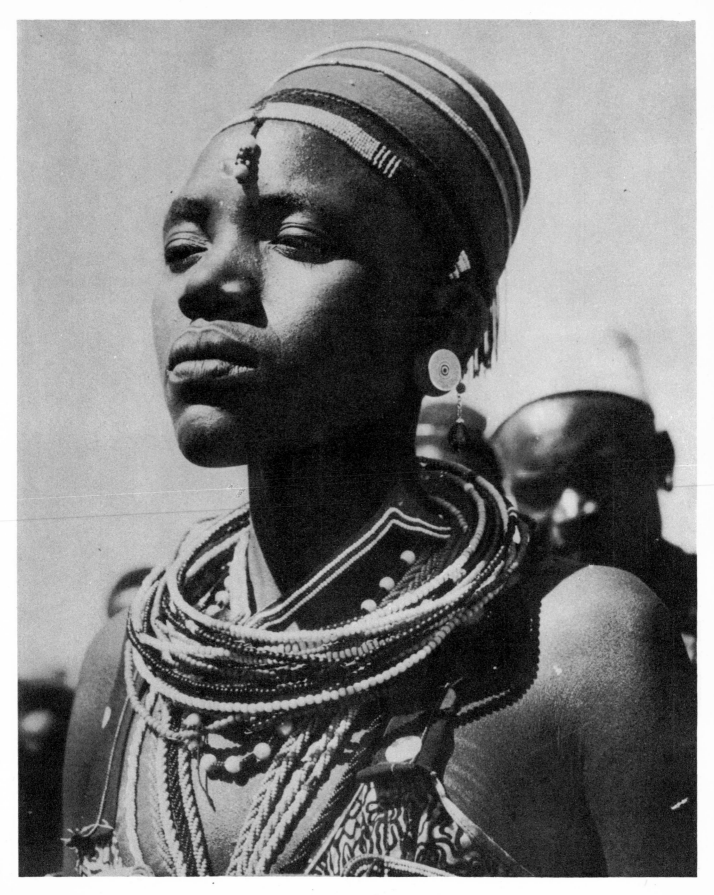

THE CREATION OF WOMAN

MALAY MYTH

After Ridjalu l'Ghabib had created the sky, the sun, the moon and the earth, he decided to populate the earth with living beings; therefore he wanted to create men.

He took a little clay and shaped it into a human figure. Then he summoned the spirits he had created and implanted one of them in the head of the clay figure to give it life. The clay figure was heavy, the spirit was unable to guide it; thus the clay man stumbled and fell, breaking into a thousand pieces; but as it had already been imbued by the spirit, every sliver of it lived. These pieces spread all over the earth and became the terrifying evil spirits whom men later named devils.

The Creator saw that he had not given sufficient life force to the being he had shaped for it to become a real man. So he made a new clay figure and this was better than the first one: for it possessed the divine strength of the triple unity: life and temperament, will and character, mind and spirit. When the Creator had implanted all these qualities in the clay shape, it came to life and the first man was born.

Again the Creator pondered and said to himself: 'I have created a man, but he alone cannot populate the earth. I'll give him a wife with which he will rejoice.'

When Ridjalu l'Ghabib wanted to shape the woman's body, he took the roundness of the moon, the pliancy of the snake, the twining embrace of the lianas, the trembling of the grass, the quivering of the cane, the perfume of the flowers, the lightness and agility of the leaves, the glance of the doe, the gaiety and charm of the sunlight, the swiftness of the wind, the tears of the clouds, the delicacy of the feather, the shyness of the small bird, the sweetness of honey, the vanity of the peacock, the slimness of the swallow, the beauty of the diamond and the cooing of the turtle-dove. He mixed all these qualities and shaped them into a female being. Then he gave this shape too, the holy power of the triple unity, and when it came to life it was more enchanting and lovely than any other creature in the world. And the Creator gave her to Man so that the earth should be populated.

A few days later Man went to Ridjalu l'Ghabib and said:

'Lord, the woman you gave me poisons my life. She chatters without a pause, she wastes all my time, she wails because of every little thing and she is constantly ailing.'

Thereupon the Creator took back his gift in order to punish Man. Hardly a week passed and the Man appeared again, saying:

'Lord, I am most desolate since you took back the woman. She was always singing and dancing. Now I cannot help remembering all the time how sweetly she looked upon me, how skilled she was in kissing me, how delightfully we played together and how she sought my protection...'

The Creator gave him back the woman.

Not even three days had passed when Man was once again standing in front of the Creator to complain.

'Lord,' he said, 'I simply cannot understand this—but if I strike a careful balance, woman causes me more annoyance than pleasure. Please, rid me of her.'

But the Creator said: 'Do what you consider best. In order to live in peace with your wife and be able to bear her presence, she shall owe you obedience from now on.'

But Man replied hopelessly: 'I cannot live with her.'

'Can you live without her then?' asked the Creator.

Whereupon Man hung his head and said sadly: 'Alas for me! I can live neither with nor without her!'

GODS AND MORTALS

Previous page: Zeus, the shamelessly promiscuous father of the gods, who adopted many novel disguises to gain his desires. Below: Europa, whom Zeus raped in the guise of a snow-white bull

Below: Leda, whom he seduced in the form of a swan. Right: Io, whom he took in the shape of a cloud

LOVE ON OLYMPUS

THE gods of the Greeks were projections of their own very real selves—with an understandable element of wish-fulfilment thrown in. They were in the image of men and women, only more beautiful and powerful than any mortals could hope to be... except in their dreams. They had blemishes and even vices; they could be petulant, treacherous, almost childish — but there was very little mystery or abstraction about them. Their motives were human motives; their appetites were human appetites. In a way we can learn more from mythology about Greek life and thought than from the philosophers, the poets and the artists. For the myths were created by the people, not by the elite; they mirrored faithfully what the average Greek thought and felt even though the ideas and feelings were sometimes wrapped in charming symbolism and delightful allegory.

And so we learn about love in ancient Greece by the exploits of their gods. Immediately we see that little respect is accorded to chastity, for there was no more wanton god in any pantheon than the father of the gods, Zeus. For Europa he assumed the guise of a snow-white bull to carry her across the seas and beget Minos, Rhadamanthus and Sarpedon. He visited Danaë in a shower of gold, and so Perseus was born. Leda he seduced in the form of a swan; though Hera chased Leto all over the place until she found refuge in Delos, the wrath of the goddess was somewhat belated—for Zeus had already fathered Apollo and Artemis. He was a very active god indeed.

Poor Hera! She was the only properly married goddess among the Olympians, for the marriage of Aphrodite and Hephaestus could scarcely be taken seriously. Hephaestus, her son, she seems to have produced with no help from Zeus—just because she was jealous that Zeus had brought forth Athena from his forehead without inviting her co-operation. Their conjugal disputes went on for aeons; once, helped by Poseidon and Athena, Hera even put Zeus into chains. But the father of the gods could not be kept a prisoner; he freed himself and beat his divine spouse soundly. Once he became so exasperated with her shrewish tongue that he hung her up in the clouds, with her hands chained and with two anvils suspended from her feet; a most undignified position for any woman, let alone a goddess. Ares and Hebe were her children by Zeus but he seems to have neglected her for centuries on end. No wonder that she persecuted all his children by mortal mothers—Dionysus, Hercules and the rest of the numerous brood.

But what of Aphrodite? She was married to

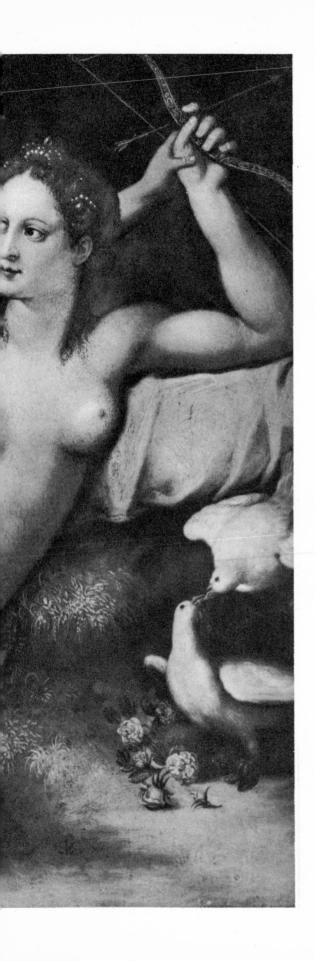

Greek amphora depicting the nuptials of Zeus and Hera

The wedding of Zeus and Hera, in an ancient sculpture believed to be the first depiction of a wedding veil

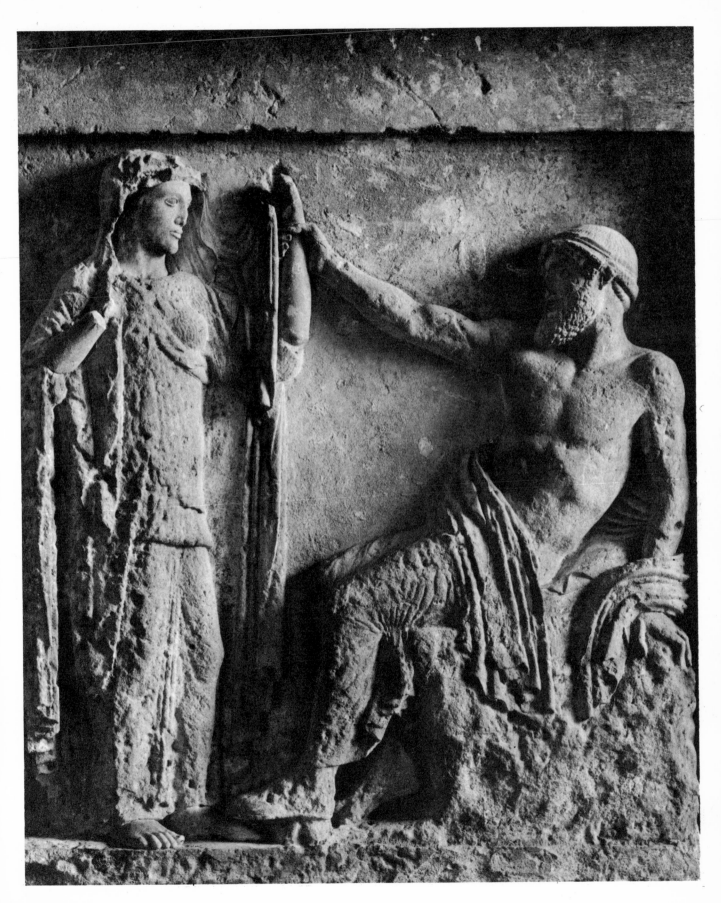

The wedding of Zeus and Hera, in an ancient sculpture believed to be the first depiction of a wedding veil

The decoration on a bowl showing the arrival of Bacchus on Olympus

Jupiter seducing Danaë in the disguise of a shower of gold

Dionysus with a bacchante

Hephaestus, whom she deceived with handsome Ares. The goddess of love was certainly not the goddess of constancy or purity.

Eros was her son, though whether his father was Hermes, Ares or Zeus, has been left delightfully vague. Eros can be playful but also deadly—especially as Anteros, punishing those who do not return the love of others.

Not as mighty as Eros but more demanding of his worshippers was the son of Aphrodite and Dionysus, the powerful embodiment of purely physical love, Priapus. His worship began at Lampsacus on the Hellespont but spread all over Greece, and then throughout the ancient world. He was the god of fruitfulness and of potency, overwhelmingly male and shamelessly sexual.

The tale of Eros and Psyche, told with great charm by Apuleius in *The Golden Ass*, has been retold innumerable times, and served as subject for countless paintings and sculptures ever since. Psyche was the Cinderella figure of antiquity, youngest of three princesses whose beauty roused Aphrodite's jealousy and envy. It was at her orders that Eros set out to make Psyche fall in love with 'the most contemptible of men'. But when he saw her, the youthful god of love was himself stricken for the first time in his divine existence. He carried her off and made love to her unseen, always in the dark.

Psyche's jealous sisters urged her to make sure that her lover was no hideous monster, afraid of the light. Trying to view the sleeping Eros by lamplight, Psyche let a drop of hot oil fall on his shoulder causing him to awake, and flee. Then came the long search of Psyche for her lover, her bitter servitude in the palace of Aphrodite, her final triumph over her mother-in-law's jealousy and hatred—and her reunion with the god who was love himself. A classic story with a happy ending which the Greeks took literally. Only later did less happy ages interpret the story as the quest of the human soul purified by passions and misfortunes, and thus prepared for the enjoyment of true and pure happiness...

THE WORSHIP OF BEAUTY

The Greek approach to love was much influenced by the fact that they considered beauty—the beauty of the male and female body alike—the equal of *virtue*. According to them the beauty of the exterior was the invariable indication of inner perfection. That is why the preservation and development of beauty was so important to them. In their constant attack on ugliness they destroyed crippled or misshapen children at birth. Expectant mothers decorated their bedchambers with the statues and images of the loveliest gods and goddesses, regard-

Hermaphrodite combines the physical features of both man and woman

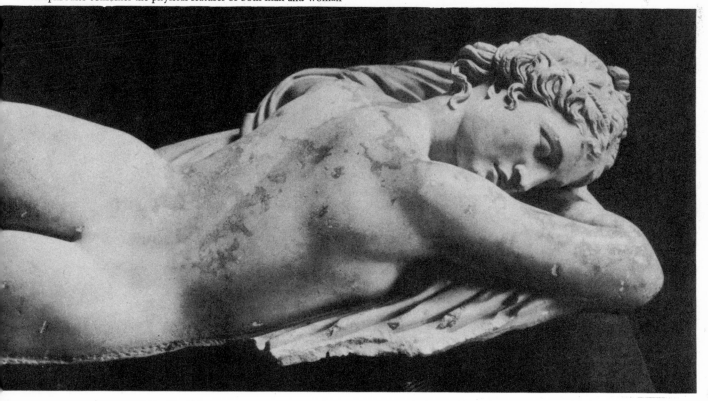

Virgil, with the manuscript of the Aeneid on his knee.
Though comprising only a small part of the book the love
story of Aeneas and Dido has been famous ever since

ing them constantly in the hope that their offspring would resemble them.

In his huge and thorough work *Sexual Life in Ancient Greece*, Hans Licht sums it up eloquently: 'The astonishingly perfect understanding of beauty possessed by the Greeks, their Dionysiac joy in the glory of the human body, ennobled for them every act of sensuality, if only it was based upon true love, that is, on the yearning after beauty... Because the fascinations of the sexual were not made still more alluring by being shrouded in a veil of mystery or branded as sinful and forbidden, and—further—because the almost unchecked sensuality of the Greeks was always dignified by the desire for beauty, their sexual life developed in overflowing force, but also in enviable healthiness. Few nations, few ages, could boast of such a happily balanced state of things.

Once the loveliest maiden of Athens, a favourite model of the sculptors, fell ill. Her life was in no danger—but her beauty was. The whole city was deeply anxious until she recovered, appearing again in her unimpaired loveliness.

Where beauty was valued so highly, it was only natural to develop its aids—to enhance Nature when she had been less generous. The Greeks knew all the secrets of cosmetics. They used powder, rouge, beauty patches; beauty culture had its own literature. The best creams were prepared with human saliva, and the maids whose task it was to mix these unguents were kept on a strict diet so that their mouths should always be clean and pleasant.

Perfumes were widely used; some women chose a different one for every day, and they were highly skilled in blending them. Men were just as ready as women to use perfume. Dry skin and dry hair were considered to be unclean. Water was softened by mixing it with soda, natron and powdered beans. The women used asses' milk to preserve the softness of their skin, and rich ladies seldom travelled without a she-ass to provide it. Mouthwashes, tooth-powders and false teeth were all widely known, though not toothbrushes. Nails were well-kept, and pedicure was just as important as manicure as the Greeks usually wore open sandals.

Fashions changed in clothing and hairstyles, though the changes were less frequent than today, and Greek statues can usually be dated by the hairstyles. Some were determined to remain fashionable even after death—so they had their busts made with removable marble wigs which could be changed according to the latest fashion by their descendants.

There were only two basic garments in the Greek lady's wardrobe—a shift and a dress, the former called *chiton* and the latter *himation*. Stockings, drawers and petticoats were unknown. The *himation* was open along one side, held only by a few buckles. In Sparta, girls usually wore nothing but the short *chiton* which ended above the knee and was slit up the side so high that in stepping along the entire thigh was exposed.

Jewellery was not merely ornamentation, for precious stones were attributed with supernatural powers. The Greeks believed there was a close kinship between a human being and the jewel that corresponded to his character; everyone had his own birth-stone, and the glitter, the shine, the colour of a jewel changed according to the person who wore it, or so they firmly held.

In an old Greek legend the wife of a rich prince was jealous of a young girl, and in her fury pierced her ears with a pin. Her husband consoled the wounded beauty; the wound healed but did not close completely and, in compensation, the prince made her the gift of two lovely pearls. Ever since, the tale concluded, Greek women asked for earrings as a pledge of love.

MARRIAGE IN EARLY ROME

Rome was the great middleman, the powerful bridge-builder between the Hellenised Orient and the pre-Christian. She had a greater political talent than the Greek states. Rome was a city state like Sparta and Athens; but she absorbed all the countries she defeated, embraced their cultures and expanded by a natural gradual process.

Founded about seven centuries before Christ, Rome was for two hundred years under Etruscan rule. Then in the fifth century B.C. she started the slow, long progress to world domination. The early Romans were peasants; stubborn, conservative, never swayed by excessive ambition or imagination. Marriage was respected as the outlet for sexual satisfaction; the refined eroticism which they practised later must have been quite unknown in these early ages. The cults of Dionysus, Venus and Priapus were entirely lacking.

Women occupied a position in no way inferior to men in the acquisition of property and money; the daughter inherited an equal share with the male children. But women, as Theodore Mommsen tells us, belonged to the household, not to the community; and in the household itself she held a position of domestic subjection.

In early Rome a marriage could not be dissolved; divorce was unknown for more than five centuries. It was in the 157th Olympiad, during the consul-

Below and right: Details from fresco depicting the Villa of the Dionysiac mysteries. The Bacchanalia was prohibited throughout Italy in 186 B.C.

The triumph of Bacchus, from a sarcophagus

ship of M. Pomponius and C. Papisus, that one Spurius Carvilius separated from his wife—being the first to do so. He was obliged by the censors to swear his wife was barren—but for his divorce, though it was necessary, he was always hated by the people.

Later in Roman history the husband lost his proprietary rights over his wife; the Roman matron was not servant, but mistress, and her main task was the superintendence of her servants.

Until 445 B.C. a regular marriage could be contracted only between patricians. After many efforts, the tribune Canuleius carried a law by which the full right of marriage between patrician and plebian was sanctioned, but inter-marriage remained rare for some time.

THE GODS OF ROME

In the Roman pantheon, which included most of the deities of nations under Roman influence, Venus was the goddess of love. And she was not only the guardian of honourable marriage, worshipped by the *matronae*, the mothers of families, she was also the goddess of harlots. Finally, in some way, she was the mother of the whole Roman nation.

Lesser Roman deities of love were Liber, Phallus, Priapus, Cybele, and Isis who had been taken over from the Egyptians. Liber was a fertility god, honoured by phallic cults; in the town of Lanuvium, a whole month was dedicated to him. Phallus, according to Pliny, was 'the protector not

only of littler children, but also of generals....' The god or its symbol served as amulets of good luck and happiness... though not necessarily of happiness in Love. Priapus, closely linked to Phallus, was both a garden god and a patron of human fecundity. As Rome declined, the festivals in his honour were distinguished by their extreme crudity.

The Bacchanalia were closely connected with the god Liber; the cult originated in Southern Italy and was introduced to Rome soon after the Carthaginian wars. But it became so destructive that a senatorial decree issued in 186 B.C. prohibited it forever throughout Rome and Italy.

Cybele, whom the Romans called Magna Mater, the Great Mother, was introduced to Rome from Asia Minor about 204 B.C. In 191 B.C. she was given a special temple on the Palatine, and theatrical shows were instituted in her honour. In aristocratic Roman houses she was honoured by banquets attended with great splendour. According to Apuleius, her priests were 'very lewd and degenerate' though later historians strongly deny the implication of a homosexual cult.

Isis, the Egyptian goddess, also had an extended cult in Rome but modern historians do not consider it a sexual one. However, it certainly had a direct influence on love because it demanded various ascetic observances from its adherents, especially the ten days chastity kept by women after they were initiated into the mysteries. Propertius complains bitterly:

'The goddess who divides such eager lovers so often is a jealous deity...

Be satisfied with Egypt's tawny children; why travel over the long road to Rome?

What benefit to you, if girls sleep lonely?'

Ovid, on the other hand, a most sophisticated explorer of the feminine heart, advised the mistress to increase her lover's ardour by often denying herself to him; and he says in his *Ars Amatoria*, the most charming and detailed handbook of love:

'Often refuse a night. Call it a headache;

and Isis sometimes makes a good excuse.'

Bona Dea was a goddess whom women often implored for help in trouble and sickness. Juvenal pictures the festival of the goddess in the most revolting terms—while Plutarch, the great satirist's contemporary, gives quite an innocent account. 'It must be admitted,' Otto Kiefer says, 'that in the cult women may have occasionally yielded to sexual excess but the cult itself had nothing to do with such depravities.'

'The Triumph of Silenus' by Van Dyke

LOVE IN THE EAST

CHINA

Until very recent times the family was the strongest influence on Chinese life. Marriage was a contract between families, often without reference to the boy and girl concerned, whether between mandarins (below) or peasants

LOVE IN CHINESE ART

THREE thousand years before the coming of Christ, the Chinese had devised an alphabet, invented gunpowder—though wisely they used it only for fireworks—built up an elaborate civil service and possessed many great poets and playwrights, painters and philosophers. By comparison, the much-vaunted culture of the West is a babe-in-arms. Three thousand years ago the Chinese spun silk; two centuries before Christ they had already invented porcelain and well before Gutenberg they knew how to print books. Confucius gave them a moral philosophy for their religion, declaring that life was a series of duties

which were much eased if man found harmony within himself. Mencius elaborated the Confucian system; Lao-Tse offered tao to the simple folk, a religion of passivity. A nation which despised the soldier and elevated the scholar to the highest position in the state was a really civilized one. Though learning and culture were the perquisite of the elite and countless millions lived in dire poverty, even a peasant boy could become a mandarin if he possessed the necessary brains.

Through ancient Chinese literature and other arts we know that this extremely civilized nation rated sex and love very highly indeed. Unlike the intricacy of most of Chinese social life, their art is usually expressed with a charming simplicity, as in the poem *Love Remembered* by Li Hou-Chu:

THEN –
> A streak of cloud
> Like a shuttle of jade,
> A pale, pale robe
> of thin, thin gauze;
> Delicately knitted moth eyebrows.

NOW –
> An autumn wind,
> A steady rain,
> A plantain tree,
> A nest or two,
> Long nights of bleak endurance.

There is tenderness, burning desire, and a fine passion for words in this eighth century poem by Li Po:

> My love was here. My house was filled
> with spring's rare essences.
> My love is gone. To me remains
> Her sweet bed's emptiness.
>
> Her empty bed her fragrance holds
> In every silken flower;
> My empty arms are empty still –
>
> My love will come no more.
>
> My love is gone. Her fragrance stays
> To haunt my heavy years
> Till yellow autumn's leaves are laid
> By winter's whitening breath.

From the *Book of Odes* by Shih Ching, the rustic swain's praise echoes still fresh after more than 25 centuries:

How lovely she is, my bashful girl!
She said she'd be here at the corner of the wall.
Hopelessly in love and not finding her here,
I scratch my head, bewildered...

The following poem was written 2,600 years later by Fann Fann Chan, the pseudonym of Fann-Cheng-Siang, Minister of Justice and Finance in the Central government of China in the 1920s:

When you take a bath, do not let your water run out which is perfumed like the cup of the roses
And when you comb your hair, let me touch it slightly with my fingers, inhaling the spicy scent of cinnamon.
I would like you to bestow upon me your perfumes; I would take them with me in my silk scarf,
To preserve them for ever upon my pillow, near my lips.

I threw away my brush. She ceased her embroidery and we stretched ourselves upon our bed.
Entwined we whispered words the meaning of which only we two understood. Then the night fulfilled our embrace.
But why do you wish me to drink of the lotus wine?
I am far more intoxicated if I can drink your orchid-scented breath.

Chinese paintings of opium smokers. Opium has long been considered a companion to the art of love

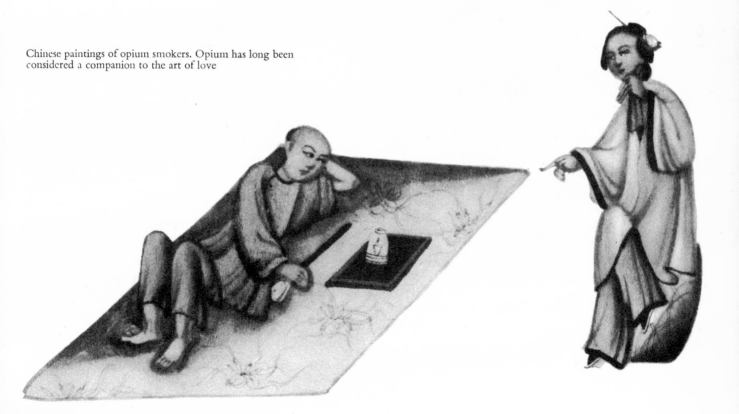

A Chinese prostitute in San Francisco watches through a window covered with wire netting

CHINESE MARRIAGE CUSTOMS

In the early eighteenth century Father Ripa, visiting China, remarked on the multitude of people, 'the swarming prolific womb' of Cathay. He ascribed this to several causes—that there were far fewer monks and nuns than in Europe; that each man married as many wives as he could support, 'not caring what may become of the children'; that bachelors were held in contempt and marriages took place as soon as the parties had attained a suitable age. 'While dining one day with the steward of the Viceroy,' Father Ripa added, 'I asked him about the number of his children. Not knowing it, he began to reckon them by name; but when he came to the eighteenth he was puzzled and called in the servants to help him count the remainder...'

From very early times, the basic form of marriage in China was polygamy. Men were 'lords of the creation' and girls considered worthless. Besides his wives and concubines (numbered according to seniority and importance) a married man could always seek entertainment in the company of 'singing girls'. There was no stigma attached to prostitution and many a singing girl married one of her rich clients—provided she possessed the necessary physical and intellectual attractions.

A young coquette of Peking

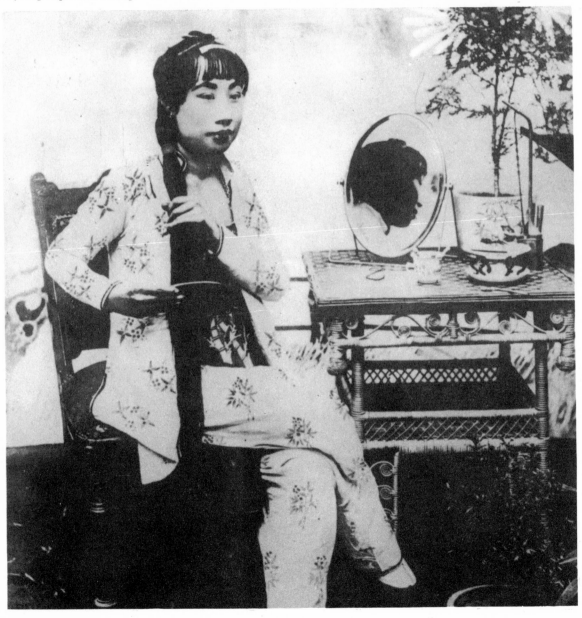

In theory men were the absolute masters; ancestor worship was extended to the reverence of age and women lived only as shadows of their sun-like lords and masters. The middle and upper-class Chinese home was a combination of a harem and a nunnery; yet women were allowed to go out, suitably accompanied, could receive visitors and attend parties and festive gatherings. And in practice this male superiority was not so bad. Many a household was ruled by a matriarch; widows had considerable powers, not only over their daughters-in-law but often their sons as well. The public humility of wives often changed to matriarchal domination in private.

There were seven grounds for divorce—disobedience to parents-in-law (this stood at the head of the list), having no son, adultery, jealousy of the husband's other wives, leprosy, thieving and talkativeness. But a wife could not be divorced if she had no family to return to, if she had shared with her husband the three year's mourning for his parents or if, having married her when he was poor, he had become rich. A highly realistic and, on the whole, extremely fair code of divorce law.

Three illustrations from *Ch'ing Ping Mei*, a classic erotic novel about a mandarin and his six wives

CHINESE WISDOM ABOUT LOVE

It is most difficult for love to last long, therefore who loves passionately is in the end cured of love.

A girl who flirts with her looks is not chaste.

A hero may be willing to lose the world, but he will not be willing to lose his concubine.

A wife is loved for her virtue, a concubine for her looks.

If heaven wants to rain or your mother to marry again, you cannot prevent it.

The walls of a city are raised by men's wisdom, but overthrown by women's subtlety.

She who is happy dies before her husband.

Don't enter a widow's house alone.

Rather patch clothes as a poor man's wife than be a rich man's concubine.

Avoid lust as you would arrows; avoid wantonness as you would an enemy.

A man's words are like a soldier's arrow; a woman's words are like a broken fan.

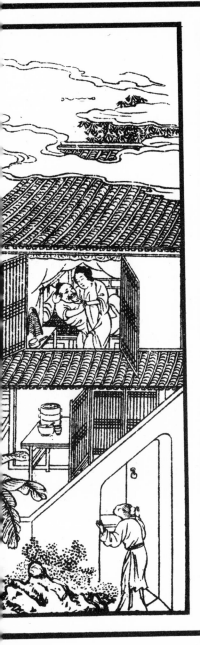

INDIA

The age-old religion of Hinduism provides the background to the Indian attitude to love. The basic trend, as far as it is possible to disentangle it from the jungle of contradictory elements, is the combination of extreme asceticism with an almost stifling sensuality. These are uneasily balanced but have achieved, through the centuries, a co-existence.

THE ROLE OF LOVE IN RELIGION

Men were expected to be 'obliging' to women in love. When Devayani, daughter of Cukra, proposes to Kaca, he refuses, for, as he pleads, she is his teacher's daughter and honourable in his sight. The girl replies angrily: 'If thou dost scorn me for love of virtue, although I have asked thee with tears, then this magic knowledge will be nought in thine hands...' (The magic which Kaca learned from Cukra, his teacher). On this occasion, Devayani's pleading is in vain.

This wooing of men by women is a recurrent motif in the *Mahabharata* and *Ramayana*, the two great religious epics of Indian literature. Svaha, the daughter of the god Dakhsha, falling in love with Agni, takes the shape of the six wives of the Rishis, one after the other, in order to seduce him.

Of their six matings, the six-headed god of war Skanda is born. In the same way Ganga woos King Pratipa, appearing before him and seating herself on his right thigh. When the startled king asks her what she wants, she replies: 'I want thee; do thou love me who loves thee? For to repulse women in love is a thing condemned by the good.' Ulupi, daughter of Kauravya, the king of snakes, tells Arjuna (who has taken a vow of chastity for twelve years): 'The distressed must be saved... if thou rescuest me, then thy virtue will not be harmed. And if, indeed, in this there be any slight over-stepping of duty, yet thou wilt win virtuous merit by giving me life, O Arjuna. Love me, who loves thee, O son of Pritha; of this the good approve. If thou doest not so, then be assured I shall die; carry out the greatest of all duties by granting me life...'

Very similar sentiments are voiced by the temptress, disguised as an old woman, of the Brahman Ashtavakra; by Carmishtha, the friend and slave-girl of Devayani, to Yayati, Devayani's royal husband; by Urvaci to the much-travelled Arjuna —and countless other women. Indeed it sometimes appears that women took all the initiative.

Love, the Indians believed, was no respecter of any person—not even of gods or kings. When the

Left: Illustration from Mahabharata
Below, left: A 19th Century painting of Krishna and Radha
in the forest
Below: The marriage of Siva and Parvati

A young husband at a wedding; child brides have been known in India until
very recent times
Below: A bride and groom

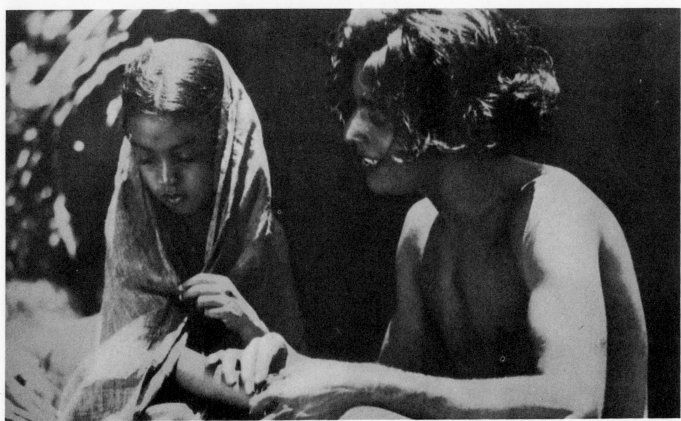

sun-god makes love to Kunti, he uses arguments
to overcome her virginal scruples which any common seducer would employ; he points out: 'All
men and women are without restraint... this is the
real nature of mankind, any other is to speak
untruly...' His plea is that love is free to all, that
no one can resist its power. Certainly he adds a
rather special, tempting point: 'After union with
me, thou wilt again be a virgin and thy son will
become strong-armed and greatly famed...' A
winning argument, for Kunti, the 'fair-hipped'
yields to his burning embrace. This story not only
parallels the Greek tradition of gods and mortals
mating, but includes the idea of virgin birth and
suggests the tale of Moses in the bullrushes, for
Kunti's child is placed into a chest and floats down
four rivers until he reaches the Ganges.

Love was the supreme good in the Hindu concept
—so much so that it was firmly believed that no
children could be conceived unless 'the husband
has joy' and the wife 'yields in passion'. Marriage
had to be sealed with love, or it was 'without
virtue'.

The temptress who works so hard to seduce
Ashtavakra speaks frankly of the terrible power of
sexual desire. 'Neither the god of wind nor he of

65

The famous Khajuraho temples in India are adorned with sculptural *mithunas*, couples in amorous embrace who symbolize the unity of heaven and earth

fire, nor Varuna, nor the other 33 gods are so dear to women as the god of love,' she tells the reluctant pilgrim. 'For to women, the pleasure of love is all. Among thousands of women, nay, hundreds of thousands, there is to be found only one that is faithful to her husband, if indeed, one at all. They know not father, family, mother, brother, husband or brothers-in-law; given up to their pleasure, they destroy families, as great rivers destroy their banks.'

To the Indian, platonic love was inconceivable; love, if it existed, had to be consummated. Those who renounced love had to do so utterly and completely; there was no middle way. No power on earth could turn a woman in love from her purpose, and the mere fact of being in love endowed her with magic virtues. Some went even further and declared that, for women, love was the first and supreme meaning of life. 'Otherwise than through love, to women there can come no rest and content from the man,' the temptress tells Rishi of the Brahmans.

Men are made differently, according to Hindu belief. The author of the *Kumarasambhaya* summed it up in a single sentence: 'The love of men which towards beloved women is unsteadfast, towards friends never wavers...' Yet when Rama loses his beloved Sita (kidnapped by Ravana) his passionate mourning (delicate, somewhat feminine, yet by no means unmanly) proves that man's love could be just as deeply-rooted and enduring as a woman's. The plaints of Rama are among the most beautiful passages in Indian and world literature. When he finds Sita gone, he runs about the forest, seeking her that is lost, wandering from tree to tree, through mountains, over rivers, asking all the trees and the beasts of the forest if they have seen 'the much loved, the wondrous fair one'.

But constancy is the exception and not the rule in Indian folk-lore. It was accepted that the dark, primeval forces of love must not be suppressed; that for the average man woman was a booty of conquest; that the ideal was the enjoyment of many women by each man, and that even virtue was rewarded in after life by the companionship of numerous wives and concubines.

THE KAMA-SUTRA

The Kama-Sutra is the equivalent of a Western manual of etiquette, except that it deals almost entirely with physical love—the opportunities, aphrodisiacs, rules on the acquiring of mistresses, and so on. Its author, as well as the age and social life it describes, have long been lost to us, but it is invaluable as an indication of the Indian attitude to physical love which still has some application

Though chiefly religious in mood the Khajuraho temples
are typical of the cheerfully erotic representation found on
temples in many parts of India

today. It displays an amazing variety and wealth of knowledge. Some of the descriptions of love-play strike Europeans as grotesque or ridiculous. Bites, scratches, kisses, embraces, an almost inexhaustible variety of attitudes and caresses, are described with a profusion that seems excessive, but was perfectly in keeping with the belief that love was the highest good, that it was all-powerful and removed all sense of responsibility, robbing those under its spell of any sense of shame. Aphrodisiacs play a considerable part in those times (and still do, as the advertisements in any popular maga-

The god Vishnu embraces his consort, Lakshmi

Relief from a temple in Nagarjunakonda

Suttee, the burning of the widow, was practised in the belief that a woman had no worthwhile life apart from her husband. Many women would go voluntarily to the pyre

zine will show). Alcohol has always been accepted as an ally of seduction, and this is one reason why the puritan prohibitionist policy of independent India has run into such determined opposition, and the laws are broken by so many people that no bootleggers are needed.

SUTTEE

The ancient custom of *suttee*, the burning of the bereaved wife, survived more than a century of the British Raj. It sprang from the ancient belief that a woman had no life of her own after the death of a husband, and most victims believed this strongly enough to go voluntarily to the funeral pyre. But it was not so frequent as generally believed and by no means did all widows accept the true *suttee* in the period before the British suppressed it.

However, widowhood was a terrible condition for an Indian woman. Even if the young widow was only 12 years old (and this could happen in a country of child marriages) she would be forbidden from ever marrying again, and would be enforced to a life of serfhood to the family of her husband.

JAPAN

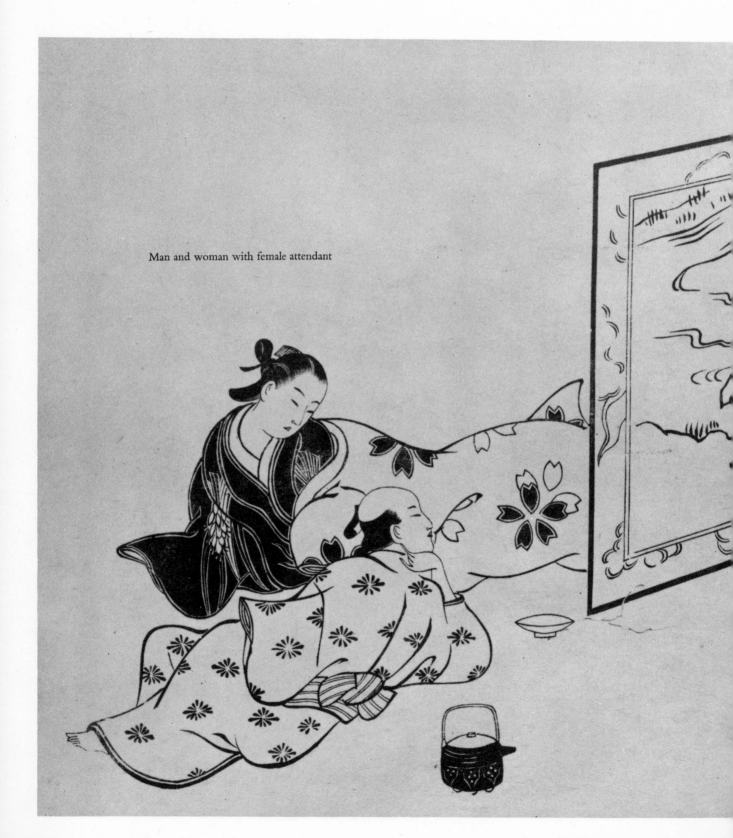

Man and woman with female attendant

大和畫師　奥村政信圖

Two illustrations from *The Book of Genji*

Courtesans of the House of Tama, from *The Mirror of Autographs of Latest Arrival Yoshiwara Beauties*, 1782. Below: At a modern 'school for brides' a woman learns to make and serve tea. The course includes flower arranging, singing, needlework and general deportment

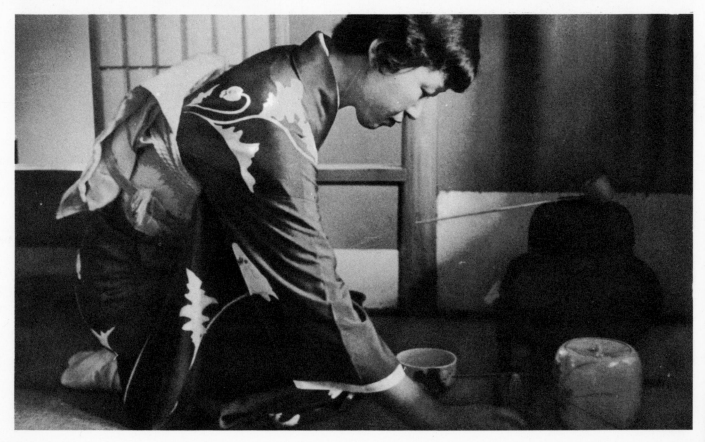

The courtesan Tsukosa of the House of Ogi in the Yoshi-wara. Accomplishment in dress was not the least of the courtesan's requirements

THE Japanese attitude to love, marriage, chastity, adultery and all problems of the relations of the sexes, reflects the behaviour of their lives generally —which seems more concerned with etiquette and manners than with religious tenets or beliefs.

Americans and Europeans have many taboos on erotic pleasure which the Japanese have never known—and are incapable of learning. In this they are utterly amoral from the Western point of view. They consider sex as a minor matter—but something good, part of the general human feelings which cannot be evil and subject to moralizing. The Western ideas of pornography and obscenity are almost incomprehensible to the Japanese (just as they cannot understand how anybody can object

to mixed bathing or to public nudity). This is one of the main reasons why Anglo-Saxons have such difficulty in sharing the Japanese attitude about love and erotic pleasure.

The most brilliant analysis of modern Japan (which has changed remarkably little in spite of two world wars and an American occupation) is probably Ruth Benedict's *The Chrysanthemum and the Sword*, dealing with patterns of Japanese culture, the work of a highly accomplished anthropologist and psychologist. Without establishing the basic ideas of Japanese social morality, it is impossible to understand the dominant attitudes.

'They fence off one province which belongs to the wife,' Ruth Benedict writes, 'from another

Guests playing games at a modern geisha party

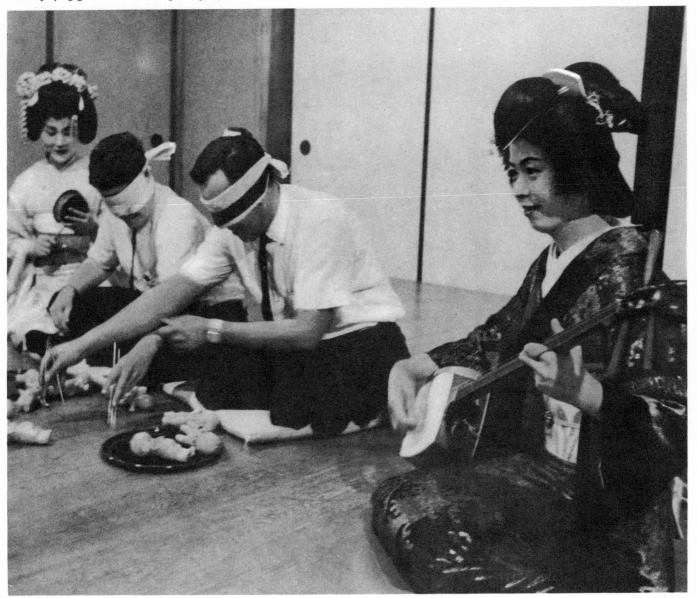

which belongs to erotic pleasure. Both provinces are equally open and above board. The two are not divided from each other as in American life, by the fact that one is what a man admits to the public and the other is surreptitious. They are separate because one is in the circle of a man's major obligations and the other in the circle of minor relaxation. This way of mapping out a proper place to each area makes the two as separate for the ideal father of a family as it does for the man about town. The Japanese set up no ideal... which pictures love and marriage as one and the same thing.... In the choice of a spouse, the young man should bow to his parent's choice and marry blind. He must observe great formality in his relations with his wife. Even in the give and take of family life, their children do not see an erotically affectionate gesture pass between them...'

And a Japanese writer adds: 'The real aim of marriage is regarded in this country as the procreation of children and thereby to assure the continuity of the family life. Any purpose other than this must simply serve to pervert the true meaning of it...'

Men can and do keep mistresses, if they can afford them. But these are not concubines—the man does not bring them into his house. Extramarital love can have three heterosexual outlets in Japan. The first is the mistress, the second the prostitute, (an inmate of the now officially abolished Yoshiwara), and the third is—the geisha.

THE GEISHA

A good deal of nonsense has been written about the geisha. She remains in modern Japan, as she has been for centuries, a courtesan who has been highly trained for her profession. That is, she is available as a companion and entertainer to any man who can afford her price—but this does *not* include sexual intercourse. If he wanted her for his mistress, he would have to become her 'patron' and sign a regular contract.

The name geisha is made up of two words: *gei*, meaning art, and *sha*, meaning person. The geisha is therefore a person whose occupation is art—or a whole variety of the arts of living.

To visit a geisha house is by no means a furtive or shamefaced matter for a Japanese gentleman. His wife may dress and prepare him for his evening of relaxation; the bill might be sent to her and she will pay it without a murmur. If she is unhappy about it, it is extremely bad manners to show the slightest sign of her resentment.

Even in the Japan of the nineteen-sixties, wives practically never mingle with male company. Any

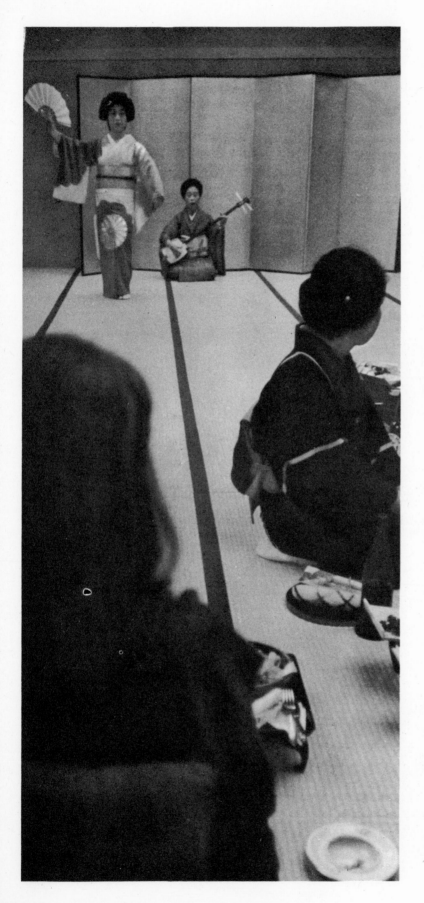

entertainment a businessman or politician has to do must unavoidably involve geishas. Only a few minutes walk from the Gina is the most distinguished geisha quarter of Tokyo, the Simbasi, a city within a city, whose houses are small and whose streets are narrow, but very clean. Here is one of the most famous geisha schools, with 350 pupils. The curriculum includes singing, history, painting, the playing of musical instruments, stage dancing, the history of literature, Chinese calligraphy, the art of conversation, painting, drawing, flower arrangement, the tea ceremony, the composition of haiku, European history, ballroom dancing, and French language.

There are, of course, hundreds of thousands who cannot afford an evening with the geishas. For them, Yoshiwara and its equivalents were built. Prostitutes are cheap and there is neither glamour nor mystique surrounding them. They live in licensed houses; their pictures are displayed outside and the customers spend a long time quite unashamedly studying them, making their choice. Most of the prostitutes are daughters of the poor, sold to the brothels by their families when they were hard-pressed for money. They are not trained in the multiple arts of the geishas. Though in 1957 the Japanese announced the closing of Yoshiwara and similar red-light districts, no Japanese government has ever pretended that it could do this.

Even among prostitutes there are girls whom a man may set up as his mistress; he then becomes her exclusive patron and a proper legal contract is made with the house which protects her. But when an ordinary girl who is not a prostitute becomes a man's mistress, this is done without any agreement and these 'voluntary mistresses' are the most defenceless. 'These are precisely those girls,' Ruth Benedict says, 'who are most likely to have been in love with their partners, but they are outside all the recognized circles of obligation.' The volunteer has no rights.

Wife, geisha, prostitute, voluntary mistress—these four represent the main varieties of Japanese women. There is a great struggle for emancipation in the first category; but the tradition and social pressures still work powerfully against its achievement. The World War and the atom bomb have brought little change in attitudes to love in the Land of the Rising Sun. 'Human feelings' still mean to the Japanese that nothing human is alien (or reprehensible) to them, whether it is homosexuality or what Ruth Benedict calls auto-erotism. And to blame them for this attitude would be just as stupid as to object to their slanting eyes of the colour of their skin.

LOVE ON THE MEDITERRANEAN

EGYPT

SOCIAL LIFE IN THE NILE VALLEY

HUMAN culture was cradled in the Middle East. One of its ancient birthplaces was the Nile Valley where, almost five thousand years before the birth of Christ, a complex and important civilization arose. This was made possible by the inundations of the mighty river which fertilized the land and gave two harvests a year.

Egyptian religion was originally a fertility cult—the earth was female, the sun male and their union created life. The bull was the symbol of male potency and bull-gods were worshipped. There was also an intense preoccupation with death; the Egyptians believed in the soul's descent into the underworld where everybody was judged by Osiris according to his merits.

Isis and Osiris, the goddess and god, were sister and brother and at the same time wife and husband. The love of Isis lasted long after Seth, the Egyptian god of love, had tricked Osiris into a wooden chest that became the unfortunate god's coffin. She did not resign herself to his death and with the help of Anubis restored him to life—first to rule only among the dead but later, in a new reincarnation, to reign over the living as well.

Life was guided by the cycle of sowing and harvesting, of birth and death. Egyptian civilization was a pyramid; the divine king with despotic powers stood at the apex; he owned all the land. A polytheistic religion still acknowledged one supreme god to whom the king had a special

These frescoes from Thebes show women using cosmetics, and holding their husbands' arms while being served by slaves

relationship. The next layer of the pyramid was the aristocracy of the priests and soldiers. The broad base was made up of the cultivators of the soil, all serfs.

The outward difference between the classes was comparatively small. The dress of the ancient Egyptians was very simple, almost rudimentary. Men wore an apron of cotton or leather fastened with a belt around the loins. Only the wealthier put on a complete loincloth while the nobles also added a lion or panther-skin. Women's dress consisted of a long, closely-fitting shift which was practically transparent; but even this started only under the breasts and reached to the ankles. The bosom was bare and the shift was held by two shoulder-straps; the chief ornament was usually a rich necklace.

During the Middle Empire—especially under the Twelfth Dynasty—there was a slight change. Men added a longer apron to the short one; women adopted a peculiar hairstyle with the hair piled on top of the head and decorated with ribbons. At the start of the New Empire (16th century B.C.) the men began to wear shirts while the women progressed to a tight dress with a voluminous cloak over it.

COURTSHIP AND MARRIAGE

Monogamy was the general rule—and the wife was addressed as 'the mistress of the household' or 'beloved spouse'. It is certain the position of Egyptian women was different from all Oriental women in the pre-Christian world. Their independence was retained even in marriage.

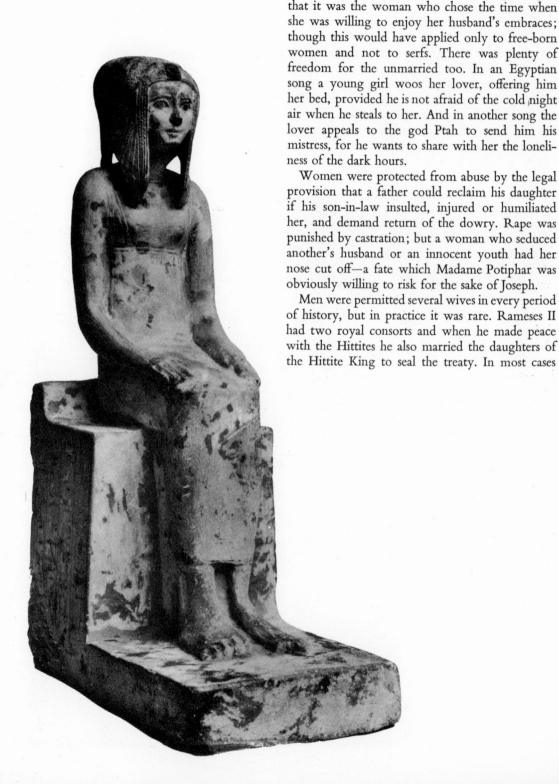

There is, for instance, a mural in a tomb (dated about 3000 B.C., the period of the Fourth Dynasty) showing the master of the house reclining on a bed while his wife entertains him by playing the harp. Archeologists deduced from this and similar pictures that it was the wife who visited the husband when she felt like granting him conjugal privileges; that it was the woman who chose the time when she was willing to enjoy her husband's embraces; though this would have applied only to free-born women and not to serfs. There was plenty of freedom for the unmarried too. In an Egyptian song a young girl woos her lover, offering him her bed, provided he is not afraid of the cold night air when he steals to her. And in another song the lover appeals to the god Ptah to send him his mistress, for he wants to share with her the loneliness of the dark hours.

Women were protected from abuse by the legal provision that a father could reclaim his daughter if his son-in-law insulted, injured or humiliated her, and demand return of the dowry. Rape was punished by castration; but a woman who seduced another's husband or an innocent youth had her nose cut off—a fate which Madame Potiphar was obviously willing to risk for the sake of Joseph.

Men were permitted several wives in every period of history, but in practice it was rare. Rameses II had two royal consorts and when he made peace with the Hittites he also married the daughters of the Hittite King to seal the treaty. In most cases

polygamy could be traced to political causes. The
northern wall of the Temple of Abidos bears the
image and name of Rameses II's 119 children—of
whom 59 were boys and 60 were girls, a nice
equitable distribution. It is reasonable to assume
that the Pharaoh, apart from his legal wives, also
had a number of concubines—but there was no
special difference made between their children and
those of the royal consorts.

Trial marriages were not unusual in Egypt.
They lasted for a year, after which they could be
dissolved by paying a forfeit.

The relations of husband and wife seem to have
been more intimate and affectionate than in other
ancient civilizations. Wherever they are depicted
together the wife has her arm twined fondly around
her husband's neck. According to the wise Ptah-
Hotep the true sagacity of a man was 'to build a
house and love his wife…'

But though they respected and appreciated women as housewives and mothers, to the Egyptian
the mistress and the prostitute were deadly dangers.
The fanatic love of order and respectability objected
to women who could seduce even the best, most
respectable man.

It happened quite often that Pharaohs could only
achieve the supreme power by marrying a first-
born princess who was heiress to the crown, and
that frequently led to the strangest feature of
Egyptian royal marriages, the union of brother
and sister.

Isis, the most famous of Egyptian goddesses, with Osiris, her brother-husband and Horus her son. Festivals held in her honour were often the excuse for sexual orgies

The bull Apis, a god of the ancient Egyptian pantheon.
He is said to represent the soul of Osiris

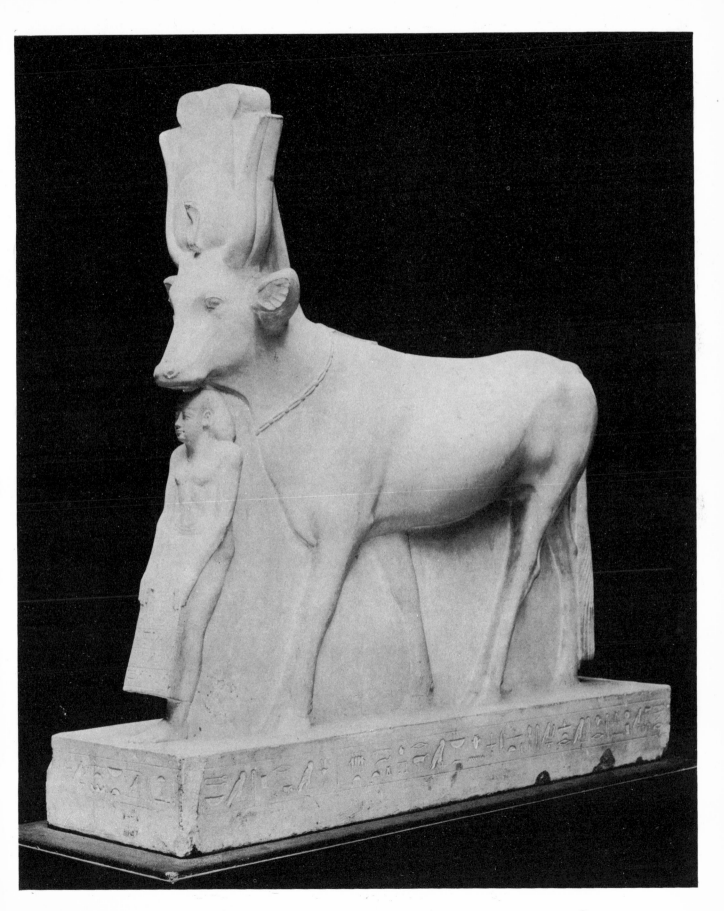

The equality between man and woman in Egyptian marriage is indicated by the familiar attitude of the wife of King Mycerinus

A tablet bearing the Hammurabi Code, which set down rules and provisions for sex, love and marriage in Babylonian culture

Thutmose III who reigned from 1504 to 1449 B.C. married his step-sister, the famous Hatshepsut. Both were children of Thutmose I who early proclaimed his daughter as his successor. Hatshepsut described herself in a somewhat boastful inscription as 'a beautiful maiden, fresher than any grass at her age; her figure resembled a divinity; her eyes and all else about her were divine...' Thutmose himself was of unknown but *not* royal birth. He married the Princess Ahmes who was the rightful ruler after the death of her brother, Amenhotep I and thereby secured his rights to the throne. Princess Ahmes was his second wife (he had married a girl called Isis first) and after her he also married Princess Mutnophret. The two princesses were clearly distinguished in the inscriptions—Ahmes was 'great royal highness', Mutnophret simply 'royal highness'. Matshepsut was the daughter of Ahmes, therefore next in succession, while Mutnophret's son, Thutmose, had no precedence even though he was a male heir.

Men were encouraged to marry very young, for in the upper classes nothing was considered more reprehensible than young bachelors seeking the company of loose-living, unattached women.

'Beware of women coming from the outside, unknown in our city.' 'The wise man marries young.' 'If you take a wife, feed and clothe her, give her jewels and treat her with the greatest tenderness, for a woman is the highest boon you can obtain in this world.' These Golden Rules were taught in the twentieth century before Christ, but it is debatable how well they were kept.

BABYLON

THE HAMMURABI CODE

Babylon arose as a mighty civilization in the valley of the Tigris and Euphrates. It colonized other countries around it until it fell finally to the might of Persia.

Perhaps the greatest achievement of Babylonian culture was the great legal code of Hammurabi which replaced tribal custom by state-law. It contained rules and provisions about marriage, sex and love and provides a pretty good idea of general moral standards.

Marriages had an element of purchase: relatives usually arranged marriages for the young and the bridegroom's father had to provide the bride-price. It varied considerably according to the standing of the families but was more than that paid for a slave. This dowry remained the wife's for life, descending to her children, if any.

At the ceremony the bridegroom said: 'I am the son of nobles, silver and gold shall fill thy lap, thou shalt be my wife, I will be thy husband. Like the fruit of a garden, I will give thee offspring...' No promises seemed to have been expected from the bride.

If she turned out to be a bad wife, Hammurabi's code permitted the husband to send her back to her parents, while he kept the children and the dowry; or he could degrade her to the position of a slave in his house. If she were left without maintenance during her husband's enforced absence, she was permitted to live with another man; but if her husband came back, she had to return to him. In such cases the children of the second union remained with their father. If the husband did make provision for her in his absence, a breach of the marriage tie was considered adultery. And adultery was punished severely—with the death of both partners by drowning. Only if the husband was willing to pardon his wife could the king intervene to pardon the lover. The Code prescribed careful investigation. Suspicion was not enough; the adulterer had to be taken in the act, or a confession in writing had to be made, before judgment could be passed.

There were other detailed and important provisions:

If a man forces his will upon the betrothed of another who has not yet known a man and lives in her father's house, being caught in the act, he shall be punished with death but the woman shall go free.

If a man accuses his own wife of adultery without her being caught in the act, she shall swear to her innocence and return to her home.

If a man sleeps with his daughter, he shall be ejected from his home and expelled from his community.

If a man sleeps with his mother, both shall be burned alive.

If a man is caught in the act of sleeping with the principal wife of his father—provided she has borne children—he shall be driven from his father's house

Monogamy was the general rule in Babylon, but in any marriage that remained childless, the husband was entitled to take a second wife. Divorce was permitted in some cases, clearly circumscribed by law. An invalid wife could not be dismissed from the household even if the husband married a second time; he had to provide for her for the rest of her life, unless she decided to leave by her own free will in which case she could take her dowry with her.

Hammurabi's Code had a strong and direct influence upon Mosaic law, though it was considerably more liberal and humane than the Hebrew code.

THE GODS OF BABYLON

The Babylonian gods included Ishtar the great 'Queen of Heaven' and chief of the Igigi, the spirits of the sky. She had, like so many Eastern divinities, a twofold aspect—good and bad. A Prayer found in Ashurbanipal's library appeals to her as 'the merciful goddess' and she was supposed to be full of pity for the sufferings of her offspring on earth. She wept at the devastation caused by the plague-god; she repented bitterly her own consent to the Flood (a myth common to the Tigris and Euphrates valley). But she was also the goddess of love and the tutelary goddess of prostitutes. She is often found dwelling in their midst—and therefore they were called not only 'samhati'—'girls of joy', but also 'harimati'—'the hallowed or holy ones'.

Ishtar was also a goddess of war, 'clad in terror', making the very gods tremble. In battle the Assyrians claimed her as their great ally; and the Philistines chose Ishtar's temple in which to hang up Saul's armour as a trophy. She was the daughter of either Anu or the Moongod and appeared as wife of some of the chief gods. Her name and Ashur's were often linked together; they were invoked together on the eve of battle, and any one who should have presumed to carry off even a single tablet from Ashurbanipal's library had their combined wrath to fear.

Among many other astral associations, Ishtar was identified with the planet Venus. Her cult was connected with that of the lover or husband whose death she caused but for whom she afterwards made her descent into Hell to seek the water of life. While she sojourned under the earth, nothing grew or flourished above ground; it was only after the messenger from Ea obtained for her the water of life and released her from the power of Allatu, the dark goddess, that she could return and the earth recovered its fertility. This particular myth linked her with Demeter and Persephone of Greece; the tilling of the soil and the cult of sex have been connected since the earliest times.

Sarpanitum, wife of Marduk, the mighty lord of Babylon, the Bel or Baal of the Old Testament, was the goddess of fertility and the protector of childbirth. Herodotus claimed that Marduk was worshipped with human sacrifices while Sarpanitum demanded the defloration of all maidens before marriage, (collecting this tribute through her priests) but no inscription or tablet ever bore out this traveller's tale.

PALESTINE

THE MOSAIC LAWS

Millions of pages have been written about the difference between the tribal laws developed by Moses and other prophets and the realities of the modern Western world.

Many of the Mosaic precepts were only applicable to a nomadic, fairly primitive people with certainly a good deal more sensuality than the average Anglo-Saxon. Half of them were not even concerned with morality but with physical and ritual hygiene.

The Mosaic law did not object to polygamy; it was the form of marriage which almost all Oriental people had developed from the primitive basis of the family. It was, however, extremely severe on adultery—which the Bible defined as 'illicit connection between a married woman and a man not her husband.' Not the other way round, it must be noticed—a married man could have sexual relations with an unmarried woman without being subject to the severity of the law. To the Jews it was a heinous sin if a woman bore children not of her husband's begetting—this preoccupation with legitimacy became an obsession.

STORIES FROM THE BIBLE

When Abraham fled from the famine to Egypt, he was worried about the beauty of Sarah, his wife—worried that it might cause his own death. The Egyptians, he thought, would kill him to make her a widow and thus gain her love. To save his life, Abraham commanded Sarah to tell everybody that she was not his wife but his sister. For a prophet and patriarch this appeared to be a rather weak deception. True, it saved his skin, but (at least for a time) he lost his wife. The Egyptians *were* struck by Sarah's beauty. 'The princes also of Pharaoh saw her, and commended her before Pharaoh: and the woman was taken into Pharaoh's house.' He must have been greatly pleased with her; for her sake he treated Abraham with considerable generosity, giving him sheep and oxen and asses, men-servants and maid-servants and camels.

Yet Jehova did not punish Abraham—but the unsuspecting Pharaoh. 'And the Lord plagued Pharaoh and his house with great plagues because of Sarah, Abraham's wife.' The Egyptian ruler must have found out the reason for his unexpected afflictions—or perhaps Sarah, long-suffering as she was, told him. He sent for Abraham, and reproached the wily patriarch. 'What is this thou hast done unto me? Why didst thou not tell me that she was thy

The first meeting between Rebecca and Isaac, as she draws water for his camel to drink

wife? Why saidst thou, she is my sister? So I might have taken her to me to wife; now therefore behold thy wife, take her and go thy way.'

Abraham went—and the Pharaoh even permitted him to take away all he possessed. Beyond a gentle upbraiding he did not seem to have taken any revenge for the trick played on him.

But this is by no means the end of the story. Abraham tried the same trick again! When he came to Gerar, he once more pretended that Sarah was his sister. Whereupon Abimelech, the King of Gerar, took her into his harem. God had to intervene once more; this time He sent no plagues. He simply appeared to Abimelech in his dreams and said to him: 'Behold thou art but a dead man, for the woman which thou hast taken, she is a man's wife.' Abimelech however had not yet touched Sarah. In his dream he even argued with the Lord, pointing out that Sarah herself had lied about Abraham being her brother. Jehovah was forced to accept the plea. 'Yea,' He said, 'I know that thou didst this in the integrity of thy heart; for I also withheld thee from sinning against me: therefore suffered I thee not to touch her. Now therefore restore the man his wife; for he is a prophet and he shall pray for thee, and thou shalt live; and if thou restore her

not, know that thou shalt surely die, thou and all that are thine.'

Early next morning, poor bewildered Abimelech rose, called together his servants and told them of his dream; then, just as Pharaoh did, he reproached Abraham. The worthy phophet's excuse was a hairsplitting one, more befitting a sophist. He maintained that Sarah was his half-sister (which was probably true) and so he had not really lied. Abimelech accepted this lame excuse, and gave him permission to live wherever he pleased in his country.

The most fantastic part of the tale is that Isaac attempted exactly the same ruse as his father, and on the same King Abimelech as Abraham had done some decades earlier. For when Isaac lived in Gerar, he introduced Rebecca as his sister, 'because she was fair to look upon'. But he was found out in a somewhat embarrassing fashion. This time Jehovah sent no plagues, appeared in no dream—perhaps He was getting a little tired of rescuing the family from trouble of their own making. 'And it came to pass' the tale is told in Genesis, 'when he had been there a long time, that Abimelech, King of the Philistines, looked out at a window, and saw, and behold, Isaac was sporting with Rebecca his

The Queen of Sheba before Solomon. According to the Bible, he gave her all that she desired.

wife. And Abimelech called Isaac and said, Behold, of a surety, she is thy wife: and how saidst thou, She is my sister?' Isaac's excuse was the same as his father's had been on the two previous occasions.

But Abimelech was seriously worried. 'What is this thou hast done unto us?' he asked. 'One of my people might lightly have lain with thy wife, and thou shouldst have brought guiltiness upon us.' To prevent this, he proclaimed throughout the land that Rebecca was Isaac's wife and that no one should touch her—or him.

According to the ancient Jewish law if two brothers shared an estate and one died without leaving a son, his widow had no right to marry into another family but had to wed the surviving brother and bear a son to inherit her deceased husband's property. This was the position in which Tamar, Judah's beautiful daughter-in-law, found herself. She had lost two husbands and had to wait patiently until Judah's third son, Shelah, had grown to manhood. But Shelah did not marry her. So she disguised herself as a harlot, waylaid her father-in-law and seduced him. She must have been an astute woman (and a clever actress) for she asked Judah for his signet ring, his bracelets and his staff as a pledge that he would send her the kid he had

promised as payment for her favours. When, three months later, she was accused of 'playing the harlot' and Judah summoned her angrily, she produced the unredeemed pledges. Judah could do nothing except acknowledge his own guilt. 'She hath been more righteous than I; because that I gave her not to Shelah my son... And he knew her again no more.'

Tamar gave birth to twins and her children flourished.

The laws against the transgressors in matters of love were draconic enough in most cases. Adultery was punishable by death whether the woman was actually married or only betrothed. Chastity was highly prized, and if a young bride's virginity was in doubt, it was the duty of her parents, to bring forth the necessary proof—nothing less than the bloodstained sheets of the nuptial bed, spreading them before the elders. If this proof was established, the complaining husband was beaten and fined a hundred shekels of silver which he had to pay his father-in-law, and debarred from ever divorcing his wife. If the accusation turned out to be well-founded, the unchaste woman was taken to the gates of the city and stoned to death. 'Because she hath wrought folly in Israel, to play the whore in

Susannah, the beautiful wife of Joachim, with two elders. When their advances
were repulsed they brought false charges of adultery against her and she was
sentenced to death

her father's house; so shalt thou put evil away from among you...'

This method was unduly weighted against the woman. The husband could make sure before he brought his charge whether the proof of her innocence was available or not; and in many cases she might have been chaste without bleeding when deflowered.

The almost pathological fear of the Jews that illegitimate children might be smuggled into a family, led to the preposterous law that decreed: 'A bastard shall not enter into the congregation of the Lord; even to his tenth generation shall he not enter into the congregation of the Lord.' How a check on a bastard's descendents could be kept for ten generations must have been a puzzling problem even for patriarchs and prophets.

The forerunner of the 'lie detector' can be found in the Bible; a strange trial by ordeal used in cases of suspected adultery. The suspicious husband could apply for this test—whether or not he had any real cause for jealousy. He brought his wife to the priest, first making a suitable offering for the trouble the servant of God had to take in such a private matter; then the woman was put through a complex ritual:

'And the priest shall bring her near and set her before the Lord; and the priest shall take holy water in an earthen vessel; and of the dust that is in the floor of the tabernacle the priest shall take and put into the water; and the priest shall set the woman before the Lord and uncover the woman's head—and put the offering of memorial in her hands, which is the jealousy offering: and the priest shall have in his hand the bitter water that causeth the curse; and the priest shall charge her by an oath and say unto the woman, If no man have lain with thee, and if thou has not gone aside to uncleanness with another instead of thy husband, be thou free from this bitter water that causeth the curse; but if thou hast gone aside to another instead of thy husband, and if thou be defiled, and some man have lain with thee beside thy husband: then the priest shall charge the woman with an oath of cursing, and the priest shall say unto the woman, the Lord make thee a curse and an oath among thy people, when the Lord doth make thy thigh to rot and thy belly to swell; and this water that causeth the curse shall go into thy bowels to make thy belly to swell and thigh to rot, and the woman shall say, Amen, amen...'

She was made to drink the water and upon the result her guilt or innocence depended. It was, of course, a psychological test; its success was deter-mined by the accused wife's mental strength or weakness. Unless, of course, the husband took good care to bribe the priest so that he put some poison into the 'bitter water'. Though these tests seem to have gone out of fashion at a fairly early stage in Israel's history, they give a fascinating insight into the psychology of the Chosen People.

The Bible is filled with love stories. There is Esther whose beauty and other accomplishments raised her above all the virgins whom Ahasuerus (as the Jews called Xerxes) gathered in his harem; and she, the shining star of Israel, frustrated the evil designs of Haman, saved her compatriots from destruction and became a heroine still commemorated in Judaic ritual. There is the moving story of Ruth in 'the alien corn' and her marriage to Boaz; the triumphant vindication of Susanna's virtue (a tale that occurs in the Apocrypha and was a godsend to artists who wanted an excuse for representing the nude female body); Hagar cast off, yet preserved by the Lord to bring up and protect her son Ishmael; Bathsheba who caused David's 'grievous sin' yet lived to bear him Solomon and three other sons—husbands and lovers, wives and concubines, provide a vivid and varied pageant of love. And the 'Song of Songs' which puritans have tried desperately to twist and force into symbolic asexual meanings, is one of the greatest hymns to the joys and torments of love.

GREECE

MARRIAGE IN SPARTA AND ATHENS

In the days of Lycurgus the lawgiver, a stranger came to Sparta and enquired what was the punishment of the adulteress, according to the wise king's laws. He was told curtly, 'There are no adulteresses in Sparta.'

The visitor, however, persisted: 'But what if there should be at least one?'

'She would be sentenced to give the state a bull that could stand on the top of Mount Taigetos and drink from the water of the River Eurotos.'

'But where could she find such a gigantic bull?' the man asked.

'But where could you find an adulteress in Sparta?' was the answer.

By and large the Greeks adopted monogamy as the chief and practically only form of marriage. In Sparta the only justification and aim of marriage were children. Women had to submit to the good of the commonwealth and accept as the father of their children the man chosen and supplied by the community.

An old husband, for instance, did wisely if he introduced his wife to a youth whom he liked and respected; and if this acquaintance, encouraged by the husband, resulted in a child, he was to accept it as his own offspring. And if an honest Spartan saw that an old fellow-citizen had a beautiful and intelligent wife, mother of lovely children, he could demand that the husband should yield her to him—for thus, and thus only, the State would be assured of a fine crop of babies. The man who remained unmarried after the age of thirty was deprived of his civic rights.

Lycurgus had a poor opinion of the marriage laws of Athens and other nations. 'For their mares they pick the finest stallions and thereby they produce the best foals—but their women they lock up in their houses, watching jealously lest anyone but the husband should father her children, though he might be decrepit, ill or an idiot...'

The freedom of Spartan women was in pointed contrast to the rigorous discipline imposed upon the Spartan men. This puzzled Aristotle who enquired about the reason when he visited Sparta. He was told that Lycurgus had tried to discipline women in equal measure with men. But they put up such a spirited resistance that the great king, knowing when he was beaten, desisted for once in his life.

The two sexes mingled perpetually and freely— a custom foreign to other Greek states. Spartan marriage began with the young husband carrying off his bride in a simulated abduction; even after that she continued to reside with her family for some time and visited her husband in his barracks in male attire and on short, stolen occasions. This was, presumably, intended to add the spice of stealth to marriage. Some married couples, Plutarch tells us, had been married long enough to have two or three children yet had scarcely seen each other by daylight.

The dowry played a very important part in most Greek marriages. It was the father's task—or if he was dead, that of the nearest male relative—to provide it. The act of marriage was a social and legal one; the religious ceremony was secondary. Some animal was sacrificed to Hera, the goddess of marriage; its gall was thrown away to symbolize that nothing should embitter the union. The bride, even if only for a little while, had her hair shorn as a sign that she would be her husband's slave and that she had no intention to please any other man.

Not even the most distinguished Greek wife was cultured; intellectually she had very little to offer. Often she hardly dared to address her husband, let alone interfere with his affairs. At family meals the husband reclined, while the wife had to sit up. 'Silence is a woman's greatest virtue,' a proverb said. A decent wife was her husband's humble slave. She supervised the servants, looked after the household, educated her children, sat at the spinning frame. The cooking was mostly done by slaves. The marketing was done by the husband, usually accompanied by slaves. Women were not skilled in cooking, so they were kept out of the kitchen.

Divorce was frequent and easy. But in some Greek city-states the divorced woman could only marry a man who was older than her previous husband.

While in Sparta the increase of the population and the production of healthy and numerous children were the main aims of any union, in Athens marital fidelity was far more important. Just as in France (at least until recently), the husband went free if he killed his wife and her lover on finding them *in flagranti*. The law even more or less obliged him to do this.

This was after marriage. The importance attached to chastity before it varied according to the periods and localities of Greek history. The Athenian Agathias, discussing the various kinds of love, warned the would-be-lover that if he approached the bed of a virgin with amorous intent, he would have to marry her or stand accused of seduction. Evidently it did not matter if the marriage were consummated before the usual ceremonies provided the lovers were united afterwards.

Athenian women were encouraged to marry very young; according to Aristotle the husband should be at least twenty years older than his wife for it was more important that the wife should respect than that she should love her lord and master. The engaged couple had no occasion to meet and fall in love before the wedding. The bride stayed at home, only going out rarely and then heavily veiled; and marriages were arranged by go-betweens. It was not unusual for the bridegroom to see her for the first time on their wedding day.

The heyday of Athenian culture and civilization was the age of Pericles. Like every great man he had numerous enemies, and as his power increased so did the bitterness of his opponents. They were not strong enough to attack him directly, so they tried to hurt him through his friends and associates. His mistress Aspasia, the philosopher Anaxagoras and the great sculptor Pheidias all suffered in turn because of these intrigues.

Aspasia was one of the company of hetaerae, or courtesans. Many of these women were quite intellectual and the most distinguished and superior among them—such as Aspasia or Theodote—appear

Spartan girls removed all clothing when playing or relax-
ing, as is seen in this bas relief of a flute player which
decorated the throne of Venus

As part of their rigorous training in self-discipline, naked Spartan youths were subjected to taunts by the girls. This may have contributed to the acceptance of homosexual love in Sparta

These Greek vase paintings show hetaerae, or courtesans, whose position in Athenian society was highly respected

In Athens an engaged couple could not meet and fall in
love before the wedding. Depicted on an ancient vase is
an engaged woman being crowned in the presence of
women only

to have been the only women in Athens who
inspired strong passion or dominated men's minds.
Aspasia was such a brilliant conversationalist that
the most distinguished Athenians were only too
glad to visit her. Socrates was her frequent guest
and several of the prominent citizens even brought
their wives when they called on her.

Pericles had chosen his wife according to the
family considerations which were almost compulsory in Athens. She was a kinswoman of his, a lady
of impeccable descent; and she bore him two sons,
Xanthippus and Paralus. But they did not get on
very well and the marriage was dissolved by mutual
consent. Pericles even arranged for another husband
to take her off his hands, and the lady seemed

perfectly happy to make the change. He then took
Aspasia into his home and though he never went
through a form of marriage with her, he lived with
her to the end of his life and had a son by her who
bore his name.

Hernippus, one of the satirists of Athens, accused
Aspasia of impiety, 'as participant in the philosophical discussions held, and the opinions professed,
among the society of Pericles, by Anaxagoras and
others...' Certainly not many women have ever
been charged with such a highly intellectual offence!
Pericles defended her so well that she was acquitted,
and the deep, enduring affection that bound these
two together was one of the most moving and
attractive examples of love in ancient Greece.

A sculpture of the charming and intellectual Aspasia, a hetaera who won Pericles' love
Below: Pericles pleading for the life of Aspasia after she was accused of impiety.
Afterwards he lived with her to the end of his life

ROME

THE FREEDOM OF IMPERIAL ROME

Rome's career of conquest began in the fifth century
B.C. By the beginning of the third century, she had
subjugated the Samnites and Volscians, the Etrus-
cans and the Gauls; then came her first clash with
the Greek colonies—the Pyrrhic wars. As she over-
came Carthage, the Macedonian and Seleucid
empires, acquired the protectorate over the Egypt
of the Ptolemies and broke the last defiance of the
Greek national movement under Perseus, the subtle
influence of the vanquished began to stir, transform
and corrupt the victor. Livy wrote sternly: 'Wealth
brought avarice to Rome and the multiplication
of pleasure brought the desire for self-ruination
and ruination of one's country by luxury and lust.'
On one side, Rome's ideal of power led her to the
gross exploitation of her conquests, and on the
other, to something more sinister—a degeneration
unknown to the Greeks—to sadism, that particular
feature of Roman sexual life so widespread in the
time of the Emperors.

Of course, this was not the only form of fulfilment and it was natural that the love-life of the
Romans should assume cruder forms than that of
the Greeks. Originally, they were uncouth farmers;
they became rough soldiers; and at last, a few of
their best and most gifted became statesmen. It was
enough for the Roman, with his primitive character, to direct his sexual instincts into simple chan-
nels. For many centuries, marriage meant to them
a severe and pure but prosaic union; it was under
the firm authority of the husband who had little
feeling for the subtler aspects of love. The only
form of prostitution was a purely physical union,
having nothing in common with the Greek
hetaerae.

Gradually, women improved their legal and
general status. They began to aspire to independence
in respect of property and rid themselves of such
male tyranny as mock marriages. 'The mass of
capital which was collected in the hands of women,'
Mommsen tells us, 'appeared to the statesmen of
the times so dangerous that they resorted to the
extravagent expedient of prohibiting the law by
testamentary nomination of women as heirs... and
even sought by a highly arbitrary practice to
deprive women for the most part of those collateral
inheritances which fell to them without testament...' The law did not work; by the last century
B.C. Roman women had made themselves eco-
nomically independent—and free from almost all
moral restraint.

Centuries had passed since the rape of a Lucretia
could cause the overthrow of the Tarquins. This

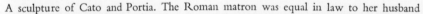

A sculpture of Cato and Portia. The Roman matron was equal in law to her husband

The rape of Lucrece, by Tarquin. From a painting by Titian

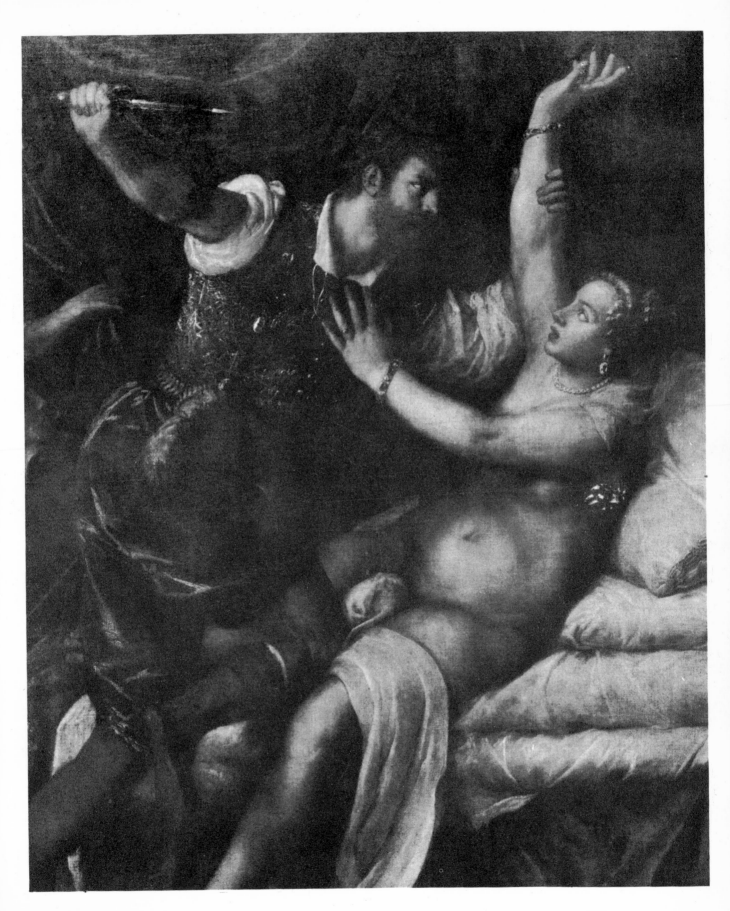

Nero looking at the dead body of his mother, Agrippina. Suetonius accused them
of committing incest

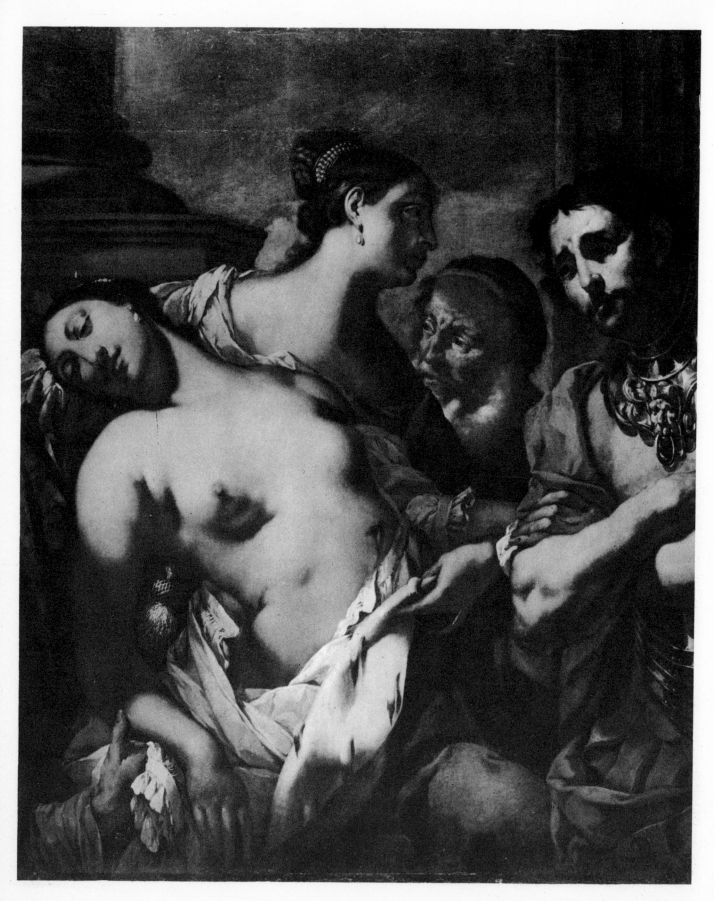

was the age of Julia, the licentious daughter of the great Augustus; of Faustina, the wife of the wise Emperor Marcus Aurelius, who was an abandoned nymphomaniac; of Agrippina, Nero's mother, who—according to Tacitus—tried to retain her son's favour by becoming his mistress.

But there were always poets to soften the crudity of lust, to record the beauty of women and the ecstasy of lovers. Here is Plautus, in the second century B.C. evoking the scenes of wild sensuality at a banquet:

'...This makes glad to be alive,
this has all pleasures, this has all life's treasures,
this is heaven itself.
When a lover holds his sweetheart, when he
presses lip to lip,
when they catch and clasp each other, tongue
with tongue,
when breast and breast are closely pressed, when
bodies interlace,
then the white-handed girl pours cups of nectar
for her love...'

Lucretius, a disappointed amorist and hedonist, glorified Venus but warned the lover from clinging to the memory of a lost love!

'... Avoid these images
and shun the food of love! distract your mind!
cast your collected seed in any body
and do not harbour it by loving one
and one alone—that brings unfailing sorrow...'

The first Roman love-poet was Catullus—the very first to give artistic (and truly national) expression to the experience of his inmost heart. The Lesbia of his poetry, in real life Clodia, was a morose, fickle, capricious woman—at least judged by the poems—yet beautiful, bewitching, cultured and capable of ardent love. She became the destiny of the poet, an unhappy destiny:

'You said you loved no other than Catullus,
Lesbia, no one, even Jove himself.
I loved you, Lesbia, not as a mistress only,
I loved you as a father loves his sons.
I know you now. My passion blazes hotter,
and yet I hold you cheap and worthless now.
How can that be? you ask. An injured lover
loves more and more, but all affection's gone.'

And there are these terrible, bitter lines:

'Now Lesbia, your faults have brought my spirit
to lose itself in devotion deep.
It cannot wish you well, were you an angel:
It cannot leave you if you go to hell...'

Horace, though he had his amorous experiences, became more and more a spectator of life and love

as he grew older and wiser. Speaking of the goddess of love, he notes with resignation:

'... she loves to
chain odd couples together—cruel are Venus'
jests...!'

The greatest or at least the most popular of them all was Ovid, who did not consider love a great and overwhelming divinity, ruining or blessing a man's life, but simply a method for obtaining transient pleasure. Yet whatever his philosophy of love, no one could sing with such eloquence and delicious wit of passion and pleasure. Ovid himself, was by no means a libertine. He obviously spoke the truth in his Tristia:

'My heart is different from my songs: believe
me,
my life is modest, though my muse is gay.
Most of my work is lies, imaginations,
and more licentious than its author was.
A book is not the mirror of the spirit –
it brings an honest pleasure, light and pure...'

That is perhaps why Ovid's *Art of Love* and *Metamorphoses* have stood the test of two thousand years—more than Petronius or Seneca, at least the equal of such masters as Juvenal and Martial. He could turn love into art, and that was the highest achievement of any mortal who worshipped Venus and Amor.

PLINY THE YOUNGER— TO CALPURNIA

A letter written by Caius Plinius Caecilius Secundus (61–113 A.D), a distinguished lawyer and a rich, well-educated patrician, to his wife Calpurnia. The affectionate husband was no longer young when he wrote this, for Calpurnia was his third wife.

'Plinius to his Calpurnia, greeting. I suffer unspeakable torments because you are not at my side. Not only because I love you so much, but also because we are not accustomed to being apart. I spend the greater part of my nights sitting in front of your portrait and when the hours arrive which I usually pass with you, I visit your apartment—it is an unconscious errand, my feet take me there without my conscious will—and when I arrive at your door and find that you are not there, I slink away sadly, sick at heart like the lover whose mistress denies him admittance. My torment only ceases when I have to go to the Forum and attend to my law cases. You can see what my life is like— work means rest for me, worry and haste are my consolations.'

Illustrations from *A Thousand and One Nights*, A collection of erotic fables and fairy stories of love and intrigue in the Middle East

ARABIA

THE PRE-ISLAMIC ARABS

According to Stendhal (more of an enthusiast than an expert) the 'model and home of true love must be sought under the dark tents of the Bedouins. Like elsewhere, here too, loneliness and the sunny climate created the noblest passion of the human heart—the passion that felt the necessity of providing the same happiness that it carried itself...'

Professor Julius Germanus, one of the most distinguished specialists in Arab literature and history, confirms this in his *History of Arab Literature* (Budapest, 1962). In the pre-Moslem tribal society of the Arabs, built on the fiction of common blood, women enjoyed a special position. The tribesmen were proud of the chastity and beauty of their women; the warriors did not consider women their inferiors—legally, and in othes ways, many a larger sphere of activity was given to her than to men. In many tribes a woman could dismiss her husband if she was dissatisfied with him. As the mistress of her home she could turn the entrance of the tent in a different direction when her husband returned from a journey—and the husband had to accept this symbol of rejection. If any stranger was adopted by the tribe, he was provided with a woman but

she could turn him away from the home at any time. The children belonged to the mother rather than the father. Polygamy was an early institution; and there were no restrictions as to marriage between blood relations. This pre-Islamic period was later called 'Jahiliya' (Barbarism) and possessed many marital traditions of which we only know through Mohammed's laws, such as inheriting the wives or concubines of deceased relatives. Arabs also practised the Spartan institution of expropriation under which an old or sickly husband would temporarily surrender his wife to some strong, virile warrior who begot children with her—children which were the property of the legitimate husband.

Among the tribes that gave up the nomadic life, the independence and equality of the woman became more and more tenuous and well before Mohammed she became subject to male domination; yet in the roaming Bedouin tribes she kept her legal rights for a long time.

THE REFORMS OF MOHAMMED

Mohammed, son of Abdallah of the tribe of Koreish, received the call to become a prophet when he was about forty. Twelve years later he fled from his birthplace Mecca to Medina and this, the year of the Hegira (622 A.D.) marked the beginning of

the Mohammedan era. Before he died, all Arabia acknowledged him as chief and prophet. The Moslem attack on the Christian world began shortly afterwards and was not stemmed finally until a thousand years later. The influence of the Koran upon the conceptions of love and marriage, sex life and the status of women has been tremendous; the Moslem attitude has also influenced many non-Moslems (particularly Spaniards and Portuguese) for far longer periods than the actual Moorish domination of the Iberian Peninsula, or the Turkish occupation of south-eastern Europe.

Mohammed was employed as a caravan agent (not as a camel-driver, as some of his enemies maintained) when, at twenty-five, he married his employer, the rich widow Khadija who was fifteen years his senior. The marriage lasted for twenty-six happy years and she bore him six children. When she died, his friends urged him to marry again; but he had loved her so much that in the end he took for his second wife a six-year-old girl, Ayesha —a union which was not consummated for at least eight years. But in his middle fifties he began to widen his scope; as Lewinsohn puts it, 'every victory over the Unbeliever was crowned by a new marriage... Mohammed's harem grew even faster than his empire...'

It is significant that in the early years of Islam,

women still enjoyed complete freedom and the bards and poets could freely declaim their love poems burning with sensuous desire in front of them. They could display their charms without veils and receive young men in their homes. The institution of the harem was unknown in the Mecca of early Islam; it was adopted later, under Byzantine influence and through the misunderstanding of one of Mohammed's sayings.

Mohammed's 'sex-legislation' was amazingly enlightened for the age. He made divorce easy— but appealed to the husbands to provide for the discarded wife, not to keep back any of her dowry; only if she was found to be pregnant after the divorce should a reconciliation be attempted—but otherwise her re-marriage should not be impeded. True, defiant or disobedient wives could and should be chastised—but if they repent and submit, all must be forgiven. The Koran proclaimed that it was wicked to kill children as the pre-Islamic Arabs used to do (by burying them alive in the sand); for 'Allah has made life holy'.

M. M. Pickthall defined the difference between Moslem and Christian ideas of marriage by saying: 'In Christianity celibacy is the strictest religious ideal; even monogamy is a concession to human nature. For Mussulmans the ideal is monogamy, the concession to human nature is polygamy.' This may be slightly over-simplifying things; the Koran by no means extols polygamy, which began after the Battle of Uhud, in which Mohammed's supporters suffered heavy losses, and the survivors were persuaded to care for orphans and widows and to marry 'two or three or four of them'. Mohammedanism was derided and abused because of this single feature far more than any other tenet.

Polygamy was not widespread among the early Moslems; for one thing, as a very simple calculation will show, there were never enough women to go round. (Nor are there enough today, with the slight statistical superiority of females over males.) For every Moslem who could afford to keep the maximum of four wives the Koran allowed, two or three would have to remain single.

Scheherezade telling Sultan Schahmah the stories of *A Thousand and One Nights*

Paribanou, from *A Thousand and One Nights*. The wedding feast of Prince Ahmed and the Fairy

FROM THE SONG OF SONGS

Let him kiss me with the kisses of his mouth:
For thy love is better than wine.
Because of the savour of thy good ointments
Thy name is as ointment poured forth,
Therefore do the virgins love thee.
Draw me, we will run after thee:
The king hath brought me into his chambers:
We will be glad and rejoice in thee,
We will remember thy love more than wine:
The upright love thee.

I am the rose of Sharon,
And the lily of the valleys.
As the lily among thorns,
So is my love among the daughters.
As the apple tree among the trees of the wood,
So is my beloved among the sons.
I sat down under his shadow with great delight,
And his fruit was sweet to my taste.
He brought me to the banqueting house,
And his banner over me was love.

My beloved spake, and said unto me,
'Rise up, my love, my fair one, and come away,
For lo, the winter is past,
The rain is over and gone;
The flowers appear on the earth;
The time of the singing of birds is come,
And the voice of the turtle is heard in our land;
The fig tree putteth forth her green figs,
And the vines with the tender grape give a good
smell.
Arise, my love, my fair one, and come away.

Behold, thou art fair, my love; behold, thou art
fair;
Thou hast doves' eyes within thy locks:
Thy hair is as a flock of goats, that appear from
mount Gilead.
Thy teeth are like a flock of sheep that are even
shorn, which came up from the washing;

Whereof every one bears twins, and none is barren
among them.
Thy lips are like a thread of scarlet, and thy
speech is comely:
Thy temples are like a piece of pomegranate
within thy locks.
Thy neck is like the tower of David
Builded for an armoury,
Whereon there hang a thousand bucklers, all
shields of mighty men.

Set me as a seal upon thine heart,
As a seal upon thine arm:
For love is strong as death;
Jealousy is cruel as the grave:
The coals thereof are coals of fire,
Which hath a most vehement flame.
Many waters cannot quench love,
Neither can floods drown it:
If a man would give all the substance of his house
for love,
It would be utterly contemnned.

How beautiful are thy feet with shoes, O prince's
daughter!
The joints of thy thighs are like jewels,
The work of the hands of a cunning workman.
Thy navel is like a round goblet which wanteth
not liquor:
Thy belly is like an heap of wheat set about with
lilies.
Thy two breasts are like two young roes that are
twins.
Thy neck is as a tower of ivory;
Thine eyes like the fishpools in Heshbon, by the
gate of Bath-rabbim:
Thy nose is as the tower of Lebanon which
looketh towards Damascus.
Thine head upon thee is like Carmel,
And the hair of thine head is like purple;
The king is held in the galleries.
How fair and how pleasant art thou, O love,
for delights!

LOVE AND CHRISTIANITY

Previous page: The start of it all—Eve offers temptation to Adam
The Story of Adam and Eve from the moment of temptation to their banishment from the Garden of Eden; from
Très Riches Heures du duc de Berry

The ideal of 15th Century German beauty represented in Dürer's demure and buxom Eve

THE INVENTION OF SIN

THE man who turned Christian faith into a religion, the teaching of Jesus into a dogma, was one of the most remarkable characters in history—Saul the tentmaker, St Paul the indefatigable apostle. He had spent a considerable time in Arabia and had become acquainted with the 'harem-ethics' concerning women. It was a grim attitude: Women must be hidden from the sight of men because women corrupted male morals. And the Jewish tentmaker, who was converted on the road to Damascus, wandered all over Southern Europe, the Greek isles, Asia Minor, Italy and Spain and composed his doctrine which forms part of the New Testament as the Letters of St Paul.

'Let your women keep silence in the churches,' St Paul advised the Corinthians, 'for it is not permitted unto them to speak; but they are commanded to be under obedience, as also saith the law...' And, writing to the Ephesians: 'Wives, submit yourselves unto your own husbands, as unto the Lord. For the husband is the head of the wife, even as Christ is the head of the church: and he is the saviour of the body.' Again, to Timothy: 'But I suffer not a woman to teach, nor to usurp authority over the man, but to be in silence. For Adam was first formed, then Eve. And Adam was not deceived, but the woman being deceived was in the transgression...'

Here was the emphasis on the belief in Original Sin, shared by all the Semitic tribes and nations.

St Paul's teaching had far-reaching consequences. *Alone amongst all religions*, Christianity regarded sexual relations outside marriage as a grave sin. Total abstinence was also considered a nobler state than marriage, and salvation was surest for those free of all physical temptation. A life devoted to God demanded undivided loyalties—to prepare for Heaven was a full-time job.

The idea that men were begotten in sinful concupiscence dominated the synods and other meeting places of Christian theologians and philosophers for many centuries. Gregory the Great declared that the lust of our parents' flesh was the cause of our being—and therefore human existence was in itself sinful. Physical love was branded as evil—whether within or outside marriage.

When general persecution began under the Emperor Domitian, the response of Christianity was a drawing together, a strengthening of the churches, a stricter moral attitude. Intemperance and wantonness became the arch-enemy which had to be defeated by asceticism. Thus the life of the hermit, of the holy anchorite retired from the world and its temptations, became the ideal. It was also

117

Adam and Eve admonished, in a mosaic in the Basilica of St Mark, Venice

Adam and Eve admonished, in a mosaic in the Basilica of St Mark, Venice

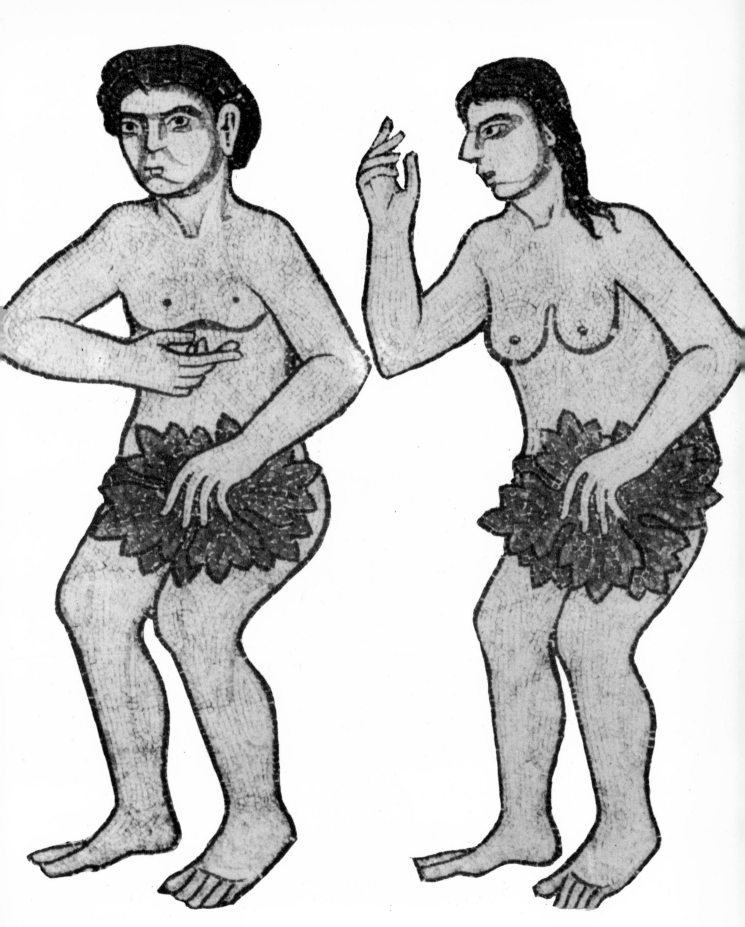

The Jewish tentmaker Saul being converted on the road to Damascus. Later to become St Paul, his doctrines formed the basis of the Catholic Church

the safest—for the Emperor's minions did not penetrate into the desert or the bleak mountains. This life had a certain fascination for people satiated with wild excess and the complete amorality that characterized the decline of the Roman Empire. Thais, the famous courtesan, renounced the world and buried herself in the desert, and there were many like her, sinners turned into saints. Sometimes it looked as if the greater the sinner, the finer the converted saint.

Several authors have claimed that chastity was not an essential part of the Christian ideal of life; for such an ideal was based on infantilism or hidden Manicheism. It could not be a basic ideal for if all lived according to it, human existence would come to an end. It would also be opposed to the divine order of things—after all, it was no mere accident that God created male and female. St Augustine's view *'magis miranda quam imitanda'* certainly applies to the majority of the early Christians—it was an ideal that they found more admirable than convenient to follow.

There was a tendency in the early Christian times to condemn second marriages—though St Paul recommended them for young widows: 'I will that the younger should marry, bear children, be mistresses of families, give no occasion to the adversary to speak evil.' But on the whole the Church did not view a second marriage with a very favourable eye and made it an impediment to the reception of holy orders. As a matter of fact, the sacrament of marriage itself was not accepted officially by the Church until the twelfth century and not confirmed until the fourteenth century. St Ambrose, one of the most highly respected Church Fathers, said in his treatise on chastity and celibacy: '... he who does not marry becomes like the angels of heaven... Naturally I do not condemn marriage ... only I consider chastity higher.... The former is permissible, the latter I admire...'

Engels said that monogamous marriages 'originated from the concentration of great wealth into one hand—a *male* hand—and from the striving that this wealth should be inherited by the descendants of this one man and not others...' And he added that 'religious weddings were nothing but special propaganda for the reactionary religious dogma proclaiming the inferiority of woman'. If this is so, then all the girls who insist on a dozen bridesmaids and the most elaborate preparations must have fallen victims to a most cunning and ancient propaganda...

Christianity had a tremendous share in making marriage a more spiritual and finer relationship. But the terrible penalties it helped to devise and

develop against fornication and adultery, refusing to accept (at least officially) the frailty of the flesh, counterbalanced much of this beneficial effect. But it is to Christianity's eternal merit that it replaced the pagan conception of marriage as a purely physical union.

WOMEN OF BYZANTIUM

The great Byzantine Empire's capital was built by Constantine the Great on the Golden Horn where it survived for almost a thousand years until the Ottoman hordes destroyed an already declining civilization.

When Constantine the Great decreed Christianity the state religion and, after centuries of persecution, the followers of Jesus could leave the catacombs,

the pure apostolic faith soon hardened into dogma and the religious tenets acquired the authority of law. But it was only in 312 A.D. that the Sign of the Cross appeared at the Milvian Bridge, proclaiming *in hoc signo vinces;* and in the three centuries that preceded this legendary conversion the followers of Jesus suffered cruel persecution. To a considerable extent this was because of their attitude to love, marriage and sex for, as Richard Lewinsohn points out in his *History of Sexual Customs*, in the age of Nero and Poppaea the moral teaching of St Paul and his successors sounded like a criticism of the private life of the Imperial family, Roman law, and the morals of Roman society. Christians were considered anarchists, subversionists and as Tacitus puts it, guilty of 'hatred against humankind'.

Augustine, after his self-confessed life of debauchery, preaching to King Ethelbert

This was, of course, a thoroughly unjust charge —for Christians loved life even if they were ready to lay it down for the sake of their faith. Indeed, one of the main differences between the pagan and the Christian idealogies was the Christian denunciation of both abortion and birth-control. There is no mention of these questions in the Gospels, but the old Mosaic law forbade the destruction of life in the womb and denounced coitus interruptus, the earliest method of 'family planning', and Christianity had embraced these principles. The apostles of the new faith did not impose continence, but they made it clear that men must not become slaves to the 'sinful flesh'.

The morals of the Byzantine Empire were not at first very high; pagan ideas lingered for centuries and even when Christianity completely permeated the Eastern Empire, kings and queens, nobles and the rich set themselves above its commandments. Society was rigid and formalistic; cruelty and lust, murder and intrigue were in many ways the dominant factors of everyday life.

Marriage, if barely tolerated by the apostles of asceticism, was at the same time considered indissoluble. The great code of Justinian, that gigantic legal system of the sixth century, regulated the public and private life of every individual and laid down the grounds for divorce with painstaking detail.

The wife could divorce her husband in five cases. First, if he was a party to a conspiracy against the State—or knew of it but did not denounce it;

The baptism of Constantine, who imposed the moral dogmas of Christianity upon the Byzantine Empire

second, if he made an attempt on his wife's life or failed to disclose plots against her; third, if he attempted to induce his wife to commit adultery; fourth, if he accused his wife falsely of adultery; and finally, if he took a woman to live in the house with his wife or, after warning, frequented a house in the same town with any other woman than his wife. Legally this put an end to concubines and prostitutes. That it achieved neither is another proof that lawgivers are seldom successful when they run contrary to human nature.

The husband had seven grounds for divorce. If his wife failed to disclose to him plots against the State; if she committed adultery; if she attempted or failed to disclose plots against her husband's life; if she frequented banquets or balls with other men against her husband's wishes; if she remained away from home against the desire of her husband (except in her parents' house); if she went to the circus, theatre or amphitheatre without the knowledge of her husband; and finally, if she procured an abortion. The husband evidently could get rid of his wife more easily than she could free herself. The papal canon law allowed six grounds for divorce: adultery or unnatural offences, impotency, cruelty, infidelity, entering a religious order, and consanguinity. The code prohibited divorce by mutual consent except in three cases: when the husband was impotent; when either husband or wife desired to enter religious orders and, lastly, when one of them was in captivity for more than three years.

This law was not very effective; declining Roman morality and the long Oriental influence made divorce by collusion all too frequent. So Justinian modified his code. Very well, he said, you can get a divorce—but if you are so anxious to get rid of each other, you must forfeit all your property. One third of the property went to the State, one third to a religious establishment and one third to the children of the marriage.

The Church was much concerned with marriage between even distant relations. Christianity argued about the union of a man and his deceased wife's sister for almost eighteen hundred years. To the modern mind it seems a rather stupid fuss over nothing. But just as there were bitter wars, causing the deaths of tens of thousands of people, over the identity or similarity (*homousion* or *homoiusion*) of Christ and God, so tiny points of dogma or practical rules for sexual, moral and social behaviour caused bishops and learned abbots, monks and lay-priests to argue long and fiercely. The Catholic Church was painfully and slowly evolved, its universal tenets gradually gaining authority over the majority of Christians.

The tale of Eudocia is a story of Cinderella—without the slipper. Her beauty raised her to the imperial throne; an apple proved her downfall. Though Gibbon is sceptical about the truth of the story, it is certainly a good indication of Byzantine morals at the time of Theodosius II who ruled from 401 to 450.

Eudocia was the daughter of Leontios, an Athenian philosopher who was still a pagan four centuries after Christ. She was very beautiful and her father had given her a classical education, a thorough literary and philosophical grounding. When he died, he left his whole fortune to his son; Eudocia, he thought, would need no dowry as she was beautiful, virtuous and learned. Thrown upon her own resources, Athenais (her pagan name: the other she took when she was baptised) decided to go to Constantinople to try her fortune. She became a maid of honour to Pulcheria, the Emperor's sister; in order to obtain this post, she also had to become a Christian. Her erudition apparently frightened off her suitors and she began to worry whether, with all her accomplishments, she would die an old maid. But Pulcheria was so fond of her that she persuaded her docile brother to fall in love with the fair Athenian. Theodosius II married her though she was seven years his senior.

Twenty years after her wedding-day Eudocia was accused of a 'criminal passion' for a handsome officer of the court named Paulinos. She was almost fifty but her passions had not cooled, and Paulinos was no youngster himself.

On the feast of Epiphany, as the Emperor was going to church, a poor man presented him with a phrygian apple of extraordinary size. Everybody admired it and Theodosius had his treasurer pay the poor man 150 gold byzants. Then he immediately sent the apple to his wife—who, in turn passed it on to her lover, Paulinos. But the courtier apparently did not appreciate the gift of the Empress and, being ignorant of its origin, offered it as a present to the Emperor. When Theodosius returned from church he found the perambulating apple on his table. Naturally he asked his wife what she had done with the apple. She replied with delightful simplicity that she had eaten it. Eudocia was exiled, and in order to keep up appearances, she went off on a pilgrimage to Jerusalem—having presumably learned the lesson that apples were to be eaten and not given away.

The most famous woman in Byzantine history is the Empress Theodora, wife of Justinian, the great law-maker and conqueror, the most brilliant organizer the Eastern Empire had known, and she started humbly enough. She was an actress—of a

Theodora, an actress and courtesan whose beauty and intellect raised her to the position of Empress of Byzantium

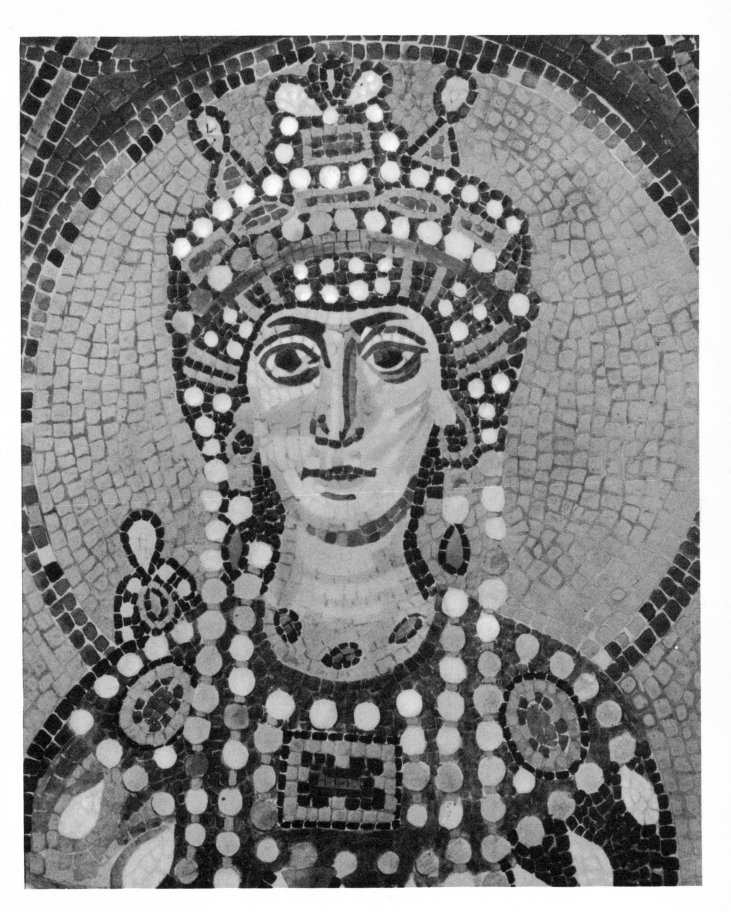

The Emperor Justinian, who changed the law so that he could marry a circus harlot

peculiar kind. 'She neither danced nor sang,' Gibbon tells us, 'not played on the flute; her skill was confined to the pantomime arts; she excelled in buffoon characters; and as often as the comedian swelled her cheeks, and complained with a ridiculous tone and gesture of the blows that were inflicted, the whole theatre of Constantinople resounded with laughter and applause.' A female clown then, but a singularly beautiful one: 'Her features were delicate and regular; her complexion, though somewhat pale, was tinged with a natural colour; every sensation was instantly expressed by the vivacity of her eyes; her easy motions displayed the grace of a small but elegant figure'—a figure she was quite willing to show off, for she appeared dressed in nothing but a narrow girdle, an early version of the G-string.

She was an actress and a courtesan of great popularity, and considerable discernment in lovers. Procopius, in his ribald and outspoken *Anecdotes*, said of her: 'After exhausting the arts of sensual pleasure, she most ungratefully murmured against the parsimony of Nature.'

Her first husband (through we do not know whether they were actually married) was Ecebolus, who became Governor of Pentapolis in Africa. But he soon discarded her (he found her both expensive and faithless) and she had to work her passage home to Constantinople. There, like a skilled actress, she assumed a more decent character. Her pretended chastity and her beauty attracted Justinian, the nephew of the Emperor Justin. And though the laws of Rome expressly prohibited the marriage of a senator with any non-patrician, particularly an actress, and though the Empress Lupicina did everything to prevent the union, Theodora did not rest until the law was rescinded and soon afterwards they were married. When Justinian later ascended the throne, the circus clown and harlot became Empress of Byzantium.

She proved a great empress; courageous, wise and far-sighted. She was cruel and merciless, but she never betrayed her husband. She lived with Justinian for twenty-four years, and died of cancer. 'The irreparable loss was deplored by her husband,' Gibbon writes, 'who, in the place of a theatrical prostitute, might have selected the purest and most noble virgin of the East.'

In a way Theodora symbolized the pagan world merging into the Christian era, the hedonist, amoral individualist becoming a staunch upholder of the Church and all she stood for. Justinian was the great lawgiver of this age; but at the same time he was the lover who cared nothing for the beloved woman's past or reputation, and defied his own

Empress Eudocia, who deceived her husband Theodosius II and was exiled for her infidelity

world and class to find fulfilment for his love. He put her on a pedestal, set her on a throne—and in exchange she helped him loyally to keep his empire.

THE CELIBATE PRIESTS OF ROME

The Roman Empire lasted a thousand years. Gibbon began his monumental work with the Antonines and ended it with the fall of Constantinople to the Turks. These turbulent centuries saw the great migrations of a dozen nations; the emergence of the Germans as partial heirs of the Romans; the development of the great Byzantine Empire with its stiff formalism, tremendous hierarchy, its crimes, glories and rather narrow culture. Vandals, Goths, Franks, Anglo-Saxons appeared on the stage of history and the Huns terrorized the West for several decades. The Franks introduced the idea of the *civitas Dei* and renewed the idea of the Occidental Roman Empire under German leadership. The Carolingians reached their great glory in Charlemagne, whose heirs became the founders of present-day France and Germany. The dark, turbulent ages made everything fluid and uncertain; the heritage of Greece was lost and only in the monasteries and nunneries did the dim light of culture and knowledge remain alive.

The now established Christian Church found that the struggle against the 'sinful flesh' could not be relaxed for a moment, even among their priests, if the principles of St Paul and his followers were to be maintained. A thousand years passed before the celibacy of clergy was established—and even then it only became the dogma of the Roman Catholic and not of the Greek Orthodox Church.

During the first three centuries of the Christian era, celibacy was not compulsory for the lower grades of the clergy. In the fourth century however, the pressure began to grow stronger; it was firmly proposed that married priests should put away their wives—or at least live in 'white' (sexless) marriages. The debate continued for another three hundred years. Near the end of the seventh century the Council of Trullo still confirmed the custom that allowed married priests to live under one roof with their wives; only when he was consecrated as a bishop must his wife take the veil. In 1018 Pope Benedict declared that children of the clergy must be perpetual serfs of the Church; a little later wives of the priests were degraded to the level of concubines. Pope Leo IX formally insisted on the chastity of all priests; those who disregarded this were to be branded as heretics. In 1059 laymen were forbidden to hear Mass from any priest who had a woman in his house. Gregory the Great's influence

Theodosius II; he gave his wife an apple—and received it
back from her lover
Below: Pope Leo IX, who demanded the chastity of the
priesthood

dominated the Council of Rome in 1074, when all
commerce between priests and women was finally
branded as 'whoredom' and all those who still
lived with their wives were commanded to put
them away at once. So it took a thousand years
for celibacy to become obligatory, and even then
concubinage continued almost openly, and the
scandals in monasteries and convents were almost
innumerable.

STATUES OF SEXUAL VENERATION

All this time the legacy of the pagan world remained
alive both within and outside the Church. One of
the strangest proofs of this survival was the trans-
formation of the god Priapus into a Christian saint.
His statue was even introduced into churches, and
barren women turned to the disguised pagan deity
for help.

The city of Lyons had a saintly bishop called
Photin. After he died, piety, not unmixed with
superstition, held him in such high esteem that
hundreds made the pilgrimage to his grave, scraping
a little fragment from his tombstone and using this
pulverized sliver as a magic potion against all kinds
of disease. Later, barren women claimed him for
their own and the pious bishop was given the role
of Priapus. In Provence he was venerated under the
name of St Foutin de Varegas; votive offerings of
wax *phalli* were made to him. The ceiling of his
chapel was filled with them and whenever there
was a strong breeze, the strange offerings performed
an even stranger dance overhead. In 1585, when the
Protestants stormed the town of Embrun in Southern France, they found among the relics of the
principal church a male member that belonged to the
statue of Saint Foutin. Barren women used to
rinse this with red wine (a survival of the pagan
libation), caught the wine in a vessel and preserved
it until it turned into vinegar. Then it was used as
saint vinaigre in the preparation of salads. In the
ancient city of Le Puy the symbol of St Foutin's
statue was a phallus-shaped stake. Childless women
scraped a bit off the wood, pulverised it with wine
and sipped it as a precious panacea.

A heavy iron post known as the Leonhardsnagel
(also phallic in shape) was set up in Innenhofen
next to the chapel of St Leonard. This was too
hard to be scraped off—the barren female pilgrims
contented themselves with embracing and kissing
it in pious transports. Replicas of this post were set
up in many other districts of the Austrian and
German Alps.

The statue of St Arnaud did not need scraping.
He was one of the truly modest saints. He wore
an apron around his middle which was lifted only

when the lady pilgrims arrived. It was sufficient to lose themselves in the dedicated contemplation of the revealed symbol; they could count on the intercession of the saint to give them babies galore.

St Gilles, St Regnaud and St Guerlichon were also supposed to be most efficient in such matters—though it is somewhat difficult to discover why.

The magic part of St Guignoles statue never wore away though it was being scraped and rubbed for centuries. This saint had his own chapel near Brest, with his wooden statue. The phallic character was represented by a stake which was pushed through the appropriate part of the image. If the projecting part wore off through the use of the believers, the stake was moved a few inches by some well-aimed hammer-blows from the back, and once again became operative for a generation or so.

The phallus procession of Lavinium was an ancient one. In the small town of Trani in Southern Italy the tradition survived until the middle of the seventeenth century. A statue of Priapus was carried in solemn procession around the town. It was an antique sculpture—perfectly unequivocal. The venerable symbol of fertility reached to its chin. It was known as 'Il santo Membro'.

The Adamites of Amsterdam, a religious sect of heretics who claimed that its members were re-established in Adam's state of original innocence

LISTS OF LOVE

KNIGHTS OF THE ROUND TABLE

A PLETHORA of myth, fact and fairy tale, told in France and England for the last few hundred years, were gathered by Malory, in the early 15th century, and presented as *Morte d'Arthur*. This classic and roisterous tale of action and intrigue among chivalrous knights, while being 90 per cent fairy tale and set hundreds of years after Arthur's death, has become startlingly real for generations of Englishmen, and represents the epitome of the age of chivalry.

In this world of 'parfait' knights and beauteous damosels there is often less morality than in a barnyard. When King Uther lay with Igraine, the Duchess of Cornwall who bore him Arthur, she was still a married woman—though Malory makes much of the fact that the Duke had been actually killed *three hours before* Igraine committed her adultery. However, at that time she did not know that her husband was dead.

But this was only the beginning. Arthur had an incestuous affair with his half-sister, begetting Mordred upon her. Again the great king could plead ignorance of this family relationship; but he certainly knew that she was King Lot's wife and not *his*.

Even Merlin's wisdom was no shield against feminine guile. For, as Malory puts it, 'he fell in a dotage on the damosel that King Pellinore brought to court and she was one of the damosels of the lake, that hight Nimue. But Merlin would let her have no rest, but always he would be with her'. The lady was getting tired of the wizard's attentions and would have nothing to do with him because 'he was a devil's son.' And in the end she tricked him into using his own magic against himself and Merlin was 'shut in a rock under a stone and there died…'

Fair women were a snare and a delusion more often than not. Morgan le Fay, King Arthur's sister and King Urien's wife, had a lover named Sir Accolon whom she 'bribed with her body' to poison her royal brother. But Sir Accolon confessed the 'foul design' and thus it was foiled. Morgan le Fay next tried to kill her husband; again she failed because her son intervened. 'Ah,' said Sir Uwaine, 'men saith that Merlin was begotten of a devil, but I may say an earthly devil bare me.' The charming and persistent would-be murderess pleaded for her life and promised to mend her ways —but her repentance did not last long. Next she set out to steal the precious sword Excalibur and though she only got the scabbard, even that was a serious loss to good King Arthur. Later—for Morgan le Fay was just as persistent as she was wicked—

Launcelot defending himself against twelve knights in Guinevere's bedchamber

she sent Arthur 'the richest mantle that was ever seen in that court, for it was set full of precious stones as one might stand by another, and there were the richest stones that ever the king saw'. It was meant as a peace-offering; but Arthur was suspicious and had the woman who brought it try it on for size. 'Forthwith she fell down dead and never more spake one word after and was burnt to coals…'

Nor were the Knights of the Round Table models of chastity; they were for ever coming upon married ladies who were about to deceive their husbands—or had already done so. Sir Gawaine was asked by Sir Pelleas to help him win the beautiful Lady Ettard. But instead of carrying out this unselfish commission, he seduced her for himself and Sir Pelleas found them in bed together. He did not harm them but 'his heart well nigh brast for sorrow'.

Launcelot was in love with Queen Guinevere, though we are led to believe that their love was blameless. But it was the same Launcelot who summed up the knightly view about love and chastity: 'Fair damosel,' he tells a lady who rebukes him because he refuses to love women. 'I may not warne people to speak of me what it pleaseth them; but for to be a wedded man, I think it not; for then I must couch with her, and leave arms and tournaments, battles and adventures; and as for to say for to make my pleasaunce with paramours, that will I refuse in principle for dread of God; for knights that be adventurous or lecherous shall not be happy or fortunate unto the wars… And so he who that useth paramours shall be unhappy, and all thing is unhappy that is about them…'

Fine words; but they were seldom put into practice. Even the great Tristam was a faithless fellow; betrothed to the Fair Isolde, he soon forgot her at the court of King Mark, his uncle. Both the old king and Tristam fell in love with the same married lady, the wife of Sir Segwarides. Uncle and nephew fought over her and almost killed each other. Tristam however, was a doughty fellow because after winning the fight, 'he and his lady supped lightly, and went to bed with great joy and pleasaunce; and so in his raging he took no keep his green wound that King Mark had given him'. He bled all over his mistress's bed which made Sir Segwarides, to say the least, suspicious. And so Tristam had to fight the husband after having fought his uncle—and all for the favours of the same lady.

One could go through the entire *Morte d' Arthur* and pick a hundred similar instances about

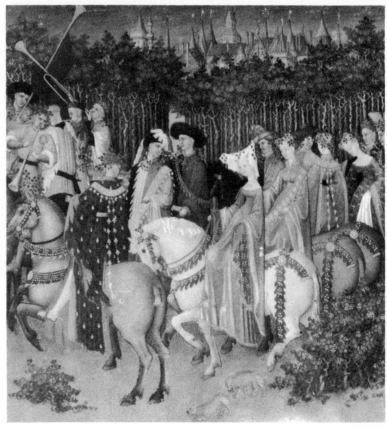

A knight's accomplishments had to include hunting: (below) bear-hunting; (right, above) deer-hunting; (right, below) hawking

the rough-and-ready moral code of chivalry. Of course it would be foolish to take Malory's book and the other Arthurian romances for gospel truth. The Arthurian morals are really the morals of the people who recorded all this; they projected them into the works of poetic imagination, bridging the worlds of Wales and Brittany, of England and Scotland. Sir Tristam and Sir Pelleas, Guinevere and Morgan le Fay were not entirely imaginary characters, because Malory and the others had their living counterparts in front of their eyes.

THE AGE OF CHIVALRY

Chivalry, with all its outward forms and manners, was born in France. No one really knows how or why it started. Many suggestions have been put forward, but none of them are really strong enough to explain such an extraordinary and isolated phase in the history of love.

The people who lived in the carefree, frivolous Provencal castles were concerned with love largely as if it were a party game—or the science of dilettantes. This tradition was adopted by the aristocracy of Northern France as well. Poets composed argumentative verses on the joys and sorrows of love. The judgments in these weighty questions were sometimes recorded; Andreas Capellanus used these to compile his *De Amore*, the code of knightly love. This was the origin of the *cours d'amour*, the tribunals of love which were supposed to hold formal hearings under the presidency of some high-born lady. Poetic practice was regulated by the same strict etiquette as the emotions of love—the Provencals actually made no difference between the two, and the textbooks of poetics were called *leys d'amore*, lays of love. The poets had no professional pride, they did not consider their poems literature (they hardly ever wrote them down) but part of the 'service of love'. Poetic conventions, like conventions of love, were part of court etiquette.

Courtly love was the idealization of woman as a superior being. It began as little more than an affection, a literary pastime — but it grew into a philosophy of love that shaped the manners of all Europe, and has had an effect on sexual morals ever since.

Woman became the adored, the worshipped; she accepted the knightly homage as a service. This service needed no reward. Whether the knight fought on her behalf, wrote her poems, or bore her colours on overseas crusades, an expectation of reward would have brought the whole façade crashing to ruins. Woman was too pure, too ethereal, to feel any amorous instincts of her own.

Gradually a hierarchy of knighthood developed;

Richard I leaving the Holy Land

but even the most distinguished feudal lord considered it a slight if he were not accepted as a knight, and various classes of knighthood were evolved.

'Seven chief virtues' were expected to be possessed by a knight. He had to be an adept at riding, swimming, archery, fencing, hunting, chess and verse-making. (A somewhat limited collection of accomplishments.) He also had to speak foreign languages—but it wasn't necessary for him to be literate. For instance, Wolfram von Eschenbach, could not write. He dictated his great Parsifal epic to his scribe.

The problem of the knight's reward might seem a delicate one for our own age. But for the medieval lovers it caused far less worry. There was not a definite convention in this regard. While most knights were willing to forego any reward other than a token, some demanded a full return of their love. It seems that courtly adultery was not considered to be serious. According to the 'laws of love' formulated by Andreas Capellanus, in most cases the knight's recompense was fairly liberal petting or 'love-play' without actual intercourse. Later the ascetic elements became more pronounced.

Jaufre Rudel, Duke of Blaya, fell in love with the Countess of Melisande without ever having seen her. He was stirred by reports of her charity and other virtues brought back by the pilgrims from Antioch. He composed beautiful poems addressed to her; then became so consumed with longing that he took the Cross and sailed for the East. On the way he fell ill; and at Tripolis was left for dead in his quarters. The Countess, hearing the story, hurried to his bedside and took him in her arms. The noble knight revived, gave thanks to God for prolonging his life until this moment, and then died in her arms. The Countess buried him with great honours in the church of Tripolis and, prostrated with grief, retired to a nunnery the very same day.

THE TROUBADOURS

One result of this courtly game was the wandering minstrel—the troubadour. There was nothing he desired, it seems, but to wander in the countries of Europe singing the praises of his adored and unattainable lady. This, of course, was supposed to be a matter of complete indifference to the lady herself. When the lovestruck minstrel sighed and sang beneath her own balcony it was not required of her that she even notice. It was reward enough for the courtly lover that he was performing in her service. The glimpse of a langorous hand and arm, were a great delight, but it would have been a presumption to expect it.

The lady could only be a married one of noble descent. There is no mention of any maiden in the poetry of troubadours. Marriage and love were unassociated and even incompatible. 'We declare and affirm that love cannot extend its domain over husband and wife,' said Marie de Champagne. 'Marriage does not absolve anybody from the duties of love,' decided Andreas Capellanus. In the eyes of medieval aristocracy marriage was a matter of practical considerations, increase of property and begetting of heirs. It could be an affectionate union, but could hardly compare with the exciting love of an unattainable object.

The essence of the troubadour's love was not hopelessness (for it could happen that the lady returned his feelings) but *distance*. It could be a physical, social or moral distance—but distance there had to be.

How did woman, the lovely creature, respond to this? Well, she liked the adoration, the thousand-and-one chivalrous services and tributes to her beauty and her virtue. She loved the love-sick troubadour sighing and singing under her balcony. She smiled graciously when her handkerchief or her scarf were carried aloft as a 'favour'. But one sometimes wonders if she did not become a little bored with all this idealization and stepped down from her pedestal rather more often than we are led to suppose.

Sometimes the troubadours forgot the laws of chivalry and the truth slipped out. In the *Roman de la Rose*, that long cautionary epic, Jean de Meung made no bones about his views on feminine chastity and constancy. In a sweeping statement he said: 'You have been harlots, you are harlots and for ever you shall be harlots...' The ladies of the court of Philip de Valois became most indignant about such free-and-easy words. Poetic licence was one thing—to call them *all* whores was quite another. For the poet had been rather unwise. If he had called only *some* of them harlots, they would have kept silent; each and every lady could have decided that it was her best friend to whom this referred. But this vile slanderer had to be punished. The ladies set an ambush for him and decided to give him the beating of his life. Jean de Meung saw there was no escape; he only asked for one favour: let him be permitted to choose the one who was to strike the *first* blow. After some hesitation, the favour was granted. Whereupon the impudent minstrel perverted the Biblical parable to his own ends. 'Let her who is the biggest whore among you strike me first,' he grinned.

The ladies exchanged quick glances of dismay—and let him go. Philip de Valois was so amused by

'A Lady Crowning her Lover', from a 14th Century French ivory work

the quick-witted, impish fellow that he had a tapestry woven to commemorate the incident.

The debunking modern historians point gleefully to the vast difference between the dreams and realities of troubadour life. Most minstrels were vassals or liegemen of their ladies' husbands; such a great lord would take the poor knight or burgher's son into his service and it became the minstrel's duty to popularize his master's policies, to increase his prestige by proclaiming his wife's beauties. For these services he was rewarded not by the lady's embraces but by far more prosaic gains: clothes, bed-and-board, cash, maybe a small fief. Under such circumstances, the historians claim, one could not take seriously whatever the troubadour sang about himself and his lady. His tribute was simply a paid panegyric. The amorous troubadours were

not such ecstatic lovers; their passion was just poetic fiction; the ladies' gentle kindness a polite lie.

This is far too harsh and unjust an analysis; much too sweeping a generalization. There were certainly poor troubadours whose social and financial position differed little from those of the despised jongleurs (jugglers)—and their love for the Great Ladies was obviously verbal juggling. But there are many distinguished names in their ranks whose bearers could not be accused of sighing and singing for gold. In any case, it would be difficult to imagine that husbands paid the poets in those days in order to make their wives the talk of the court. The lists of love were real enough, as a hundred reasonably well-documented tales bear witness. And even legend and fanciful imagery have been found to have their roots in fact.

The chastity belt, a gruesome contraption, has drawn the attention of humourists since its invention. In a Dürer engraving, (below) the locked-up wife steals from her husband's purse to purchase a spare key; (right) the husband receives the key while behind the bed a servant sells a duplicate key to the wife's lover

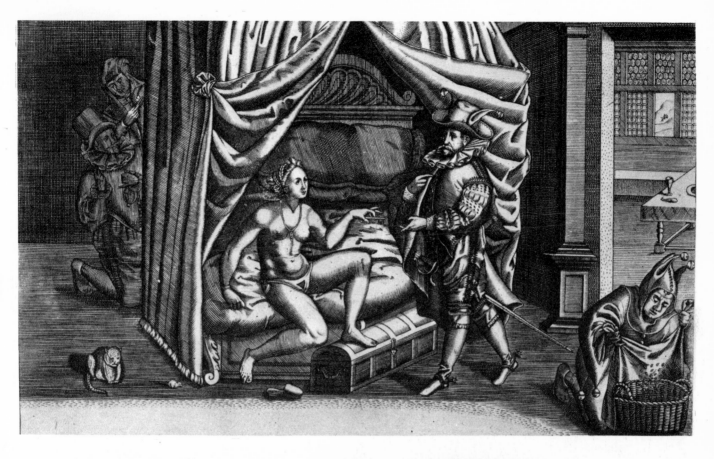

THE GIRDLE OF VENUS

The crusading knights were no plaster saints; and if a few of them set out with a high aim, a pure heart, for every one of this sort there were maybe a score who used the opportunity of indulging, as Villehardouin puts it, in 'robbery, whoring and the gratification of their selfish lust'. Many of the crusading armies had married Syrian, Palestinian, Byzantine, Egyptian wives, and Hilaire Belloc ascribes the degeneration of the Crusaders' Empire to their union with 'half-breed women' and the loss of fertility which climate and dissipation caused.

But if the valiant knights misbehaved under alien skies, what about the wives they left behind? Not being particularly honourable themselves they ascribed none to their wives. And so was born the idea of the chastity belt. It was a metal girdle, encircling the pudenda, which left only a small opening for the woman to perform her necessary non-sexual functions. It was closed over the hips by a lock to which only the husband possessed the key.

This barbarous contraption derived straight from the *Odyssey* in which Homer described how Hephaistos forged a girdle to prevent his wife Aphrodite from deceiving him—*after* she had cuckolded

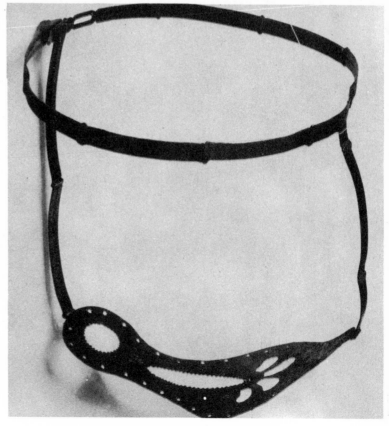

Philip I, excommunicated for living with another man's wife, made his peace
with the Pope—and continued to live with her

Philip I's grandson, forced to honour his marriage to Ingoberg, kept her in prison for thirteen years

him with Ares. But the Greeks did not dream of turning the fable into fact. Two thousand years later the Florentines did so, however; and it spread from Italy throughout Europe under the name of the 'girdle of Venus' or 'Florentine girdle'. In Spain, always conservative, it was still in use early in the nineteenth century. There were, of course, innumerable jokes about spare keys and the ways ingenious ladies found to rid themselves of such inconvenient shackles.

With or without chastity belts, women would not be denied the pleasures of love. When King Boleslav II of Poland took his nobles to campaign in Russia, he stayed away so long that the wives began to fret and grumble. When this did not help, they decided to seek consolation where they could find it—in the arms of their menservants. The news of their infidelity reached the camp of the king. Jealous and worried husbands began to desert in droves. The king, who had an important war on his hands, became furious and rushed home to clean up the situation. The knightly families all had a bastard or two to show by then. King Boleslav gathered all the babies and had them taken to one of the nearby forests there to perish or survive as luck would have it. For the adulterous women he designed a peculiar punishment: to mark their shame, they had to nurse puppies! Nor could they leave the house without carrying a small dog in their arms.

The Polish ladies suffered in silence. But with typical feminine ingenuity they turned their punishment into fashion. Soon all women, guilty or not, were going about with small dogs. Naturally they chose the smallest breed available. True or not, some historians maintain that this was the origin of lapdogs.

LOVE AMONG THE ARISTOCRACY

All we know of burghers and serfs must be based on general implications; few, if any of them, were important enough to be recorded individually in the chronicles unless they were criminals or heretics. The medieval history of love is unavoidably the history of the great, the famous, and therefore that of a comparatively small group.

Philip I of France decided to discard his wife Bertha. They had been married for almost twenty years when Philip fell wildly in love with Bertrada, the daughter of Simon de Montfort. Bertrada was married to Fulk Rechin, but this was no impediment to the king who simply carried off the lady and decided to marry her. The French bishops refused to attend such a sacreligious ceremony—but a priest was found to perform it. Whereupon Pope

William the Bastard came to England to claim the crown. The Battle of Hastings has been immortalized in the Bayeaux Tapestry

Urban II excommunicated the king. Bertha died soon afterwards but as Bertrada's husband was still alive, the papal ban could not be withdrawn. For ten years Philip lived with the lady who was the wife of two men—and then, for merely political reasons, he made his peace with the Church. The Pope had to save his face—so he made the king promise that he would never meet Bertrada in the company of 'non-suspect' persons. Philip was quite willing to make the promise—as long as he was not expected to keep it. Not only did he continue living with Bertrada but even took her on a visit to her first husband who must have been a very complaisant one.

Philip Augustus, the great-grandson of Philip I, found himself in the same quandary as his ancestor.

His first wife died and he married a Danish princess, Ingeborg, mainly in order to acquire the Danish claims against England and to spite Richard I whom he hated. But the Danish lady must have had the same effect on him as Anne of Cleves had on Henry VIII—one look and he said: 'I can't bear this woman'. This happened on the morning of their wedding-day; not without difficulty, Philip Augustus was persuaded to go through with the ceremony. But a few years later he fell in love with Agnes, daughter of the Duke of Meran. He defied the Pope, who refused to annul his union with Ingeborg, and married Agnes. He was immediately ex-communicated—and Philip Augustus must have taken this more to heart than his great-grandfather, for he agreed to put Agnes away and recognize

Ingeborg again as his lawful wedded wife. He did it with bad grace, for he kept her in prison for thirteen years. The Danish princess, however, must have been rather tough for she survived her husband by a further thirteen years. Agnes of Meran, if we are to believe Drury, died of grief when she was discarded.

THE NORMANS IN ENGLAND

The greatest man of those times was William the Conqueror—known as The Bastard. His father, Duke Robert of Normandy, had seen Arletta, the daughter of a tanner of Falaise, washing linen in a little brook under the castle walls and fell in love with her. She bore him his only son, out of wedlock.

William was often taunted with the shame of his birth, but never twice by the same man. When the rebellious townsmen of Alencon hung out raw hides along their walls in scorn with cries of 'Work for the Tanner!', William replied by tearing out the eyes of the prisoners he had taken, cutting off their hands and feet and flinging them into the town. He was rather touchy on the subject of his parentage. But the tanner's grandson conquered England and established his dynasty for centuries.

William's second son, Henry, married Matilda, daughter of King Malcolm of Scotland. This marriage had to overcome a certain difficulty—Matilda had taken the veil. However, the lady was more than willing to forget this trifle. She had been veiled in her childhood, she asserted, only to save her from the insults of the rude soldiery who

Robert of Normandy, whose affair with a tanner's daughter
produced the conqueror of England

The Conqueror's son Henry, who married Matilda of
Scotland undeterred by the fact that she had taken the veil

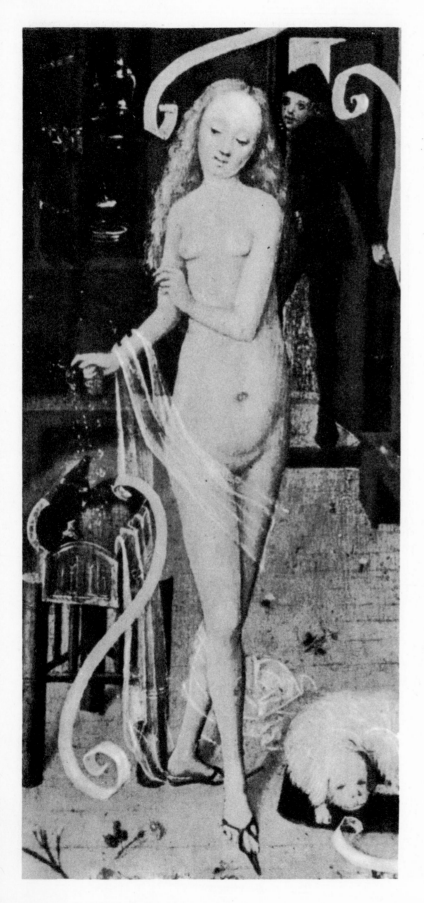

infested the land; she had flung the veil from her again and again and had yielded at last to the unwomanly taunts of her aunt, Christina, Abbess of Romsey. Pleading her case in the presence of the saintly Primate Anselm, Matilda said, 'I wore the veil, trembling as I wore it with indignation and grief. But as soon as I could get out of her sight I used to snatch it from my head, fling it on the ground and trample it under foot. This was the way and none other, in which I was veiled...'

So, probably, were thousands of other girls, whether of noble or common blood. Matilda was declared free from the bonds of the nunnery and married to Henry. But the majority of girls who disappeared in the cloisters ended their lives without a husband—though not necessarily as virgins.

During the first three centuries after the Norman conquest of England, there existed the strange constitution of 'double monasteries', which put rather too great a trust in self control. One of the most famous institutions was the Gilbertine, founded in 1148. Gabriel d'Emilianne recorded: 'He (Gilbert) in a short time got thirteen cloisters built which 700 monks and 1,100 nuns lived together, separated only by the thickness of a wall. This hermaphroditic order, consisting of both sexes, soon produced worthy fruit. For these holy virgins, nearly all of them, became pregnant...'

Nunneries were far from safe and tranquil heavens. More often than not they were invaded by soldiers, and the nuns turned into doxies.

The marriage customs of these Norman times embraced many of the native traditions. 'Nowhere has marriage by purchase assumed such repulsive forms as in England,' Ivan Bloch declared. 'The origin of this barbarous custom goes right back to the Anglo-Saxon era.' According to Jeaffreson, in his *Brides and Bridals* this was due to the economic value a daughter represented. She not only did the cooking, but made her father's clothes and helped on the farm. Marriage by purchase, therefore, was in the interests neither of the woman, nor the suitor, but solely in those of a father with marriageable daughters. The law fixed a girl's value according to her rank. A widow, understandably, was worth only half as much as a virgin. But she was obliged by a law of Canute to remain unmarried for at least twelve months after the death of her previous husband; otherwise she lost whatever she had inherited.

A young husband might return his wife to her father, a law that King Ethelbert had proclaimed, and demand the repayment of the money spent if, on 'close inspection' he found her in a different condition from that which the seller had admitted.

On the other hand breach of promise meant that the bridegroom not only forfeited the wedding price—he had to pay a fine as well. King Alfred had decreed that whoever had intercourse with a virgin was obliged to buy and marry her; or in the event of the father not agreeing to the marriage, at any rate pay her value in money. If a free man dishonoured the wife of a free man, he was forced to pay the full 'weregeld' and also *to purchase another wife* for the wronged husband and bring her to the house. Unscrupulous fathers sometimes sold the same daughters to a dozen different men!

After the Norman invasion public morality declined even further. Anglo-Saxon simplicity and crude but straightforward customs yielded to vice of all sorts. 'Neither the morals of Englishwomen were much more restrained, nor was their character much more modest than that of the Frenchwomen,' remarks Alexander. 'The same indecent familiarity was remarked in their public and unbridled excess in their private behaviour. During the Christmas festivities nearly every nobleman entertained his vassals of both sexes, and a neighbouring clergyman was usually appointed by him to preside over these

According to the Jena Codex, the dignity of priests was not always in evidence

extravagantly lustful and indecent revels. He was, according to the character of his office, usually designated the 'Abbot of Misrule'. In the houses of the great were usually to be found rooms for the sewing and embroidery maids. The name that was given to these rooms, in accordance with the use that was made of them, became in time synonymous with that of a brothel. Indeed, so shameless were all men of position in those days that even the clergy did not hesitate to have inscriptions put over the doors of these rooms, plainly showing their purpose...'

According to an account in Fox's *Acts and Monuments*, the English priesthood kept for itself more than 100,000 harlots (who in the medieval dialect were known as Lemmans from the French *l'ammante* beside the 'numerous women they seduced in the confessionals'. Of the English Kings of this period, it is said that Henry I, Henry II and Richard I lived in open polygamy and had more illegitimate than legitimate sons and daughters.

When knights were bold in Britain, it seems, they jousted with equal zeal in the tournaments and in the bedchambers.

An ivory mirror case of the 13th century is decorated with an allegorical scene of *a cours d'amour*. In the top section, Cupid, the god of love, wounds with his arrow those who render homage to him. In the lower section lovers discourse together.

REBIRTH OF VENUS

Previous page: 'The Birth of Venus' by Alexandre Cabanel

Below: Flemish illustrations to *Roman de la Rose*, circa 1500. Venus and her team of doves; the Lover attains the Rose; God of Love, and Lover

ROMAN DE LA ROSE

THE most important poetic form of the late Middle Ages was the amorous allegory, and its final convention was shaped in the 13th century by the *Roman de la Rose*. The first quarter of this didactic poem was written by Guillaume de Lorris early in the century; the rest by Jean Clopinel de Meung in the second half of it. Guillaume de Lorris respected the conventions of courtly love, but (as befitted an intellectual) he did not depict them in lyrics or an epic; instead, equipped with Ovid's *Ars Amatoria*, he set out to write a text-book of love dressed in allegory. His characters became deeply rooted in the consciousness of his age: Hope, Sweet Thought, Ugly Mouth, Favourable Reception and their companions formed the mythology of the late Middle Ages, and one of

'The Sleeping Venus' by Giorgione

them, *Leal Souvenir*, was the subject of Jan van Eyck's famous painting.

Jean de Meung, who completed this textbook of love, was more interested in teaching than in love, of which he held no high opinion; he had the sober burgher's contempt for such knightly fancies. He valued women very low; only the mendicant friars, the constant targets of the late Middle Ages, stood lower in his esteem. He used the allegory of love to expound his philosophy of life. The celibate monks and nuns, Meung declared, sinned just as much against Nature as the lechers—all were sinners who did not fight against universal mortality by serving the survival of the race. The *Roman de la Rose* ends with Venus setting the fortress of love on fire, and the Lover plucking the Rose—chastity yielding to the flames of passion.

Today, having lost the taste for allegory and didactic poetry, we can hardly understand the amazing popularity and influence of this work. Churchmen argued for and against the poem, which had thousands of partisans and permeated the imagination of the age. It was one of the bridges that led from medieval darkness into the light of the Renaissance.

DANTE AND BOCCACCIO—SACRED AND PROFANE LOVE

One of the greatest men in the dawn of the Renaissance was Dante Alighieri, and his *Vita Nuova* is a monument of this new chapter in the history of love. In order to clarify the meaning of his verses, he told the strange story of his life and of his love for Beatrice with a peculiar mixture of allegory

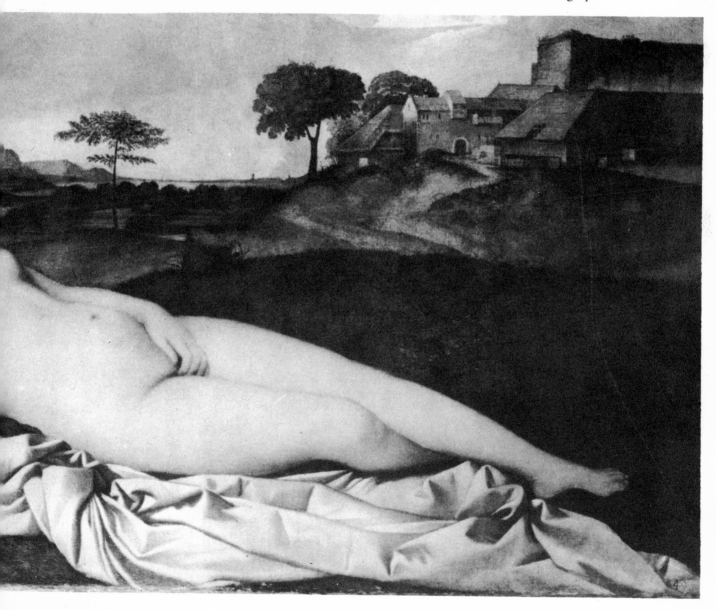

and biographical truth. Beatrice is at one and the same time the teen-age daughter of the Florentine Folco Portinari, and the symbol of some immense, indefinable idea. When she walked down the street, said Dante, she ennobled all who met her; whoever she greeted was atremble; the sinner paled and sighed over his guilt. When Beatrice died, Dante wrote a letter to the princes of the earth to notify them of the great loss the world had suffered.

The Divine Comedy was also begun by him to sing the praises of Beatrice, placing her among the saints. The transcendental emotionalism of the medieval soul, of medieval love poetry, reached its highest expression in this extraordinary allegorical story. Dante's beyond-the-grave desire remains the great symbol of spiritual love—a love so pure that its partners could meet only in eternity.

But Dante was not typical of the Renaissance, and most poets and artists were beginning to reject the idea of spiritual love. Earthy sensuality and freedom in love was the new fashion. Husbands were born to be cuckolded; women to be embraced. There is no need to look far for proof of this conviction; a quick look at the contents of Boccaccio's *Decameron* amply furnishes it. Here are synopses of three of the stories:

'Sacred and Profane Love' by Titian. It is interesting that the clothed woman represents profane love, whilst the naked one depicts sacred love

Dom Felice instructs Fra Puccio how to attain blessedness by doing a penance. Fra Pucio does the penance and meanwhile Dom Felice has a good time with Fra Puccio's wife.

Madonna Filippa, being found by her husband with her lover, is cited before the court, but by a clever and jocund defence acquits herself, and brings about an alteration of the statute.

Tedaldo, being in disfavour with his lady, departs from Florence. He returns in the guise of a pilgrim, and manages to make his lady see her fault. Her husband who had been convicted of slaying him, he delivers from peril of death, reconciles him with his brothers—and thereafter discreetly enjoys his lady.

For every tale with an unhappy outcome, there are ten that end happily—usually for lovers. Never is the slightest blame attached by the author to any lady for bestowing her charms upon a lover, and much fun is made of the deceived husband. Ladies are, however, denounced if they are hard-hearted and withhold the pleasures of love from their gallants. Boccaccio presents a gay, reckless, amoral world, full of humour and pleasure-seeking

Dante sees Beatrice for the first time

Below: Rossetti's painting 'Dante's Dream' shows the sentimentalism of his attitude
to love

cynicism that has come a long way from Dante's tormented spirituality. He recognized, long before Kipling, the truth about the Colonel's lady and Judy O'Grady being sisters under the skin.

Boccaccio himself met the great love of his life in the Church of San Lorenzo, Naples. She was a striking beauty with glorious red-gold hair—Mario d'Aquino, illegitimate daughter of Robert I, King of Naples, and the Countess of Aquino. The meeting of Fiammetta, the Little Flame, as Boccaccio promptly named her, with the French-Italian adventurer was the beginning of one of the most famous romances in history.

Fiammetta was of royal blood, even if born on the wrong side of the blanket. Her grandmother was Queen Maria, a Hungarian princess, wife of Charles II, King of Naples. Boccaccio was alarmed when he discovered the high birth and even higher connections of the woman he loved. But Fiametta was quite pleased with the handsome and well-educated poet's wooing. Their affair was no secret; she introduced Boccaccio into her father's court and the young man became one of King Robert's favourites.

When after 17 years of happiness his aging father recalled Boccaccio to Florence to look after his business interests, he left Naples filled with foreboding. He felt it was the last time he would hold her in his arms. And his fear proved well-justified. By the time he returned to Naples in 1348—it was longing for the Little Flame that brought him back—Fiametta would have nothing to do with him. She left the city and kept away during the whole of his visit.

So Boccaccio returned to Florence. Here he became an envoy of the Republic. Once he was sent to Ravenna to take ten Florentine gold pieces to Sister Beatrice, daughter of Dante, who lived in a convent. On another occasion he was sent as special representative to the Pope in Avignon.

In 1362, almost fifty, he still dreamed of the bitter-sweet memory of his Fiametta. Once again he set out for Naples. There was no trace of his Little Flame. Sadly, in remembrance of those happy days, he began to gather the old, spicy stories he had used to entertain the court. He had 'borrowed' most of them from the Indian Panchatantra, the Arabian Nights, and especially from the works of a Portuguese Jewish physician named Moses Sepharda, who later turned Catholic and became a missionary among the Jews. But if the stories were old, the way of telling them, and the spirit animating them, were entirely new and delightful.

Fiametta's memory persisted. Boccaccio was almost sixty when he visited Naples for the last

DOMINVS IOHANNES BOCCACCIVS

Confuetuer? et
e ferme et aure
ronifeur qui
font aucun ·
long et fabou
rieur eternin · ont de couftu
me foy arrefter et a fune ·
foie torcher la fueur de fe
vifage · et a fantir foie met
tir uu feuue fardeaulr w:
affegier fe corps a fantir
foie prendre fe vent frez et

fouef et boire vin ou eaue
vour amufer fa foif · et
fi ont de couftume preferme
ce ronifeure de vouir et a
venter combien if ont fait
de eternin apree ce quif; de
tonine fe de aucun no
table lien vont if fe font
puitie · If recordent entre
eulv fe nombre et fee noms
de chifteaulr de rumere
de ulfece · de montampice

Boccaccio also wrote the book of *Famous Women:* The two illustrated are Thisbe,
with the dead Priamus, and Sappho

Charles the Sixth, in one of his fits of madness, being calmed by his mistress Odette de Champdivers

time. Perhaps he was lucky that once again he missed his old love; the contrast between the passionate past and the dreary present would have been painful. The aging poet roamed the city, trying to invoke the scenes of his youth and his love. And when he died in December 1375, it was Fiametta's name that trembled on his last breath. Not even death could quench the Little Flame.

INTRIGUES IN FRANCE

Louis, Duke of Orleans, was a warrior and politician, but he was far more famous as a lover. He had a special liking for married women, and courted them as assiduously and professionally as he hunted boar and deer.

One afternoon he happened to entertain a high-born lady. Unfortunately her husband walked into the apartment to pay his respects to the Duke. He had come at a very inopportune moment, for the lady was as naked as Eve. But Louis, never at a loss for a daring strategem, probably remembered what ostriches were supposed to do in moments of danger. In a single swift movement he covered the lady's head with the silken coverlet and threatened the husband half-jokingly that he would fare ill if he tried to unmask the lady's incognito. The courtier, of course, swore to respect the Duke's amorous secret; but he did use the opportunity to inspect the lady with close interest.

The same evening, in bed with his wife, he told her that he had never seen such hidden charms in his life. And he spent a long time in trying to guess who the mysterious beauty might have been. Probably the lady helped him in the guessing-game. If it was dark in the conjugal bedchamber she would not even have had to keep a straight face.

After Charles VI had gone mad, having exhausted 'all the pleasures, all the emotions, from those of debauchery to those of the field of battle', the royal power was exercised by his two brothers, the Dukes of Burgundy and Orleans. These two were deadly rivals; they both thirsted for power—and their ambitions were bound to clash sooner or later. But the French court whispered of a 'non-political jealousy'. The Duke of Orleans was a famous lover—he belonged to the 'kiss-and-tell' sort, and liked to brag of his conquests. One day he complained that all the walls of his bedroom were covered, not an inch of space remained; for it was his custom to have a miniature painted of every lady whose favours he had enjoyed.

One day the Duke of Burgundy paid this voracious lover an unexpected visit. And as he looked around in his co-regent's bedchamber, one of the portraits he noticed bore his own wife's likeness.

The Duke of Burgundy was assassinated on the Bridge of Montereau, at the end
of a long family feud following his cuckolding by his brother

He was a man of considerable self-control; he swallowed hard and said a polite goodbye. But not much later, on a dark November night, as the Duke of Orleans left the Hotel Montaigu mounted on a mule, a group of assassins fell upon him suddenly. They stabbed him to death; and the Duke of Burgundy, wearing a red cap which hid his eyes, came out of a nearby house to make sure that the blow had not failed.

The feud of the two great families that followed this assassination split the whole of France; the two parties of Burgundians and Armagnacs killed, tortured and plundered each other. The English, called in to help, added to the devastation; and the unhappy country almost went under in the long civil war. The Duke of Burgundy himself, invited to an interview with the Dauphin at the bridge of Montereau, was stabbed to death by Tannerguy Duchatel and the prince's servants.

This was the dark side of Renaissance love, recurrent tragedy born of passion and hate.

CHAUCER'S ENGLAND

In the Middle Ages England was called the 'Paradise of Women'. Not because they were entirely free to do as they pleased (the moral standards of Britain in the 13th and 14th centuries were infinitely higher than those of France and Italy), but because they were considered far more as human beings than their continental sisters. When the Merchant Guilds rose up, women were freely admitted to them, and many guilds had as many women members as men. Breweries were almost entirely in the hands of women—just like the sale of beer at inns.

Women enjoyed considerable freedom even in the nunneries. They must have, otherwise the prioress of the convent of Appleton in Yorkshire would not have been asked to see to it 'that none of your sisters use the alehouse nor the waterside, where scores of strangers daily resort'. The Roman Church had gradually developed the indissolubility of marriage as a sacrament, but in England this principle was applied for only a comparatively short period before Henry VIII broke away from Rome. And as the king set the fashion in changing wives, on the introduction of Protestantism divorces again became daily occurrences.

Prostitution was well developed in medieval England. William Walworth, mayor of London, owned a good many *bagnios* (most of the bath-houses in England had developed into brothels, hence their name) in the reign of Richard II and 'farmed them out' to Froes of Flanders. Both Lord Mayor and the Flanders 'entrepeneur' enjoyed fat profits. During Wat Tyler's rebellion the brothels were

An open-air theatre occupies the top storey of a medieval house of prostitution, whilst the inmates are soliciting on the street below; Below: An illustration from Chaucer's *The Merchant's Tale*

destroyed; but Henry VI again passed ordinances for the same places and houses. Henry VII closed them for a season but even that grim Tudor king could not fight human nature and they were opened up again. They were all sign-posted with colourful names; one was called *The Cardinal's Hat*, perhaps in honour of the priests who frequented them.

On the whole sex was a healthy and vigorous preoccupation of the British in this period; there was little perversion or effeminacy. Their sensuality was unashamed and it was not until the Restoration began that an appalling coarseness became general in sexual relations. The English writers of pre-Elizabethan times preferred to call a spade a spade, an adulteress a wanton woman without much embroidery. 'From Chaucer to Marlowe and Shakespeare,' as Ivan Bloch pointed out, 'there was a great deal of obscenity but it was naïve obscenity…' Thomas Wharton, in his *History of English Poetry*, said that in England all through the Middle Ages 'not only were the worst offences against chastity allowed and taken for granted, but even the most shameful evils were regarded as harmless. It was only the conscious improvement in living that led to the discovery of new evil pleasures; at the same time, it led to the prevention, in the matter of sex, of the enormities that occurred in the Middle Ages.'

A 15th century engraving of mixed bathing in Holland, with musical entertainment provided

Bawdiness, both frank and implied, is well represented in *The Canterbury Tales*. The Wife of Bath's Tale tells the story of the woman who had buried five husbands.

'For God so wisely be my salvation,
I loved never by no discretion,
But ever folwed min owne appetite,
All where he shorte, longe, blake or white;

I toke no kepe, so that he liked me,
How poure he was, ne eke of what degree..'

She was angry with her fourth husband for deceiving her—not because he loved another woman but because he witheld from her what she considered her due:

'My fourthe housbond was a revelour,

The Wife of Bath and the Miller, (opposite) from Chaucer's *The Canterbury Tales*

This is to say, he had a paramour,
And I was yonge and ful of ragerie,
Stubborne and strong, and joly as a pie..'
Metillius, the foule cherl, the swyn,
That with a staf by raft his wyf hir lyf
For sche drank wyn, though
  I hadde ben his wif,
Ne shuld he nat have daunted me fro drinks:
And after wine of Venus most I thinke.

For al so siker as cold engendreth hayl,
  A likorous mouth most han a likerous tayl…'

Yet when the erring husband returned to her,
she could not resist his amorous advances—confess-
ing naïvely the reason:

'But in our bed he was so fresh and gay,
  And so well therewithal he ciude me glose,

When that he wolde han my belle chose,
That though he had me bet on every boon,
He coude win agen my love anoon.'

Edward III succeeded his murdered father when he was fifteen and reigned fifty years over England. He was a great king and a highly amorous one. Froissart tells us how, when the king visited the castle of Wark during the absence of its owner, the Earl of Salisbury, he was fascinated by the charms of the Countess and started immediately to woo her. Froissart declares that the Countess found the right way of keeping the royal suitor at bay. 'Ah, right noble prince, for God's sake, mock nor tempt me not,' she pleaded. 'I cannot believe that it is true what you say: nor that so noble a prince as you would think to dishonour me and my Lord my husband, who is so valiant a knight and hath done your Grace so good service…'

At that, according to the chronicler, 'the king departed, all abashed'. But Jean le Bel, in his

Chronique, has a different tale to tell. 'That night,' he relates of Edward III, 'he entered the chamber of the lady. He locked the door of the ante-chamber so that her maidens could not come to her aid. Then he took her and stopped her mouth so violently that she could but utter two or three cries and treated her as evilly and grievously as any woman had ever been villainously treated. He left her as one lying in a swoon and bleeding at the nose and mouth: then departed the next morning without a word.'

Whether it was Froissart or Jean le Bel who had the story right we have no way of telling. But both versions of the truth show the crudeness and violence of manners among the 14th century English and make us wonder whether the various rules and laws about morals and marriage were much applied or possessed any real force. The pious chroniclers said that the Black Death which scourged Europe more than five centuries ago was the punishment for the lechery of some of the rulers and nobles.

Pious chroniclers said that the Black Death which scourged Europe in the Middle Ages was the punishment for the lechery and immorality of those times

NEW HORIZONS

THE BORGIAS

THE woman who for centuries personified the lasciviousness and licence of the Renaissance was Lucretia Borgia. Countless tales have preserved her beauty, wit, cruelty and lewdness. There are, unavoidably, many contradictions in her story —for the Borgias had very articulate enemies who slandered them even when the truth itself was bad enough.

Roderigo Lanzol y Borgia, a soldier who later became Pope Alexander VI, was said to have seduced a widow called Vanozza dei Cattanei *and* her two daughters. One of the daughters bore him four sons, Francis, Cesare, Louis and Gottfreid, and one daughter—Lucretia.

According to some stories, Roderigo was not a soldier but a lawyer who deserted law for the Church when his maternal uncle became Pope in 1455. He was made a Cardinal a year later—a young, handsome most amiable man of 26 with polished and courtly manners. His tutor, Gaspare da Verona declared, 'He is a fine-looking, smiling, bright-eyed young man, with a distinguished manner of speech and winning ways. It is almost amazing how he can make the prettiest women fall in love with himself—attracting them as a magnet attracts iron.'

On June 11, 1460, Pope Leo wrote to him: 'My dear son, four days ago several Sienna ladies, inclined to light-hearted dalliance, gathered in

Cesare Borgia, son of the Pope, was made a cardinal on the same day as Alexander Farnese, who had procured his sister Guilia for the aging Pope

'He is a fine-looking, smiling, bright-eyed young man, with a distinguished manner of speech and winning ways. It is almost amazing how he can make the prettiest women fall in love with himself—attracting them as a magnet attracts iron'—Roderigo Borgia's tutor

Giovanni Bichi's garden...' The ladies and their escorts, including Cardinal Borgia, amused themselves with 'lewd dances', the Pope said, and 'did not forget a single variety of amorous seduction.. All Sienna talks of nothing but your behaviour. They invent innumerable pleasantries; it is a general topic in the bath-houses. You are the Chancellor of the Church, in charge of the See of Valencia and a member of the Consistory of the Cardinals. A Cardinal's life must be a model for everybody....'

But the young prelate did not reform. A few years later, at a meeting of the Consistory, Cardinal Jean Balue accused him loudly: 'You are a drunkard and you lead a scandalous life!'

Yet in spite of these excesses, the active industri- ous and highly intelligent Cardinal acquired a wide knowledge and an amazing practice in the affairs of the Curia. The fat livings which Popes bestowed upon him made him in time one of the richest Cardinals—and, at the age of 62, he was elected to succeed Innocent VIII in the Holy See. This elevation in no way curbed his sexual appetite, and his next mistress was the beautiful Giulia Farnese, whose blonde hair reached to her heels. She was procured for him by her brother Alexander, who was rewarded by being made a Cardinal on the very day that Borgia's own son Cesare was invested with the same high dignity. Later, Alexander Farnese himself became an occupant of the Holy See.

Lucretia was married off to Alfonso, Duke of

A rather oddly-dressed Lucretia Borgia dancing before her father, in this painting by Kaulbach

Bisceglia. Later, the Duke was murdered (Lucretia was said to have been implicated in the crime) and she wed the Prince of Ferrara.

The Borgias have been accused of every crime under the sun. Incest is one of them. Both the Pope and Cesare are supposed to have enjoyed Lucretia's favours. The Pope was said to have begotten a child upon her, both son and grandson to his happy father.

Burckhardt, a servant to Alexander VI, said in his diary that the apostolic palace had become a brothel, and a far more shameless brothel than a public one could have been. Lucretia was described as wife, daughter and daughter-in-law of Alexander. The last accusation was based on the alleged fact that one of her many husbands happened to be another son of the Pope.

Was this a true picture? Orestes Ferrara, a modern Italian historian, has produced an impressive array of documents and references to show that neither Cesare nor Lucretia were Pope Alexander VI's children. He denied that she was married to three different men before Giovanni Sforza. The three Spaniards who popped up in her life were only suitors, Lucretia's champion declared. And he dismissed the terrible charge of incest rather contemptuously.

'It originated in the sordid conflict between Giovanni Sforza and the Borgias, when the Pope, wishing to annul Giovanni's marriage with

Roderigo Borgia was elected to the Holy See at the age of 62—and shortly afterwards took the beautiful Guilia Farnese as his mistress

Provisions for the Convent by Jacques, illustrating behaviour which was 'entirely unpunished, except perchance by a small and secret fine...' (in a petition to Henry V)

'I spread my plumes, as wantons doe,   Agreeing to my wanton minde
Some sweete and secret friends to wooe;   At last my name in court did ringe
Because chaste love I did not finde   Into the ears of England's king.'

Lucretia, declared him impotent. Sforza replied with an abominable phrase, reflecting upon the aged pontiff's *intentions* towards Lucretia. But, grave as the subject was, the offended husband did not allege any actual fact. His outburst was meant to be an insult, not a calumny.'

To some people this might be too fine a distinction; but of course there is no proof for or against the horrible accusation of triple incest. According to Farrara, Lucretia never took part in orgies—she just loved 'innocent fun'. But there are no reliable witnesses, after five centuries, to decide what is the truth.

We *know* that Lucretia's first marriage was dissolved because of her husband's impotence. This was officially announced and the Pope even assembled the Consistory. It must have been a strange scene: Elderly Cardinals discussing whether Lucretia was maid or matron. Giovanni Sforza fought the suit vigorously; but by November (the proceedings started in June) he officially admitted his impotency. On December 19 the marriage was declared null. Lucretia was once more a maid. Six months later she married 17 year-old Duke Alfonso d'Aragon. The Pope appointed the young bridegroom Governor of Spoleto, Foligno and Nepi. They lived together for two years and she bore him a son. Then the Duke was assassinated. The crime was ascribed to Cesare; Ferrara defends him against the charge though he does not offer a solution to the mystery. Duke Alfonso was stabbed by hired assassins, nursed almost to recovery in the Vatican, then suddenly died. Contemporary records said that as he refused to bleed to death he was strangled in his bed.

Lucretia seems to have loved her second husband and was griefstricken at his death. She retired to the Castle of Nepi, but a few months later she was summoned back to Rome for she was to marry again. Her third husband was another Alfonso, Duke d'Este, eldest son and successor of Ercole, Duke of Ferrara. The marriage, according to all accounts, was happy. Lucretia died at the age of 42, in childbed.

Was she a monster, without honour and shame, this woman whose name still conjures images of lust and intrigue after so many centuries of history? Or was she a victim of her family's all-devouring ambitions? Or was she an innocent plaything of circumstance? We do not know. All we know is that she was lovely and clever; and in her the Renaissance of Italy became personified with all its glory and lust, all its murderous intrigues and shining examples of faith. Perhaps she was all of these things because she was a woman.

EDWARD IV AND MISTRESS SHORE

English monks of the 15th century were no better than their counterparts of the 14th, and there was much complaining about their wickedness. John Bromyard recorded with scathing anger in his *Summam Predicantium:* 'I will say plainly that they are consumed in gluttony and drunkenness, in couches—not to say in uncleanness—so that now the assemblies of clerics are thought to be brothels of wanton folk and congregations of play-actors....' And in 1414 the University of Oxford petitioned Henry V: 'The carnal and unchaste life of the priests scandalizes nowadays the whole Church, and their public fornications are entirely unpunished, except perchance by a small and secret fine...'

How much sympathy the victor of Agincourt had with such complaints we do not know. Certainly Edward IV, the first of the Yorkist kings, couldn't have been too much of a moralist—at least not according to Philip de Comines, who reported in his *Memoires:*

'Lovers' from 'The Ages of Man', a set of prints by Crispin de Passe

'An Allegorical Love-feast' by P. Pourbus

A syphilitic and (below) the treatment of syphilis. Two of the earliest known drawings on the subject

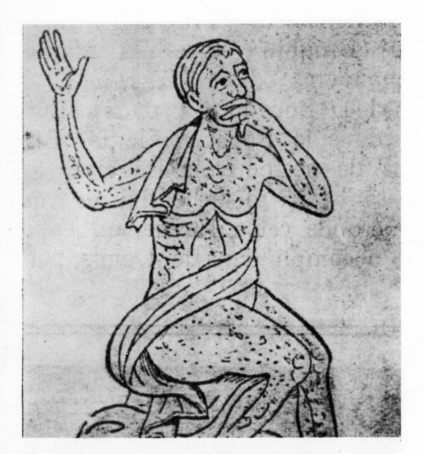

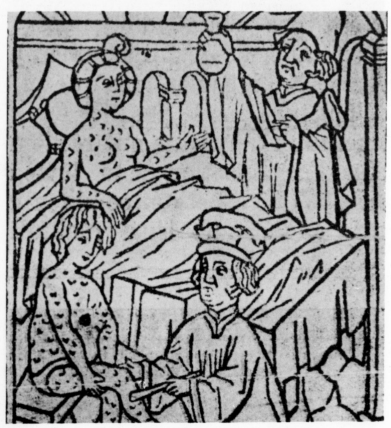

'That which greatly contributed to his entering London as soon as he appeared at its gates was the great debts this prince had contracted—which made his creditors gladly assist him; and the high favour in which he was held by the citizen's ladies, into whose good graces he had frequently glided, and who gained over to him their husbands, who, for the tranquility of their lives, were glad to depose or raise monarchs. Many ladies and rich citizen's wives, of whom formerly he had great privacies and familiar acquaintance, gained over to him their husbands and relations…'

This certainly must have been both a pleasant and efficient way of winning friends and influencing people.

Of Edward's many love affairs, the most lasting was with Jane Shore, wife of a London mercer. This was described with considerable gusto in songs and ballads, in one of which Jane is made to tell her own story:

'To Matthew Shore I was a wife
Till lust brought ruine to my life;
And then my life I lewdlye spent,
Which makes my soul for to lament.
In Lombard Street I once did dwelle,
As London can yet witness welle;
Where many gallants did beholde
My beautye in a shop of golde.
I spread my plumes, as wantons doe,
Some sweete and secret friends to wooe;
Because chaste love I did not finde
Agreeing to my wanton minde.
At last my name in court did ringe
Into the eares of Englande's king.
He came and liked and love requir'd,
But I made coye what he desir'd.
Yet Mistress Blague, a neighbour neare,
Whose friendship I esteemed deare,
Did say, I was a gallant thing
To be beloved of a king.'

Jane was easily convinced by the arguments of her procuress friend and became the King's mistress. Her husband left England in order not to be witness of her shame. Jane attained considerable influence at Court and was a lavishly charitable lady, so that the widows and orphans of London adored her. When, however, her royal lover died in 1483, Richard III persecuted her with grim tenacity. She was stripped of her possessions and her friends all turned against her. Even her old crony Mrs Blague showed her the door. Only one man, whose life she had once saved, stood by her—but was hanged for his pains. Finally, Jane Shore had to earn her living as a beggarwoman in the streets of London.

The ballad concluded with the following 'warning to wantons':

'You wanton wives that fall to lust,
Be you assur'd that God is just,
Whoredom shall not escape his hand,
Nor pride unpunished in this land...'

Towards the end of the century, a book published in Italy, *Relation of England* showed what Italians thought of the English as lovers.

'Although their dispositions are somewhat licentious, I have never noticed anyone, at Court or among the lower orders, to be in love. Whence one must necessarily conclude that the English are the most discreet of lovers in the world, or that they are quite incapable of love. I say this of the men, for I understand it is quite the contrary with the women who are very violent in their passions. Howbeit, the English keep a very jealous guard over their wives, though anything may be compensated in the end by the power of money...'

A pretty slander, hinting that English women did not find satisfactory lovers in their husbands and preferred foreigners; and if an English husband discovered his wife's infidelity, he could be bought off with money!

THE CLAP AND THE POX

The end of the 15th century introduced the most terrible scourges of love in all history. In December 1494, less than two years after Columbus and his crew returned from their first voyage to America, a new plague struck Naples. The first cases that were properly observed and described occurred among the French garrison—so that the illness was called *morbus gallicus*, the French sickness.

The real origin of syphilis has remained one of the unsolved mysteries of medical history. Early in our century a thorough attempt was made to discover the truth. Ivan Bloch's theory was that it originated in the New World, probably in what is called Haiti today; Karl Sudhoff claimed that it had existed in Europe before Columbus sailed on his voyage of discovery. But neither school of thought has provided completely convincing arguments. It is certain that the new plague (for it was new to all practical purposes) was introduced to Europe via the Mediterranean before it crossed the Alps. By August 1495 the Emperor Maximilian was forced to issue a proclamation about the *pose plattern*, the bad pox which he ascribed to divine punishment for human wickedness. Within three years, as the *Monumenta Medica* records, ten lengthy treatises were published about the new scourge. It was the Veronese physician Girolamo Fracastoro

Diane de Poitiers, mistress of Francis I and Henry II of France.
Below: Her bed at the Château d'Arnet, decorated with the initial and crown of Henry II

who gave the new disease its name in his didactic medical epic *Syphilieds, sive morbi gallici libri tres* (Verona, 1530). Characteristically, for little was really known about it, the very name was due to a misprint. Fracastoro took it from Niobe's son, Sipylus—whose name was spelled as 'Siphylus' in one of the editions of Ovid's poems. In the poem the Veronese doctor described how the shepherd Syphilus rebelled against the Sun-god because of the terrible drought that devastated the island of Haiti—whereupon Apollo sent this new plague of which the shepherd was the first victim! The French called it *mal de Naples* or simply *verole* (pox) until Jacques de Bethencourt suggested *morbus venereus*—and in time all diseases derived from sexual intercourse were called 'venereal' from their source. It was a long time, however, before syphilis and gonorrhea were recognized as separate illnesses.

This affliction provided the moralists and killjoys with a powerful weapon, though the primitive conditions of hygiene and medical knowledge made it possible for innocent girls and children to contract the disease. Still, those suffering from it were more often than not treated as criminals rather than sick people.

KINGS AND COURTESANS

The *Memoires* of Seigneur de Brantôme hold up a perfect mirror to the kings and courtesans of the 16th century. They could not be published until forty years after his death because they were so frank. Brantôme was an honest man; he did not flatter and he did not suppress. Almost one-third of his book on the *hommes illustres* and *dames galantes* is devoted to 'amorous ladies and cuckolded husbands'. Even so, he excused himself for being unequal to his work, for according to him the entire paper supply of the Paris Office of Records would be insufficient to relate even half of the available stories. 'If all faithless women and all cuckolded husbands would form a chain by clasping hands, this chain would circle the earth,' he wrote. And, having lived after Columbus, Pierre Brantôme already had some inkling of the length of the equator.

The first section of his '*Vie des dames galantes*' is devoted to '*Mari pardonnant à sa femme*'. In this he tells the story of a worthy Frenchman who returned from a long journey unexpectedly and found the conjugal bedroom door locked. By the time he managed to get in, his wife's lover had jumped out of the window and he found only the lady kneeling at the bedside, pleading for mercy. She argued and begged so sweetly that the revengeful husband dropped his naked sword, and by the

time dawn arrived they were on the best terms
possible. Brantôme evidently approved of such
leniency. He quoted the example of King Menelaus
and Helen of Troy as one that should be followed.

But if the husband had not yielded to the wife's
pleas, if he had killed her, he would have gone
unpunished. A French husband possessed this right
of taking the law into his own hands, and the
notorious Paragraph 324 of the *Code penal* preserved
the medieval spirit even up to our own day. A
woman taken in adultery can be killed and so can
her lover; it counts as justifiable homicide; the same
rule applies to the wronged woman, who can
execute her faithless husband and is hardly ever
condemned.

The great Renaissance king of France, Francis I
was often unlucky in war but always very lucky
in love. Gay, sensual, a patron of arts and literature,
he was a glorious monarch indeed. And Brantôme
says he cuckolded more husbands than any other
king of France.

Of course, there were husbands who did not like
this. But the courtiers usually resigned themselves
to the inevitable, and a good many were even
happy to have been chosen for such royal favour.
The motto of the French court was *royal blood
does not defile*. But there were simple burghers living

Henry IV meeting Margaret of Valois in the Gardens of Alençon

beyond the glittering circle of the court, who believed in old-fashioned morality and straightforward loyalty. They were less ready to accept the royal *droit du seigneur*.

There is a beautiful da Vinci portrait in the Louvre known as *La belle Ferronnière*. According to tradition it depicts a famous beauty, a smith's wife, heroine of a tragic adventure in the lovelife of Francis I. Actually, the model of this portrait had nothing to do with the smith's delightful wife; she was not even French but Italian. Some art critics claim that it represents a Princess of Mantua, others that it is a portrait of Lucrezia Crivelli, the mistress of Lodovico Sforza. The false legend arose because of the jewels worn by the lady in the painting: her forehead is circled with a narrow golden band from which hangs a small diamond. (This is said to have hidden a tiny scar.) Such ornaments are called in French ferronnières—and the singular of the word might also stand for the wife of a smith.

Modern authorities have dismissed her story as a fiction, yet writers of the 16th century proclaimed it as gospel truth. It seems that Francis I caught sight of the beautiful woman in the doorway of her husband's shop. This husband was either an artist in wrought iron or a merchant selling such wares, not an ordinary smith. Next day a courtier called at the shop. He tickled the lady's vanity by telling her that the Queen of France had noticed her remarkable beauty and would like to make her acquaintance. Would she call on Her Majesty at the Louvre. The inexperienced young wife swallowed the bait and set out with the courtier for the palace. Of course, the carriage took her instead to the Bois de Boulogne where Francis I had one of his secret hide-outs, a pavilion equipped for love's adventures. He was a handsome man and a king—the lovely Ferronnière did not cry for help. When she returned a few days later she told her husband the tale she had been taught to tell—that the Queen had found her much to her liking, kept her at court and that she could not defy royal wishes. The husband pretended to believe her. But he began asking questions and soon discovered the true state of affairs.

What could he do against the all-powerful King of France? Helpless, bewildered, he roamed the Paris streets for nights on end. And one of the daughters of the night gave him the answer. In the past, he had been a clean-living man. But now he bought love where he could find it, the more sordid the better. And before long he acquired the weapon of revenge. The gift of the back alleys of Paris soon reached the King—through *la belle Ferronnière*.

Historians are still wondering if Francis I died

of venereal disease at the age of fifty-three. Dr Cabanes, in his *Cabinet Secret de l'Histoire* denies it on the basis of the original records; but he quotes the words which the dying king repeated constantly: '*Dieu me punit par on j'ai péchè.*' (God is punishing me wherewith I have sinned.) The puzzle is still unsolved.

The difference between aristocratic and plebian love was described by Brantôme quite simply: 'Let the women of lower classes be like fixed stars —they must be always seen in the same place and remain constant. If such a woman moves and seeks variety, she deserves contempt and severe punishment like any other wanton. But a noble lady must be like the sun—she must give her warmth and her light to all...' Such a benevolent sun in the sky of the French court was Margaret of Navarre whom they also called Marguerite of Valois, the wife of Henri the Fourth.

When the Catholic princess wed Henri—at that time still a Protestant—Charles IX, her brother, hoped that their union would establish religious peace. 'Giving Margaret to Henri,' he said, 'I give her to *all* Huguenots.'' French courtiers quoted widely the royal words. Only they interpreted them in a different way. Margaret *did* belong to all Huguenots, they snickered—providing they were men.

This was an exaggeration—but if Henri was famous for his amorous adventures, Margaret repaid her husband's escapades with compound interest.

She had no difficulty in finding lovers; for she was not only beautiful, but witty and learned. Brantôme said that all the goddesses of antiquity could have been, at the best, only handmaidens to Queen Margaret's beauty. Whatever her style of dress, she always left her lovely neck and beautiful bosom bare for she knew that she had no right to deny the world the pleasure of seeing her charms. The most distinguished nobles of Europe visited the French court just to catch a glimpse of her; some waited two months before they were admitted to her presence. Don Juan d'Austria said of her: 'Though her beauty is more divine than human she is far more likely to lead men to damnation than guide them to salvation.' She was the undisputed arbitress of fashion. Once she used a material embroidered richly with gold. A single ell cost a hundred ducats, and fifteen ells were needed to make the whole dress—it was so heavy that, as Brantôme records, 'some ordinary little princess would have been crushed by it'.

Her individual taste was also applied to her sleeping habits. She had black silk sheets which set

Finally, Henry IV divorced Margaret and married Maria de Medici — for political reasons

off perfectly the dazzling whiteness of her body— she slept naked—and her bed was surrounded by hundreds of candles.

It was she who introduced to France the *verdagado*, the ancestor of the crinoline.

A rather doubtful story is that Margaret preserved the memory of her dead lovers by embalming their hearts, placing them in a golden box and keeping them in a secret pocket of her skirt. Gradually they increased in number and a whole chain of pockets had to be sewn into her skirt. When she undressed, she hung up these amorous relics near her bed.

There was little basis of fact for this story. Margaret had one tragic love affair with La Mole, who was beheaded for high treason. She got hold of his head—some say she collected it herself from the charnelhouse—and had it embalmed. She kept it constantly in her room in a special cupboard, took it out again and again and even kissed the dead lips. According to another version of this story, it wasn't La Mole but one of his accomplices, Coconas, who was also beheaded, and the embalming was done not for Margaret but for the Princess Nevers, the mistress of Coconas. Dumas described the double tragedy in his picaresque *La Reine Margot*.

Henri Quatre was just as amoral and amorous

as his wife; they understood each other perfectly. Once they stayed together at a provincial chateau. Henri smuggled in a certain Mademoiselle Fosseuse who was his current mistress—and very near her time of bearing a royal bastard. One night Margaret was awakened by her royal husband who offered a thousand apologies for the unexpected visit. But Mlle Fosseuse was suffering from birthpangs and he, as a mere male, could not help her. If Margaret would be so kind.... The understanding wife did not hesitate, but had the girl brought to her own apartments.

Later, when for political reasons Henri wished to marry Maria de Medici, Margaret herself smoothed the way to divorce. Henri was most grateful and wrote a letter bubbling with appreciation: 'Your kindness and understanding have moved me deeply. I hope God will bless our remaining days and we both shall be made happy by our love in God and the prosperity of France.'

There was plenty of love in Margaret's remaining days—even if it was not King Henri's. As the years passed, she had to use many aids to beauty, and all her footmen and lackeys had to be blond in order to supply her with hair for her wig. Among her later lovers were two pages, properly jealous of one another, and during a quarrel one of them was

stabbed to death. Even in her declining years Margaret could bring pleasure and pain into the lives of men.

THE PRIEST TAKES A WIFE

During the Reformation and Counter-Reformation the celibacy of the Roman Church again came into question; Protestants claimed it as a main cause of the Catholic Church's decline at this time. Melanchthon preached against celibacy; Zwingli, a secular priest at Zurich, actually married at forty, the first priest of the Roman Church who had dared to do so in five centuries. Martin Luther added insult to injury, when, as an excommunicated monk, he married a nun, who had deserted her convent with eight of her companions after reading Luther's books. It was a happy marriage that lasted 21 years and from which six children were born.

Within a single generation celibacy in the clergy disappeared from all the Protestant countries of Europe, though not without protest from the more orthodox. Erasmus, the great humanist who stayed in the no-man's-land between the two embattled religious camps, did not like married clergymen; he said that the great drama of the Reformation seemed to end in a stage comedy with monks and nuns casting off their habits and rushing off to weddings. In his *De Scandalis* Calvin accused Luther and others of starting a whole series of Trojan wars for the sake of women. Luther was regarded by his enemies as a sex-fiend, though by all available evidence he was only a healthy man who enjoyed a normal marriage, after a life of chastity. He saw in marital intercourse both a right and a duty for the partners; and he recognized divorce if the husband proved impotent or the wife sterile.

THE LUSTY TUDORS

England's rise had been continuous ever since the decline of the Holy Roman Empire began in the 14th century. The Hundred Years War only steeled her strength; and though the English Reformation began with a king's lust for a lovely woman, it ended in something stronger and far more important: the Anglican Church.

King Henry VIII was handsome, jovial, a lecher and a supreme egotist. That he had fundamentally a poor view of women is shown by the rather callous answer he gave when he was asked whether Jane Seymour's life or her child's should be spared. Henry replied that it should be the boy's, because he could easily provide himself with other wives.

But if he did not attach too great an importance to their survival, in other respects Henry was certainly a ladies' man. Raubutaux tells us that there

The two wives of Henry VIII who died on the scaffold. Anne Boleyn (left) and Catherine Howard

was a room in the royal palace with the inscription 'Room of the King's Prostitutes'. Gentlemen of considerable property did not blush to bear commissions for being Marshals of 'the king's whores'. Copying his royal master, Cardinal Wolsey had these words inscribed over the door of a similar apartment in his palace: 'The house of the harlots of his Excellency the Cardinal'. True to the ecclesiastical spirit, however, the inscription was in Latin.

Of Henry VIII's six wives, he had two executed for adultery; the first divorced because he suddenly discovered religious scruples (and also because he wanted Anne Boleyn); from Anne of Cleves he separated because she did not please him. Jane Seymour died in childbirth and only Katharine Parr survived him without coming to grief.

Only a few weeks after Anne Boleyn had a miscarriage she died on the scaffold. Chapuys, the Imperial Ambassador, sent a remarkable report to his master:

'The King (Henry) said that he believed that more than an hundred had criminal relations with Anne Boleyn. The newly created bishops encouraged her and taught her that according to their sect, it was allowable for a woman to

Anne Boleyn receiving proof of Henry's passion for Jane Seymour.
An engraving by George Cruikshank

'A LETTER WRITTEN BY HENRY VIII TO ANNE BOLEYN'

In debating with myself the contents of your letters I have been put to a great agony; not knowing how to understand them, whether to my disadvantage as shown in some places, or to my advantage as in others. I beseech you now with all my heart definitely to let me know your whole mind as to the love between us; for necessity compels me to plague you for a reply, having been for more than a year now struck by the dart of love, and being uncertain either of failure or of finding a place in your heart and affection, which point has certainly kept me for some time from naming you my mistress, since if you only love me with an ordinary love the name is not appropriate to you, seeing that it stands for an uncommon position very remote from the ordinary; but if it pleases you to do the duty of a true, loyal mistress and friend, and to give yourself body and heart to me, who have been and will be your very loyal servant (if your vigour does not forbid me) I promise you that not only the name will be due to you, but also to take you as my sole mistress, casting off all others than yourself out of mind and affection, and to serve you only. Begging you to make me a complete reply to this my rude letter as to how far and in what I can trust; and if it does not please you to reply in writing, to let me know of some place where I can have it by word of mouth, the which place I will seek out with all my heart. No more for fear of wearying you. Written by the hand of him who would willingly remain your

H. R.

ask for aid in other quarters—even among her own relatives—whenever the husband was not considered suitable or sufficiently strong enough to satisfy her sexual desires… At the Bishop of Carlisle's house, whilst supping with several ladies, he (Henry) showed great joy at the Concubine's arrest, and said to the Bishop: 'For a longe time back had I predicted what would be the end of this affair; so much so that I have written a tragedy which I have kept by me.' Saying which, he took out of his breast-pocket a small book all written in his own hand, and gave it to the Bishop, who, however, did not examine the contents.'

Chapuys' task was, of course, to paint a black

Mary Stuart and Chastelard

The Earl of Leicester with his wife, Amy Robsart...

... and with Queen Elizabeth. A favourite of Elizabeth for years, he was generally believed to have murdered his wife

picture of his Imperial master's arch-enemy. The story of a king who put himself at the head of his country's church in order to be able to marry his lady-love, only to end up by writing a tragedy about her alleged multiple adulteries, is very hard to accept. Francis Hackett, in his admirable biography of Henry VIII, claims that Anne was indicted 'not for unchastity but for unpopularity....' She was a true representative of the new generation of free-thinking women, which included Anne of Beaujeu, Isabella the Catholic and Catherine of Aragon; they were not cut out to be heroines and preferred playing with love to the mortal passions; and she cared more for variety than for the rigid self-possession and massive maternity of the old school.

There were no such doubts about Katherine Howard, whom Henry had called the Rose Without a Thorn.' On the scaffold she proudly proclaimed her love for Thomas Culpeper—a moving and beautiful defiance of those about to kill her:

'Brothers, by the journey upon which I am bound I have not wronged the King.

But it is true that, long before the King took me, I loved Culpeper. And I wish to God I had done as he wished me; for at the time the King wanted to take me, he urged me to say that I was pledged to him.

If I had done as he advised me, I should not die this death, nor would he.

I would rather have him for husband than be mistress of the world. But sin blinded me, and greed of grandeur, and since mine is the fault, mine also is the suffering and my great sorrow is that Culpeper should have to die through me. I die a Queen but I would rather die the wife of Culpeper. Good people, I beg you, pray for me...'

Henry was determined to make quite sure never to be cuckolded again. By an Act of Parliament any lady whom he might marry—if she was a subject— was bound on pain of death to declare any charge of misconduct that could be brought against her; and so was anybody else who knew or suspected anything, within twenty days on pain of perpetual imprisonment and confiscation.

The Counter-Reformation began with the great conclave that lasted, with interruptions, for eighteen years and sat in Trent and Bologna. It was this Council that made marriage a 'public and solemn act' and introduced the threefold calling of the banns and the three witnesses. Even more important, it demanded the consent of the parents, which gave them much greater authority over children than they had previously enjoyed. The civil autho-

rities backed up this Church policy by a number of laws, especially in France; sons and daughters marrying without paternal consent were automatically disinherited—and later such marriages were pronounced equivalent to rape, the penalty for which was death.

The Council of Trent reaffirmed the celibacy of the clergy and took steps against pornography and loose living; the representation of the nude in visual art was outlawed. This was why Michelangelo had such a fight with the would-be censors of the Sistine Chapel over the nudity of his gigantic Last Judgment: and he was only one of the many great painters who had to submit to ignorant and narrow-minded critics and patrons.

The second half of the 16th century was dominated by two women—Mary Stuart and her great, victorious rival, Elizabeth, the Virgin Queen.

Mary Stuart was surely one of the loveliest and most enigmatic women in history. The strange story of Pierre de Bocsozel de Chastelard who was sent over from France 'by permissions of distinguished position' in order to compromise the young queen, shows that Mary's weakness was known to her friends and enemies alike. After a life of amours, secret marriages and political intrigues, Mary was executed by her cousin Queen Elizabeth, in order to remove the only rival to her throne.

But to kill in order to achieve one's ambitions, political or social, was not so unusual in Elizabethan times. The Earl of Leicester, for many years Elizabeth's favourite, was generally believed to have murdered his own wife, Amy Robsart. It was also felt that the 'spouses of ladies in whom he took an interest had a strangely convenient habit of dying,' as Vaughan Wilkins put it. The Virgin Queen was the greatest riddle of the age. Was she virgin or wanton? Her enemies accused her wildly of 'unspeakable lust'. Cardinal William Aleen identified her with the 'Whore of Babylon' and called her 'an incestuous bastard, begotten and born in sin of an infamous courtesan.'

'With the aforesaid person (the Earl of Leicester)', thundered the Cardinal in his *Admonition to the Nobility and People of England*, 'and divers others she hath abused her body—against God's laws, to the disgrace of princely majesty and the whole nation's reproach—by unspeakable and incredible variety of lust, which modesty suffereth not to be remembered; neither were it to chaste ears to be uttered how shamefully she hath defiled and infamed her person and country... She could never be restrained from this incontinence, though the principal peers of the realm and others of high authority, as deputies

Gertrude Elliott as Ophelia. Shakespeare's heroines almost without exception show devotion and faithfulness to their husbands and lovers

from the whole parliament and estates, made humble suit and application to her, that she would marry and procure lawful heirs of her body to inherit her dominions after her...'

Elizabeth did not marry though she kept a whole string of royal suitors dangling. She had favourites, though no proof has ever been conclusive enough to discover how close she let them approach the royal bedchamber. Did she die a virgin? We do not know. Gaston Baty, the French playwright, offered the ingenious theory that in her girlhood she was so frightened by attempted rape that she could never bring herself to love any man physically. D. H. Lawrence had an even grimmer theory. According to him the royal families of England and Scotland were syphilitic—both Edward VI and Elizabeth being born with the inherited consequences of the disease.

'Edward VI died of it while still a boy, Mary died childless and in utter depression. Elizabeth had no eyebrows, her teeth went rotten, she must have felt herself utterly unfit for marriage, poor thing. That was the grisly horror that lay behind the glory of Queen Bess...'

Did this grim hypothesis explain why the Virgin Queen would or could hot bear children? Lawrence extended his theory to wider implications:

'England traded with the East and with America; England, unknowing, had opened her doors to the disease. The English aristocracy travelled and had curious tastes in love. And pox entered the blood of the nation, particularly of the upper classes who had more chance of infection. And after it had entered the blood, it entered the consciousness, and it hit the vital imagination....'

SHAKESPEARE'S WOMEN

By and large, Shakespeare's heroines are true to their chosen mates. Desdemona, accused of wantonness, might have been foolish in championing Cassio, but in reality she was as pure as the freshly-fallen snow. The lovers in *Midsummer Night's Dream* change allegiances during that wonderful and confused night; but it is the spell Puck puts on them, not their hearts that causes the change. Lady Macbeth might be an evil accomplice of murder but her loyalty to her Thane remains unshaken. Shylock's daughter turns against her father but not against her lover. Kate gives a lot of trouble to Petrucchio but the shrew is tamed in the end. Constancy in love is the true characteristic of Shakespeare's women—from Juliet to Ophelia, from Viola to Portia. Almost the only example of an adulterous wife is Hamlet's mother—and she seems to have little joy of it.

FROM DON JUAN TO CASANOVA

THE TRUTH OF THE LEGEND

DON JUAN was the Julius Caesar, the Alexander, the Napoleon of sexual conquest. Love, as such, did not interest him; he was concerned only with seductions—the more the better.

A romantic writer of the nineteenth century said: 'The lovely white bodies of women dying of love writhe around him. Across the corpses of their husbands, brothers, fathers, they crawl to the feet of this terrible conqueror—with their arms, sheathed in brocade, their beringed white fingers, they embrace the feet trampling on love and try to wash with their tears the blood from the merciless hands....'

This is a striking piece of purple prose. But was there ever such a superhuman master of women? Or, if his figure was purely legendary was there some basis for the belief that his type, the professional seducer, really existed?

The great myth of Don Juan was evolved from the real-life stories of two men—Don Juan Tenorio and Don Miguel de Manara. A Seville chronicle tells the story of the first.

'Don Juan Tenorio, a member of one of the most distinguished families in Seville, one night killed the Grand Master Ulloa, after raping his daughter. The Grand Master was buried in the Monastery of St Francis where the family had its vault. The Franciscan monks had been watching Don Juan's profligacy for a long time, and as there was no way of punishing him legally because of his high connections, he was lured into the monastery and killed there. Afterwards they spread the rumour that Don Juan had mocked at and insulted the Grand Master's effigy on the tomb whereupon the Statue dragged him off to hell.'

There was a Tenorio family in the 14th century, at Seville, and one of its members, Don Juan was an intimate friend of King Don Pedro the Cruel, sharing his orgies and wild adventures. But there is little more evidence than that. The original of the quoted chronicle has never been traced... and it sounds most unlikely that pious Franciscan monks would have punished a wrongdoer, however evil, by such extreme means. If that semi-legendary Don Juan really disappeared in the monastery, he was probably enticed there to be murdered by kinsmen of the Grand Master. And the frightened monks, in order to escape the blame, might have invented the story of the Statue. The importance of the two families involved probably encouraged people of the time to accept the story of the ghostly revenge without further investigation. The Don Juan of the Seville chronicle could only be described

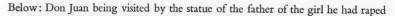

Below: Don Juan being visited by the statue of the father of the girl he had raped

A scene from the comedy *Don Juan* by Molière, which evoked violent disapproval and was suppressed within a month of its first performance

as an immoral, profligate savage who met his deserved punishment after one of his outrageous crimes. This story alone would not have been enough to give rise to a romantic legend.

Don Juan was reborn three centuries later. Tirso de Molina, the Spanish dramatist, published *The Seducer of Seville and the Stone Guest* in 1630. It was this play, probably based on historical sources and oral tradition, that created the Don Juan who has survived in literature and tradition. But it would not have survived without the story of the Count of Manara.

Don Miguel de Manara was beyond doubt a real, flesh-and-blood man. He was born in 1623, and at his death in 1679 was Abbot of the Santa Caridad monastery in Seville. He was a distinguished Seville nobleman who had led a spendthrift life and was especially famous for his amorous adventures. The details of his love affairs are little known; tradition has it that during his stormy career as a lover he succeeded in seducing a total of one thousand and three women. He kept a famous list of his conquests on which women of all classes figured in great variety. Those who believe the story maintain that the list still exists in the possession of the Manara family, but they refuse to publish it.

His list contained all classes of women from peasants to princesses. He even succeeded in seducing the mistress of the Pope. But he had still not achieved the highest conquest, so he decided to kidnap and seduce a nun—the bride of Christ. On the fateful night when he had prepared everything for the elopement, while waiting for the hour to strike, he fell asleep on a stone bench. Suddenly he woke to the strains of a funeral hymn; a grim, mournful procession approached him by torchlight. Hooded monks carried the coffin, and he asked one of them who was being buried. 'Don Miguel de Manara!' came the ghostly reply. He lifted the shroud in horror—and saw himself in the coffin. This was the turning point of his life. He repented of his sins, left the world and entered the Santa Caridad monastery. There he spent 17 years in mortifying his flesh, praying for divine forgiveness. For his exemplary piety he was elected abbot. When he died, miracles began to happen around his coffin; and it was even proposed that he should be canonized.

There are few authentic records of Don Miguel's love-life. A few words in his last will and testament were enough to build up the figure of a great lover. In this remarkable document the penitent sinner confessed that he had 'served Babylon and its prince, Satan, with a thousand abominations, pride, adultery, blasphemy, scandal and wickedness'. He asked to be buried under the threshold of the church and that his epitaph should read: 'Here rest the bones and ashes of the most wicked man who ever lived in this world.'

These moving and humble words only proved that Don Miguel had lived a sinful life before he turned to God. It does not particularly specify what these sins were. Adultery is mentioned, but without any emphasis; he merely included it among his 'thousand abominations'.

Was it this figure of a thousand (certainly a figure of speech) that provided the basis of the legend about the one-thousand-and-three victims of Don Miguel's amorous appetite? It is a question that cannot be answered with any certainty. For that notorious list is certainly a fiction.

Let's look at the facts. Don Miguel turned monk in 1662, at the age of 36. Let us assume that he began his career as a grand-scale seducer at the age

of 20, and so had 16 years to win one-thousand-and-three ladies. This meant 62 every year. Five women every month. Six days or less in which to gain the favour of each mistress, humble or proud, maiden or matron! An achievement that would have taxed the resources of a Hercules.

No, the thousand-odd frail ladies must be relegated to the realm of legend.

THE AGE OF GALLANTRY

The 17th century was the age of gallantry, born of the Renaissance and the romantic ideal of chivalry. Gallantry was a special relationship between men and women. Bedier-Hazard defined it as a special ideal of life—to turn love into a human and humane passion. Montesquieu called it 'a light and delicate pretension of love'. A less witty but more thorough analysis was: 'Gallantry is manifested by the constant attention that must be paid to the desires and

Louis XIII did not believe in gallantry. Once he expressed his dislike of a lady's dress by spitting at her

A scene from *Les Précieuses Ridicules* by Molière which mocks at the affected manners of the age
Below: 'It was my firm belief that it was impossible to win a lady's love until you had spent the regular amount of time in sighing, tearful lamentations, pleadings, and the writing of love letters' — Comte de Bussy

small whims of all females without exception, to strive incessantly to win their approval by proper flattery and services, by interesting and amusing them—finally to make oneself worthy of female company by elegant and tasteful raiment...'

The essence of gallantry was perhaps the polite fiction that polished and civilized courtiers were a little in love with *all* women, and behaved accordingly. It was during the reign of Henri IV (1589—1610) that the first French novel appeared, based on the idea that the most important thing in human life was not fighting but love. (Honoré d'Urfé: *Astrée*, Paris 1607). The characters in *Astrée* were peaceful shepherds who longed to lead a serene and happy life. According to them love was the supreme feeling, the mother of all that is good and beautiful. *L'Astrée* had a very considerable effect on French life and literature. According to Brunetière, whenever the writers of later centuries depicted love as a noble passion, purifying and ennobling souls, it was as a result of d'Urfé's influence. The book became the code of good manners, polished behaviour and gallantry towards women.

Louis XIII (1610–1643), was not exactly a follower of these principles. Once, during a court banquet, he expressed his dislike of the dress of a lady-in-waiting by spitting at her. But under Louis XIV one of the most perfect incarnations of the gallantry ideal, it became the general rule of life.

The Queen of France had an exceptional position. In most other courts, the sovereign's wife could not share her husband's table on ceremonial occasions. At the French court it was otherwise. When Christina, Queen of Sweden, visited Paris in 1656, the King seated her on his right. When Anne of Bavaria, Louis XIV's future daughter-in-law, arrived in France, the King would not let her kneel in front of him and made her sit beside him in the royal carriage, while the Dauphin was relegated to a minor place. And he doffed his hat to all women—including peasant girls.

Perhaps the best setting in which to observe *galanterie* was the Palais Rambouillet in Paris. The first *salon* was opened very early in the 17th Century by the young Marquise de Rambouillet, who had been disillusioned by the corruption of court life and created her own court. An intelligent woman, the mother of seven children, she succeeded in gathering the best of French society, and in her salon French intellectual life was given shape and guidance. But when the Marquise de Rambouillet died, her far less talented daughters inherited her famous salon, which soon became the headquarters of the *precieuses*. The gallantry of the drawing-room became nothing but an excessive sophistication carried to the extreme of stupidity, ornamented and elaborated by the fashions of the age. According to the *precieuses*, 'women were the ornaments of Nature born to be adored and surrounded by great emotions in exchange for which they offered friendship and respect'. And the cavaliers—at least in the salons of the Rambouillet ladies—seemed well content with this meagre fare. Their ladies were very fragile and sensitive, and some of them would faint away when any vulgar expression was used in their presence. Commonplace words were banished from the conversation and replaced by new, more refined synonyms. An outsider could never understand their talk, and Claude de Saumaise, the French classical scholar, compiled a dictionary of their language. For instance, the word *hand* was considered most vulgar, as ordinary people used it for manual labour. Therefore it was renamed *la belle mouvante* (the beautiful mobile). The word *mirror* was replaced by the much prettier expression *le conseiller des Graces*. An *armchair* was much too common—it had to be called *commodité de la conversation*.

The talk in these salons was exclusively about the perfection of ladies, and the totally satisfying

happiness pervading mankind through worshipping at their feet. Here is a letter which Guez de Balzac, one of the most respected writers of the age, addressed to Madame Rambouillet on the pleasant occasion of receiving a gift of perfumes from the lady:

'Roman poets have sung of the perfumes of Venus. But my gift has come from a more exalted hand than that of this common goddess; from the truly heavenly goddess of love, virtue itself which has now manifested itself to humanity by descending from the sublime heights. I cannot cease bragging about it to all and sundry. All human things, all the treasures of earth are dwarfed by it. And just as there can be no greater glory than your gift has created for me, there is no gratitude in the world that can be compared to mine. I can only express a small fraction of my emotions in words and most of them have remained within my heart.'

The ladies of the *precieuse salons* were playing a bloodless game of love, finding its expression in a literature of euphemistic and empty hyperbole. But many inexperienced and romantic youths accepted this literary game as meaningful. Bussy-

Louis XIV, the Sun King, with members of his family. Madame de Maintenon, the 'old procuress', is on the left

Three of the Sun King's mistresses: Maria Mancini, (below, right) La Vallière, (below, left) Louis persuading La Vallière to be untrue to her vows, (right) two pictures of Madame de Montespan

Rabutin, who in his maturity travelled a great distance from all this platonic nonsense, described his youthful passion for a pretty widow:

'I had such a ridiculous conception of the respect due to women that my beautiful widow might have died of a broken heart at my side if she had not realized my folly and hadn't encouraged me. For a long time I didn't even dare to acknowledge this encouragement. It was my firm belief that it was impossible to win a lady's love until you had spent the regular amount of time in sighing, tearful lamentations, pleadings, and the writing of love letters....'

THE COURT OF THE SUN KING

In his *Age of Louis XIV*, Voltaire describes the early loves of the Sun King. The nieces of Cardinal Mazarin, seem to have played an especially important part in Louis' youthful years, especially Maria Mancini. 'He was sufficiently in love with her to be tempted to marry her, and yet sufficiently master of himself to abandon her,' Voltaire says, and adds, typically, 'The victory gained over his passion was the earliest sign that he was born with a great soul.'

After the Mancini sisters, Louis had a series of mistresses. Most of them were married before they

won his favour, or were married off to some complaisant husband soon afterwards. Voltaire tells us about one suitor of Mlle de la Vallière. 'He had offered Mlle de la Vallière 200,000 livres, but she had indignantly rejected the offer before even she had any design on the king's affections.'

Saint-Simon relates in his memoirs the story of the Marquis de Montespan whose wife was another of the Sun King's mistresses. He was deeply in love with his wife and felt desperate when the lovely creature could not resist the royal Don Juan and yielded to Louis. In his bitter despair de Montespan put on deep mourning and asked for a royal audience. The King was not a very sensitive soul, and asked why his courtier was dressed in that fashion?

'Sire, I mourn my lost honour,' replied the Marquis.

This was tantamount to high treason; for some months the Marquis found himself in the Bastille, and afterwards was banished to his estates. But some years afterwards Louis XIV was gentlemanly enough to settle Montespan's debts to the tune of 200,000 francs.

Behind the façade of Versailles the precious conversation, the sonorous lines of Corneille and Racine, there was much naked lust and commercialized fornication. Mme Maintenon (whom Louis XIV married secretly) was nicknamed 'the old procuress' and she always had a whole harem ready for the Sun King's pleasure. Princesses did not scruple to act as 'mediators' between gallants and the ladies of the court. The royal bed was not often empty, though few of the royal mistresses succeeded in keeping the King's favour to the end of their lives. The liaisons often lasted several years however, and resembled, in many ways, normal marriages. Louis had four children by La Vallière and eight by Mme de Montespan. The children, like their mothers, were given high titles.

It was in France that the institution of 'kept women' was born and developed. They were called *mignonnes*, and they were passed from hand to hand until they retired with a fortune into 'private life'. They were much respected, received in the best company and had not the slightest difficulty in finding husbands. There were two types of *mignonnes*. The first were kept women who received their official lovers in the homes provided for them. The others were call-girls, who were summoned at any time, and often arrived in most luxurious carriages.

THE GLOOMY COURT OF SPAIN

In Don Juan's own country, under the centuries-long Moorish influence, women lived in an almost

Louis XV. He had seven children, and many mistresses. One of them was the Marquise de Pompadour (below)

harem-like atmosphere. When the husband was unable to watch over his wife he appointed a chaperone, a *duenna*. The daily existence of the Spanish court was frozen rigid by one of the strangest inventions of the human mind—Spanish etiquette. It was devised by Philip II in the second half of the sixteenth century. He bequeathed it to his successors together with an empire already bursting at the seams.

Spanish etiquette turned the persons of the King and Queen into divinities. And gods did not smile. All laughter and fun were banished from court. It was recorded of Philip IV that he laughed only three times in his entire life.

There was an elderly lady-in-waiting to the Queen known as Chief Lady Chamberlain. Her task was to watch over her Majesty with iron severity from morning till night, to see that etiquette was observed. 'The Queen of Spain must not laugh,' sounded the warning when the young Queen burst into laughter at the clowning of the court jester. 'The Queen of Spain must not look out of the window'—even though the window opened only on to the lonely garden of a monastery. When the Queen found much pleasure in her parrots and their idle chatter, the Lady Chamberlain wrung the necks of the unfortunate birds

Ninon de Lenclos, one of the Paris *mignonnes*

with her own hands. Once only did this old crone come to grief. During pregnancy Spanish custom permitted the young mother-to-be to satisfy any whim or appetite. The Queen took advantage of this and, when the hated woman presented herself for the usual hand-kiss, she slapped her twice,—and hard. 'I couldn't resist it...' she excused herself demurely, and the Chief Lady Chamberlain couldn't say a word.

In such an atmosphere ladies-in-waiting almost died of boredom. They also had their supervisor, the *Guardadama*, who, with suitable aides, watched over their morals. They had to live in the palace; but, to make their lives more bearable, the court rules permitted them to have one or more 'official admirers', whose official name was *galanteos de palaceo*. Such a cavalier could be married or single, old or young—it was all the same, for there could be no hope of any tangible reward for his services. His rights were simply to adore and serve his lady. In the whole year there were only a few days when he was permitted to enjoy the company of his *adorata*. The ladies-in-waiting were seen in public only on rare occasions at great court receptions, when the official cavalier was allowed to stand beside his lady and court her—naturally only within the limits of strict decorum. This wooing was given a peculiar official character by the privilege of such *galanteos* to keep their hats on in the lady's presence. This privilege, so it was said, was granted to the cavalier because he would be so dazed in the presence of his lady that he would have dropped his hat had he tried holding it in his hand.

For the rest of the year the *galanteo* was permitted to lurk around the palace and wait until his lady appeared for a moment at a window. Then he was able to declare his love, but only by signs. This sign language, according to Spanish tradition, consisted of the *galanteo* touching his handkerchief first to his lips, then to his forehead and finally to his heart. According to the memoirs of the Comtesse d'Aulnoy, the cavalier moaned so loudly on such occasions that he was heard at quite a distance.

In spite of all this, such an official courtship was considered a great honour. Old and young men alike intrigued and fought for the privilege; and those chosen heaped expensive gifts upon their ladies. The Comtesse d'Aulnoy asserted that during her visit to Spain more than one *galanteo* was completely ruined by this mania for giving presents.

LOW LIFE IN THE HIGH COURTS

Meanwhile England was passing through a bawdy phase of her history. After the reign of Elizabeth, and even during it, court morals were at a very

low ebb. One of the greatest scandals of 17th Century England was the murder of Sir Thomas Overbury, the poet and courtier. The great Francis Bacon led the prosecution for the Crown against Frances Howard, Countess of Essex, and Robert Carr, Earl of Somerset. Somerset, being in love with the Countess, planned to have her marriage annulled so that he could marry her, but Overbury, who up to this time had been Somerset's confidant in the amorous intrigue, opposed it. She was good enough as a mistress, Overbury told his friend, but unworthy as a wife. This led to a violent quarrel between the former friends, and Somerset and the Countess decided that Overbury had to die.

To achieve their purpose, they chose a somewhat complicated method. Overbury was appointed to an ambassadorship. In those days such a post was very unpopular, being costly and underpaid, and Overbury refused it. Somerset himself encouraged him to do so. Thereupon he was charged with contempt of the Crown, arrested and taken to the Tower. Somerset arranged for the Lieutenant and the underkeeper of the great fortress to be replaced, and through his minions he proceeded to have Overbury poisoned slowly and carefully with blue vitriol.

Their punishment seems to have been rather lenient under the circumstances. Lady Frances was pardoned; Somerset was sent to the Tower for seven years and afterwards released.

The 17th century poet Sir Thomas Overbury and (right) Robert Carr,
Earl of Somerset, with the wife for whom he poisoned his friend

K: Charles ẙ 2ᵈ. &
his Queene

Charles I, unlike his son Charles II, led an exemplary moral life. However, one could not say the same of his subjects. Mervin, Lord Audley, Earl of Castlehaven, was accused of forcing his wife to have 'frequent sexual intercourse' with a footman in his presence, and of using the same footman for sodomy. His trial opened in April, 1631 and unfolded with sickening detail.

'The Countess, on being questioned, said that shortly after her marriage to the Earl, Amptil, a footman, came while she and her husband were in bed; and on this occasion Lord Audley spoke obscenely to her and told her that her body was his property, that she was to love Amptil in the same way as himself; that he would willingly take responsibility if she slept with other men. She was forced to obey. He then attempted to force another footman on her. On another occasion a servant, Broadway, was obliged to rape the Countess while the Earl himself held her arms and legs. Afterwards the Countess wanted to kill herself with a knife which Broadway wrenched from her hand. Skipworth had to do the same thing with her. And his master often told him he would be pleased if a son were the result of this intercourse...'

The 'noble' satyr was sentenced to death by strangling—his peers were unanimous—but the sentence was modified to decapitation which was carried out at the Tower on the 14th May, 1631.

Charles II was grief-stricken when his sister, the Duchess of Orleans, died. The French, realists and good politicians, thereupon sent him an enchanting little mistress, Louise de Querouaille, who managed quickly to console him. She had rivals, of course, among them Nell Gwynne, the 'Protestant whore'. The King divided his attention between the two, and Nell was wildly jealous. 'This Duchess,' the former actress declared, 'pretends to be a person of quality. She says she is related to the best families in France. Whenever any person of distinction dies, she puts herself in mourning. If she is a person of quality, why does she demean herself to be a courtesan? As for me, it is my profession and I do not pretend to be anything better.'

DUC DE RICHELIEU

The Duc de Richelieu, Marshal of France, was the most famous seducer of the 18th century; almost a symbol of his age's *galanterie*. When he died in 1788, at the ripe age of 92, they found five unopened love letters at his bedside, in which high-born ladies asked him for a rendezvous. No doubt most of these meetings were concerned with financial affairs, for even the Duc had become a prey to the infirmi-

Charles I. Unlike his son, he was a fond husband and father and his moral life was exemplary

ties of age around 85; but in his younger years he could have boasted a record in *affaires*. The husbands he had cuckolded could have formed a fair-sized regiment; two of his biographers published a list of his conquests on which the brightest, most glorious names of France glittered.

When he was Governor of Bordeaux, he charmed the city with lavish festivals. One of his ideas was to invite 29 distinguished ladies to supper—he was the only man to complete the company of 30. They sat down unsuspectingly and nothing happened until the very end of the meal. Then the Duc toasted his pretty guests and told them the secret of selecting them for this particular occasion. In various states of indignation and amusement they departed according to seniority—not in age, but according to the length of time each had been the *Duc's* mistress.

Richelieu's petite maison at 5 Rue de Clichy, where today the Casino de Paris stands, was a perfumed haven of love—quite literally— for the Duc used scent in tremendous quantities. One of his smaller palaces was bought by the Neapolitan ambassador who could not bear this excess of perfume. The only way to get rid of it was to use the rooms as a stable for sheep. Their strong smell

Below: 'Les plaisirs palpables' by A. Bosse, circa 1630

The Duc de Richelieu, who lived for 92 years and was an
accomplished seducer for most of them

finally neutralized the over-sweet perfume the Duc had used.

But even the Duc did not have it all his own way. One day he happened to enter his wife's bedroom when she was in bed with her riding master. They had every reason to be blind and deaf to the world. Thereupon the *Maréchal* retired tactfully to the hall and began to shout: 'Isn't there anybody to announce me to the Duchess?' He created quite a scandal—*outside* the bedroom. The lovers *inside* had ample time to emerge from their trance. When the *Maréchal* knocked at the door and entered, he found the Duchess alone and perfectly composed. 'Madame,' he said 'forgive me for breaking in on you like this, but your lackeys seem to be very remiss in their duties; I advise you to get rid of the rascals.'

CASANOVA

Casanova was one of the most remarkable men of the 18th century. Thought he is chiefly famous for his 12 volumes of *Mémoires*, he was known in his day for a career of adventure and intrigue far more amazing, because believable, than anything in his books.

He was born in Venice, and at the age of 16 was sent to the seminary of St Cyprian, from which he was expelled for scandalous and immoral conduct. He travelled widely, being by turns journalist, preacher, diplomatist, musician, alchemist, gambler and financial wizard. When he returned to Venice in 1755 he was imprisoned as a spy. The following year he escaped from prison, and went to Paris. There he first became famous as director of the state lotteries. He went off on his travels again in 1759 and never really settled again anywhere for long. He visited many countries, was expelled from at least two of them (Florence and Spain) and fled from two others, from France where a *lettre de cachet* awaited him, and Poland, after a scandal and

a duel. From 1774 he was a spy in the service of
the Venetian Inquisitors of State, but in 1782 went
into exile once again after a libellous attack on one
of his patrons. He ended his life as a librarian to
the Count Waldstein in Bohemia.

His *Mémoires* were brilliant and witty, but not
very trustworthy concerning his amours. Love
affair follows love affair with such regularity as
to be almost monotonous. Their style is shamelessly
frank, and they have never been published in a
completely unexpurgated form.

TEEN AGE DON JUAN
The other archetype of 18th Century lovers was
created by the French revolutionary politician
Louvet de Couvrai, a fearless adversary of Robes-

pierre who survived the Terror but died at the
early age of 37. His *Adventures du Chevalier de
Faublas* is a forgotten and unjustly neglected classic
—like Casanova's *Mémoires* it is usually issued in
garbled and severely cut versions. Faublas, the hero
of this extraordinary four-volume novel, is barely
17 when his adventures start. Nearly all these
adventures are centred around seduction; either
Faublas being seduced, or doing the seducing. He
is so young and smooth-faced that he can disguise
himself in girl's clothing, a stratagem that gets him
into hilarious and spicy situations. He has affairs
with a dozen women—marquises and chamber-
maids, courtesans and nuns—and it is characteristic
of the age that most of the women come to grief.
They are killed by their husbands, die in childbirth,

Empress Maria Theresa of Austria, mother of 16 children, created a Commission
of Chastity to stop the habit of adultery. It didn't succeed

are locked up in nunneries or suffer similarly cruel
fates. But *not* the young hedonist, the teen-age Don
Juan. Though at the end he has what we now call
a nervous breakdown, his faithful Sophie nurses
him back to complete health and they live happily
ever after. Louvet de Couvrai seems to say that it
is always the woman that pays—but that she has
only herself to blame for running up such a very
heavy bill!

THE OFFICIAL MISTRESS

In Prussia, it was Frederick William II, successor
of Frederick the Great, who introduced the institution of the *maîtresse en titre*. The Countess Lich-
tenau remained for 11 years the royal paramour.
These 11 years, as Colin complained in the last

year of the 18th Century, turned the morals of
Berlin upside down.

'Women are so dissolute that the aristocracy
have become common procuresses, enticing their
daughters and wives of the best families into fornication and adultery. Some band together and take
an apartment where they meet their lovers and
celebrate orgies. Ladies of the best families do not
scruple to sit in the theatre among prostitutes in
order to meet men. As Berlin is the capital of
Prussia, all that is good or bad in Berlin is zealously
imitated by the other cities of the kingdom. The
cavaliers of Berlin, these regular disturbers of
peace, trample on everything that had been sacred;
religion, conjugal fidelity, domestic chastity. Their
own wives have become common property, they

223

A police raid on prostitutes, 1780

are bought and sold, bartered and seduced. A decent burgher cannot find a wife who has not been defiled by these scoundrels; and if he finds a chaste bride, very soon she turns him into a cuckold....'

AUSTRIA'S VICE SQUAD

Only one ruler in Europe attempted to stem 'this flood of adultery, this spreading canker of immorality'. The Empress Maria Theresa of Austria bore sixteen children to her husband and, the prototype for Queen Victoria, was most definitely 'agin sin'. It was she who created the famous *Keuschheitskommission*, Commission of Chastity, in her capital city of Vienna. The good Empress meant well, but the results were most disappointing. She planned an efficient, incorruptible anti-

vice squad; it turned out to be an over-zealous, terroristic police force.

The police roamed Vienna streets day and night, trying to snuff out immorality. The least suspicion was enough for an unfortunate matron or girl to be dragged to the police station, so that women did not dare to go out without a prayer book or rosary prominently displayed. The bushes in the Prater park were cut down so that they should not offer a haven to sinful lovers. The Commission entered private homes, sometimes at night; turned the furniture upside down, forced open drawers and confiscated letters. If a police spy saw a woman enter a house he waited to question her when she emerged. If she could not give a satisfactory reply, he took her to the police station and shamelessly

After her husband was assassinated Catherine the Great had many lovers. Two of the most famous were Prince Potemkin (below, left) and Grigori Orlov (below, right)

blackmailed her. Whoever paid—in cash or by surrender—was freed. Those who could not, or would not, were brutally treated. The better class women were sent to nunneries—the prostitutes were put on a boat and taken down the Danube to Hungary. Twice every year, in the spring and in the autumn, these transports sailed with two or three hundred of them. Quite a few of them managed to sneak back within a month or so. And chastity by no means increased, however hard the *Keuschheitskommission* worked at it.

THE LOVERS OF CATHERINE THE GREAT

The Empress Maria Theresa tried to set a good example to her male and female subjects and stamp out vice, but another Empress had very different ideas on love. Catherine the Great has been compared to Messalina. In one of the many films made about her she confessed to 17—or maybe 70—lovers, but if we can believe Georges Oudard who discovered Catherine's love letters in the Soviet archives, the Empress loved only a dozen times. She may have had a few more passing affairs but the number of her 'officially recognized' lovers was only 12.

She married the deranged Peter III, nephew of the Empress Elizabeth, but soon became separated from him. When Elizabeth died Peter became Czar, but only reigned six months; then Catherine, with the help of her lover, Grigori Orlov, deposed and imprisoned him. A few days later the ex-Czar was assassinated, and few people doubted that this was done, if not at the express order, at least with the connivance of his wife. No retribution followed. Catherine lived and reigned undisturbed for 34 years.

She was 44 when a poor Guards officer named Potemkin, ten years her junior, became her lover. She lavished presents, honours and affection on him. Once she gave him four expensive watches—and he was so proud of them that he wore all four at the same time, each on a separate watch-chain. One of the Czarina's 'wedding presents' was a collection of diamonds worth 60,000 roubles. Catherine seemed equally grateful to Potemkin's predecessor. When she removed him from his post of her '*maitre en titre*' she presented him with 100,000 roubles in cash, a huge silver dinner set worth 50,000 roubles, an annuity of 20,000 roubles and 7,000 serfs. Such a golden handshake must have made it easier to lose the love even of a Czarina.

None of her lovers did as well as Orlov and Potemkin. Orlov was made Viceroy of Poland.

Potemkin became a prince, a Field Marshal, Grand Admiral of the Black Sea and one of the richest men in Russia.

MORALITY IN ENGLAND

In England, where the Stuarts had yielded to the Hanoverian dynasty and the century of the four Georges had begun, Dr Johnson bent his mighty mind to the problem of morality. To him, chastity was necessary because all property depended on it. But he argued that a woman ought not to resent a husband's affairs with a chambermaid. 'I would not receive home a daughter who had run away from her husband on that account,' he said in the fullest smugness of male superiority.

Dr Johnson believed, with many other utilitarians, that the restrictions placed on sexual conduct were, basically, no different from restrictions placed on any other mode of living. Enough drink, food and work were essential and should help to mould character. Too much of anything produced harmful results. It was only reasonable, therefore, that certain restrictions should be placed upon sexual conduct.

Georgian England did not accept this principle. George I imported his seraglio with him from Germany. All his mistresses were married ladies, following the French tradition. His weakness was for one particular type of feminine beauty. 'No woman came amiss to him,' Lord Chersterfield recorded, 'if they were very willing and very fat. The standard of his Majesty's taste made all those ladies who aspired to his favour, and who were near the statutable size, strain and swell themselves like the frogs in the fable to rival the bulk and dignity of the ox. Some succeeded, others burst.

Horace Walpole painted this picture of the Baroness von Kielmansegge who, when George I brought his menage to Britain, became Countess of Darlington: 'I remember as a boy being frightened of her enormous figure. The fierce black eyes, large and rolling beneath two lofty arched eyebrows, two acres of cheek spread with crimson, an ocean of neck that overflowed and was not distinguished from the lower part of her body, and no part restrained by stays. No wonder that a child dreaded such an ogress....'

It was an age of considerable vulgarity. It found its outlets in promiscuous sexual intercourse, in wild drinking, gargantuan eating, and practical jokes of the most questionable taste. It was also the century in which the 'Englishman who sells his wife' became, instead of a French libel, a tangible reality. Jouy says that in the 18th Century 'most often husbands sold their wives; fathers sold

George I. 'No woman came amiss to him if they were very willing and very fat' — Lord Chesterfield

their daughters more seldom than in earlier days'. But wives were not valued very highly. A farmer in 1722 advertised the loss of his horse in a London newspaper and offered a reward of five guineas to the finder. The next day his wife ran away—whereupon he advertised again and offered for her recovery the princely sum of four shillings. A journeyman carpenter in London sold his wife to a mate—who got far the best of the bargain as a few weeks later his new wife inherited an unexpected legacy of £1,500. A donkey-driver in Westminster sold his wife and donkey together

An anti-clerical cartoon. 'Friar Bald Pate's Absolution to his Fair Penitent'

for 13 shillings and two pots of beer to another donkey-driver.

Scandals in low and high life were numerous. As late as the 1780's Horace Walpole could write about Archbishop Blackburne of York: 'He lived within two doors of my father in Downing Street and took much notice of me when I was near man.... I often dined with him. His mistress, Mrs Cruwys, sat at the head of the table and Hayter, his natural son by another woman, and very like him, at the bottom as chaplain. Hayter was afterwards Bishop of London....'

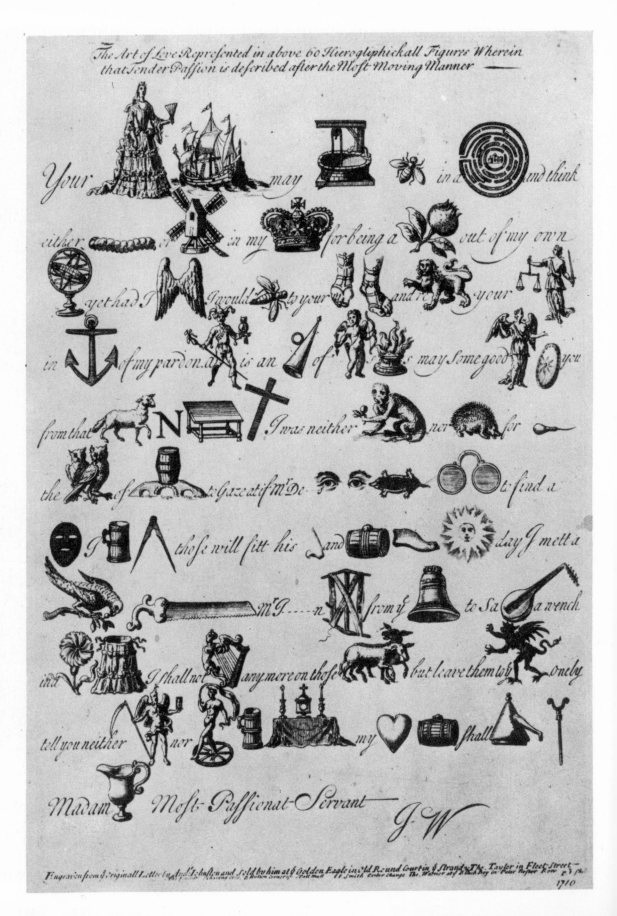

THE GOOD OLD DAYS

Previous page: Napoleon, the military genius of Europe, was deceived many times by wives and lovers

Two mistresses of Napoleon—and others. The Countess Walewska, and (below) the actress Mademoiselle Georges

BONAPARTE'S PARIS

NAPOLEON, in spite of his martial glory and world-embracing genius, was perhaps the worst-deceived lover in the world. Nor did he fare much better as a husband. The Milan singer Grazzini, the lovely actress Mademoiselle Georges, the charming Polish Countess Maria Walewska, and many others granted him their favours; but Josephine de Beauharnais and Marie-Louise, Archduchess of Austria, both provided themselves with a substitute. Josephine's lover *after* her marriage to Napoleon, was the lively Captain Charles. Marie-Louise, frail and attractive, had at least three known *amants*.

Yet when the great Bonaparte dictated his last will, the preamble of the third clause began: 'I have always been proud of my dearly beloved wife, Marie-Louise; I have preserved my most affectionate feelings for her to the last moment.' He enjoined Marchand, his chief valet, to have a bracelet made of his hair to be sent to the Empress.

During the Napoleonic age, a type of woman reigned in France who, according to Maurice Barres, was 'only woman from the girdle down....' The first pages of Alfred de Musset's *Confessions of a Child of the Century* provide a good idea of sexual morals in Europe in the early years of the 19th century. A purely physical union, without the mind or the heart participating in it, was the main characteristic of these years. Eros had been degraded to the level of a procurer.

Napoleon's immediate circle seemed proud to set society a shining example of sexual licentiousness. The Corsican's cousins and sisters and in-laws generally danced happily in the lustful ballet of court life. The Emperor's generals, his handsome staff officers, the civil servants of the aristocracy, the world of art and all its ladies, joined the mad whirl. There was hardly a general in Napoleon's armies who could have felt indignant when General Laclos, author of the *Liaisons Dangereuses*, mocked at chastity.

While Bonaparte's armies spread over Europe, Paris was kept breathless by a series of exciting scandals in high society. Women like the Princess de Fleury were blunt and unashamed. This aristocratic lady, who fled to Italy to escape the Revolution, returned to Paris after the proclamation of the Empire. She was justly famous for her amorous adventures. The reputation of a sinful, but in no way penitent Magdalen preceded her and reached the ears of Napoleon. When she was received at court, the Emperor asked her brusquely, 'Well, Madam, do you still like men?'

The Princess gave him a deliberate stare and

replied: 'Certainly, Sire, if they are well mannered!'

Napoleon walked on, abashed and silent.

MARQUIS DE SADE

The amazing Marquis de Sade survived almost until the end of Napoleon's reign. The man who gave his name to the deliberate exercise of sexual cruelty was more of a 'pervert of the pen' than an actual practitioner of his black love-magic—though in his youth he had been guilty of two rather grotesque sexual crimes. One involved kidnapping a prostitute, another a couple of harlots he tried to poison. For these he spent 17 years in prison, was released in 1790 and seven years later found himself once again in jail. He died in a lunatic asylum. His three novels *Justine ou les Malheurs de la Vertu* (in which vice is rewarded and virtue crushed), *Juliette, ou Les Prospérités du Vice* (part pornography, part political satire) and *Zoloë et ses deux acolytes* (a barely disguised romance about Madame Tallien and Josephine de Beauharnais) earned him neither money nor fame—until he was re-discovered at the end of the century and fully exploited by psychopathology and psychoanalysis. His basic contention that the shortest way to pleasure was through pain, that sex equalled violence,

hardly deserved to be elevated into a comprehensive
conception of the world.

MIDDLE CLASS ROMANTICISM
Sooner or later a reaction had to set in against the
crudely materialistic conception of love. This took
the form of romanticism, born of the longings of
the age—it burst the framework of literature and
art and had a decisive influence upon the forms of
early 19th century life and love.

Its effect was by no means immediate. During
the reign of Napoleon's successors the spicy songs
of Beranger and others were still widely popular
and booksellers still made fortunes from the sale
of obscene novels. But the romantic, idealistic
trends in social and sexual evolution seemed to
gain more and more ground. The *grande passion*,
for which no one seemed to have time during the
Napoleonic age, once again became fashionable.
A flood of lyrical enthusiasm spread everywhere;
love became an idolized, spiritualized emotion.
It was no longer the prerogative of the aristocracy.
The officers and diplomats yielded to the deputies,
the journalists, the bankers and industrialists. Signi-
ficantly, Louis-Philippe no longer called himself
'King of France', but 'King of the French'; the
reign of the middle-class began.

The wildly passionate dramas of Victor Hugo,
the sweet elegies of Lamartine, the pseudo-platonic
pathos of Chateaubriand's rather bloodless lovers
held this society in their spell. And they did not
only do it through their works. In the Paris salons
there was much gossip about the love-affairs of
George Sand, Musset, Theophile Gautier, Alphonse
Dumas, and the great tragic actress Rachel.

DIVORCE IN BRITAIN
In a sordid divorce trial that lasted for three months
in 1820, George IV tried to rid himself of his
Queen. The attempt to prove Caroline an adultreress
failed, and she died in the following year. Her death
was due in great measure to the mental and physical
humiliation she had suffered. Shelley, in his brilliant
satire *Oedipus Tyrannus or Swellfoot the Tyrant*,
erected a lasting monument to 'the hypocrisy of
the royal husband, the shameless harrying of the
Queen on the subject of her purity....'

Another famous divorce was that in which Ed-
mund Kean had to pay £800 damages to a Robert
Albion Cox whose wife the great actor had seduced.

Lady Cavendish was the sorry heroine of still
another case in which a series of love-letters were
read in open court, some of the most obscene ever
written. Their author was the young Count de la
Rochefoucauld, who wrote them when he was

attached to the French Embassy in Rome. When their love affair had ended, the Count begged Lady Cavendish to destroy them. 'But, with the strange short-sightedness of her sex,' as Ivan Bloch put it, 'she kept them, and they formed the only proof by which she lost her position in society and was ruined....' She was 45 and the mother of several children—but 'it is just these undisciplined and licentious matrons who are most attractive to a young man who feels flattered and proud to have conquered a woman in society. It was certain that she was no novice in depravity and had probably passed through many hands before he won her....' As a result of these obscene letters (some of which were published in the notorious *Romance of Lust*, issued in 1873–76) Lady Cavendish became a social outcast.

Lord Campbell accused his wife of having committed adultery with four men, including the Duke of Marlborough; while she counterclaimed that His Lordship had deceived her with Mary Watson, her maid. Lord Colin lost his case because it was proved that he had infected his wife with

venereal disease and the medical testimony showed that her illness 'precluded the possibility of co-habitation'. The costs of the case amounted to £15,000.

Lord Lyndhurst protested against the publicity given to testimonies and reports. 'No European country would tolerate it,' he declared. 'At least I have talked with many expert foreigners on this subject and have never heard another point of view expressed.' Another contemporary moralist complained: 'The husband shamelessly pockets the damages. The publicity in which these cases necessarily take place, and all the details and evidence about the accusation, are in the highest degree scandalous and improper. For instance, the evidence of servants, young ladies' maids, which they give in details before the public in open court—what they saw, heard or guessed—is no less than a kind of prostitution, even lower than the common form....'

Only very gradually was this gloating in public over private disgrace eliminated from England's divorce trials.

Lord Byron, and right with his mistress. His poetry
was the epitome of sad and unrequited love

Below: The early 19th century was the age of suffering for love; two of its greatest interpreters were Heinrich Heine (below left) and (below right) de Musset

BIRTH CONTROL

In the two decades before young Victoria came to the throne, much thought was given in England to the problems of population and eugenics. Francis Place, a tailor, followed in the tracks of Malthus, by proclaiming in 1822 through his *Principle of Population* that birth control was by no means disreputable and that if it were systematically applied, 'vice and misery, to a prodigious extent, might be removed from society....' At the same time he asserted that early marriage was the cure-all for social evils, and that late marriage was bad for women, for 'very few women can live single lives for any considerable length of time with impunity from physical evils.... If all women were to live unmarried and chastely until 28 or 30 years of age, there would soon be a lamentable deterioration of the human race....' And though women, by and large, were prepared to let the human race take care of itself, they certainly agreed with the learned tailor's views about the evils of spinsterhood.

LOVE IN LITERATURE

The remarkable Lord Byron's poetry was the epitome of sad and unrequited love. His influence was world-wide and endured for several decades—an influence deeper than his rather uneven genius warranted. Heinrich Heine, whose lyric gifts and pure melodic talents were greater than Byron's, poured his awareness of the everyday tragedies into some of the greatest short poems of world literature. Alfred de Musset and Alfred de Vigny were both worshippers of suffering; though they wrote even before the birth of Leopold von Sacher-Masoch whose name provided the eponym for *masochism*, they were, in effect, prophets of self-humiliation in love. 'A poet had to suffer inwardly, or he was no true poet,' Richard Lewinsohn pointed out. 'This masochistic feature attaches to the whole generation that was born round the turn of the century and was setting the tone about 1830.'

In his classic *L'Amour*, first published in 1826, Stendhal invited his readers on a tour of love, visiting the various European countries which this much-travelled soldier and diplomat knew so well. He was an amiable cynic, never entirely serious in his analyses, but with a penetrating wit and a deep understanding of human nature.

In Italy, he said, public opinion was a humble servant of passions. The power which was elsewhere in the hands of society belonged here to tangible pleasure.

'Only in Rome is it possible that a married woman, driving in her carriage, should speak thus to another married lady as I heard her this morning—who was only a new acquaintance: "My dear, whatever you do, don't start an *affaire* with Fabio Vitteleschi; it would be better if you loved a highway robber than him. With his kind and reserved manner he is capable of pushing a dagger into your heart, and while he twists it in your breast, he will ask with a gentle smile: *Does it hurt, little one?*" And this she said in the presence of a pretty 15-year old girl, daughter of the lady whom she addressed!'

After the fall of Napoleon, Vienna became the 'world's biggest love-market'—according to contemporary statistics *five per cent* of the Austrian capital's 400,000 inhabitants were prostitutes! They worked primarily for the 'tourist trade' and were also exported—for visitors to the city on the Blue Danube could hire and take away 'free girls' for long periods. The police, far from persecuting them, encouraged this traffic—for the prostitutes acted as unpaid informers and stool pigeons.

Vienna ladies, however, were faithful to their lovers if not to their husbands. Stendhal reported:

'The loveliest lady in Vienna, a married woman, bestowed her favours on Captain M. who was attached to Imperial G.H.Q. He was a pleasant, witty young man though by no means exceptional in appearance. The general staff officers searched every corner of Vienna but could find no one to surpass the mistress of the captain. They tried every ruse and stratagem to gain her love; her house was practically besieged. Pages and colonels, generals of the guards, even princes wasted their time under her window and their money on her servants. At last, one of them asked her why she was so hard-hearted. "Hard-hearted?" she repeated with a laugh. "But good God, don't you gentlemen realise that I *love* Captain M.?"'

Two young men who belonged to the entourage of the Emperor at Schönbrun never received anyone in their Vienna lodgings. They were often sneered at because of their lack of hospitality. At last one of them told Stendhal, 'I have no secrets from you. A young Viennese lady, wife of a well-known banker, became my mistress but only under the condition that she would never have to leave my lodgings and that I would receive no one there without her previous permission....'

It is questionable how much influence all this romantic literature had on everyday life. Girls in the Romantic Age wept over the pages of *Werther*, devoured the Waverley novels and sighed at the poems of Heine and Byron—but they married the man their parents chose, or at least submitted *their* choice to their parent's approval. Money was a

An illustration from *The Sorrows of Werther* by the greatest of all German poets, Johann Wolfgang von Goethe

A romanticized drawing of the Ojibway Indians by Miss F. Corbaux, published in 1845
Below: Manners and morals of the frontier people, while often crude, never resembled the corruption of the early 19th century Old World

A romanticized drawing of the Ojibway Indians by Miss F. Corbaux, published in 1845
Below: Manners and morals of the frontier people, while often crude, never resembled the corruption of the early 19th century Old World

mark of social distinction and young lovers were expected to choose their mates within their own class and financial setting.

WHEN LOVE WENT WEST

In North America the young Republic consolidated its territory and began its westward expansion. The colonial woman gave place to the frontier woman. Morals and manners, while often crude, never resembled the corruption and sophisticated amorality that characterized France and a good many other countries in the 18th and early 19th centuries. Life was too hard, the Indian menace too real, women too active, to follow their sisters in dalliance and inconstancy. For many decades there were only two kinds of American women, the 'nice' and the 'other sort'; and men kept the two categories strictly apart. How deep and lasting this cleavage was is shown in Dreiser's *Jennie Gerhardt*.

The wife of a frontiersman in America, Ernest R. Grove tells us, was 'no servile follower who, contrary to her inclination was pushed into an alien environment. If she belonged, as she usually did, she was as much committed as the male. If she found herself through Indian warfare, disease or accident, a widow, she usually did not turn her back from the wilderness, seeking security in some thickly settled section of one of the colonies or later of a state, but instead she usually accepted a second husband and carried on as a pioneering woman.'

On the frontiers young people courted early and married young. There were many more men than women, which enhanced the value of the latter.

'Marriage was expected, and for the woman at least there was little else except the spinster's career in some other person's household.... Marriage was literally an investment, for the

single man or woman found it almost impossible to become established on the frontier.... Often precociously matured, the young people resented interference from any quarter, once their thought seriously turned towards the finding of a mate.'

All this meant that there were few possibilities of extramarital sexual experience; women found husbands readily and in most cases settled down with them for life. Families were isolated, visitors few and far between and conjugal fidelity not difficult to preserve. There was a small proportion of men who went into the wilderness and married Indian women, or lived with them temporarily. Often this seemed expedient for the trapper and especially for the trader with the Indians. But even those white men in North America who had no aversion to sex relations with the natives did, as a rule, wince from the thought of marrying them.

Between the Revolutionary and the Civil Wars industry was established and grew rapidly in the Northern States. Thousands of women worked in the mills. Their moral standards were carefully watched and in the boarding-houses which many mill-owners established for their unmarried female workers, no one was tolerated against whom any complaint of irregularity could be made. 'Bad' women were no longer treated with the severity

Queen Victoria married at the age of 20, having herself had to propose to Prince
Albert of Saxe-Coburg

The wedding of Queen Victoria and Prince Albert was the beginning of a change in the reputation of the British monarchy from ineptitude and lax morality to private virtue and public honour
Below: The Queen and Consort with some of their children. They had nine children in all

On Prince Albert's death Queen Victoria went into widow's weeds, never to take them off again. During this part of her life the public attitude known as 'Victorian' compaigned for the suppression of sex in art and literature

of the Puritan age but they were still social outlaws without any rights; the woman of virtue was supposed to have the respect and protection of every man.

The same period in the Southern States saw complete male dominance over women and a family system which was patriarchal in spirit. 'In the South,' Groves says, 'we find not only the division between the sexes but a separation of social experience. This habit of maintaining a man's world and a woman's world appears to have evoked no impressive protest from either individual women or men.' Here, too, young people became interested in courtship at an early age. Unmarried women, however, were supervised more than was customary in the North. Sometimes this supervision was so irksome and so severe that young people rebelled against it. Greensboro, North Carolina, became a Gretna Green for Virginians who entered upon clandestine marriages against their parents' will.

Marriages were so early that in the South, grandmothers were found sometimes at only 27. Childbearing began as soon as possible and European observers were struck by the early aging of American women.

When Lola Montez, after her numerous European love affairs, marriages and scandals, betook herself to America, she was received with an equal share of abuse and admiration. She was a Countess, and American society had a snobbish curiosity towards the titled courtesan. But when she appeared in a ballet called *Diana and the Nymphs*, a female theatrical critic protested violently against such goings-on.

'When a certain piece first presented a partly unclothed woman to the gaze of a crowded auditory, she was met with a gasp of astonishment at the effrontery which dared so much. Men actually grew pale at the boldness of the thing; young girls hung their heads; a death-like silence fell over the house. But it passed; and in view of the fact that those women were French ballet-dancers, they were tolerated...

In other words, the distinction between 'good' and 'bad' women still endured—and if someone appeared on the stage in the scantiest costume, it was all right for she was 'only a French ballet-dancer'. To their own ladies, if they were guilty of indiscretion, the American were less lenient.

'In the stalls, which were occupied by a number of ladies and gentlemen in full evening costume,

Illustration from *Illustrated Police News*. A policeman returns home to find a colleague kissing his wife

and of established social position, there was to be observed a woman whose remarkable lowness of corsage attracted much criticism. Indeed, it obviously scandalized the audience, among the feminine portion of which a painful sensation was abundantly perceptible. At last, their indignation found tangible expression, and a voice from the pit was heard to utter in measured accents a stern injunction that could apply to but one individual. Blushing with embarrassment, the offender drew her shawl across her uncovered shoulders. A few minutes later, she rose and left the house, amid well-merited hisses from the gallery and significant silence from the outraged occupants of the stalls and boxes....'

There was a good deal of hypocrisy in the United States, but the yellow press had not yet been born. Often silence was the wage of sin, and America had to travel a long way to Reno.

'VICTORIANISM'

The young Victoria came to the throne in 1837. She married at 20, having herself had to propose to handsome Prince Albert of Saxe-Coburg because a queen could not be wooed like an ordinary blushing maiden. It turned out to be a model marriage: nine children in quick succession, idyllic and industrious domesticity; and when Albert died of typhoid after 21 years of marriage, Victoria put on widow's weeds—never to take them off again.

Cover for a music score by H. Walker. The lighter side of an increasingly hypocritical age

'Man of Feeling', a satirical cartoon by Rowlandson

This picture is a fanciful one. Jack the Ripper was a murderer of women in London between 1888 and 1891 who multilated his victims, and was never discovered

Below: An 1864 sketch entitled 'Disgraceful Scene at a fancy house near St James's Street'. Note the woman smoking!

One of Edouard Manet's most famous paintings, 'L'Olympe', representing the age of the French courtesan of the 1870s

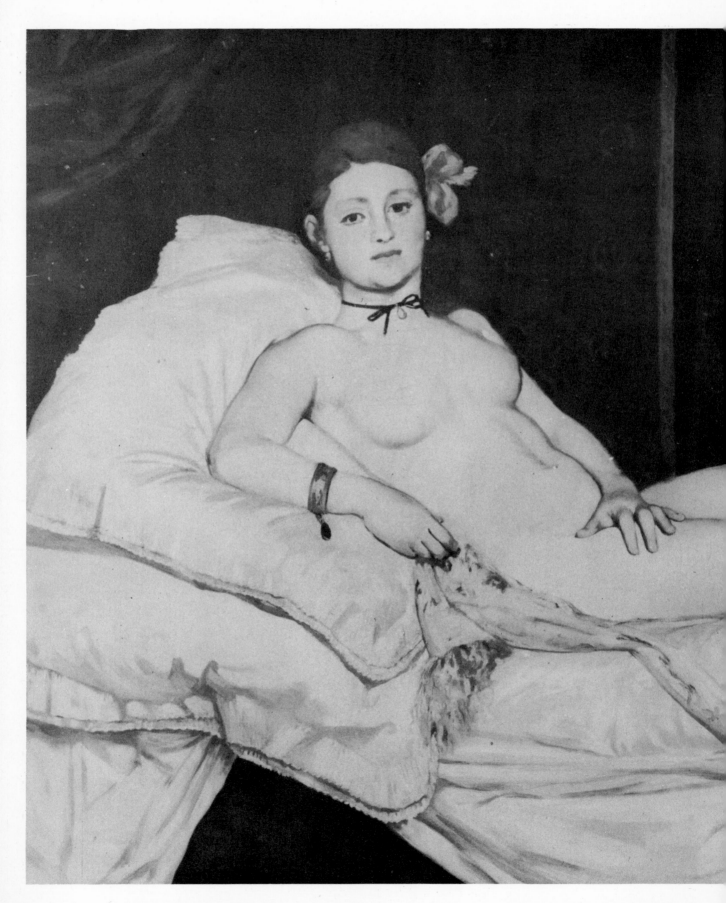

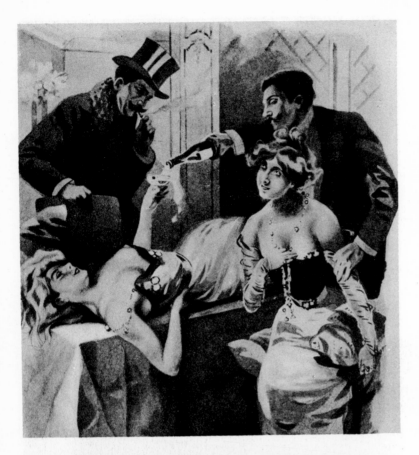

Now, Victorian morality was not as severe as one would judge by the debunkers of Victorian greatness. Divorce, true enough, was extremely difficult and divorced people could not be received in court or achieve certain high offices. Sex had to be discreet; but if a man kept his passion between four walls, no one demanded that he should become a celibate. Victorian England adopted the motto 'always do it—never talk about it!' Hypocrisy was the individual's protection against inquisitive society, and by and large the majority got away with it. Prudery having had to discard its ancient, barbaric weapons, found equally effective ones through social pressure. Victorian censorship's victims included Dumas and (*La Dame au Camelias*), Zola, (*La Terre; Germinal*) and several other books; Shakespeare and Defoe were bowdlerized. As always happens when sex is suppressed in art and literature, it went underground and became pornography, and obscene publications had never been so numerous.

A city of about two million inhabitants, London could boast almost a thousand brothels and about 850 'houses of ill-repute' while the number of prostitutes was officially put at 7,000. (The actual figure was much higher). Typically the moralists' campaign was waged against the street-walkers and not against the harlots who kept 'decently out of sight'.

Prudery dominated fashions—like the Queens of Spain, Victorian ladies were supposed to have no legs and even the thought of the anatomy of the lower half of a woman's body was shocking. Doctors could examine women patients only in the presence of a husband or female relative and touch her body only through a cloth or underclothing. Sexual hygiene was practically nonexistent and the most barbaric contraptions were devised against masturbation. It is remarkable that this sex-ridden society kept its illusions about love being sexless. Victorian writers became masters at sublimating the basic urge, of using euphemisms for bodily functions or intimate garments. Yet the strong sensuality of Dickens pulsates in many of his characters and Thackeray could create in Becky Sharp a heroine who was the equal of Tolstoy's Anna Karenina or Flaubert's Madame Bovary in flesh-and-blood immediacy. Parnell and Oscar Wilde were destroyed because of their unorthodox love-lives; others like Dickens survived because they kept their sexual lives much more discreet.

THE FABULOUS COURTESANS OF PARIS

In France there was an amazingly rapid recovery from the '*annee terrible*' of 1870–1871, a year of defeat and Russian occupation. As the flow of money restored the conditions for living in style, it was only natural that the creature of luxury, the very essence of the orgiastic, hedonistic society, the *courtesan*, should step into the limelight. All contemporary records agree that the '*filles galantes*', the courtesans and cocottes had a remarkable power of endurance; they defied age and time. The Second Empire had disappeared—but the ladies of pleasure still glittered and triumphed over a new set of hearts and pocketbooks. The Paris wits were right to declare that these lovelies belonged to the 'Old Guard'; they differed from the Imperial Guard at Waterloo only in one essential respect—they surrendered quite regularly and with pleasure.

Many of these great courtesans achieved quite extraordinary careers and became fabulously wealthy; they married aristocrats, gained influence, riches, fame, respectability. A good example was the career of La Paiva. Her real name was Therese Lachmann and—after a life of famine and feast, the wildest ups and downs— she became the Marquise de Paiva. She had already divorced one husband—ruined her second—and then her real career began. It was obviously a successful one for she soon built a palace on the Champs Elysees, a marvel of architecture, decorated with murals by the foremost painters of the age.

Her fortune was the subject of much speculation. She pretended to despise money though she loved spending it. Once a young politician started to woo her. 'Have you ten thousand francs?' asked La Paiva. 'No,' replied the young man, 'I'm poor...' 'You're lucky,' she smiled. 'If you had said yes, I'd have demanded twenty or a hundred thousand francs for a night. But I'll be content with ten thousand—which we are going to burn together. And I'll be yours until the last note has gone.'

The politician agreed. Next day he returned with ten thousand-franc notes. While he embraced her, she burned one banknote after the other in the flame of the small bedside lamp. The notes soon turned to ashes and the lover was sent packing. He turned on the threshold to explain: 'I think I ought to tell you... those banknotes were forgeries. One of my friends, an artist, was kind enough to fake them—after all, what difference did it make as they were to be burned anyhow?' He was one of the very few to outwit the lady.

La Paiva later married a kinsman of Bismarck and became Princess Henckell. She became involved in rather obscure political intrigue, and was expelled from France.

La Paiva was by no means the only famous cour-

tesan in Paris. Marthe de Vere managed the remarkable feat of spending five million francs a year while her salary as a chorus girl was 150 francs a month. Anna Deslions aided Prince Demidov considerably in wasting his large fortune. These, and many other ladies considered their occupation as a profession and were by no means ashamed of it. The famous demi-mondaine, Louise Guimont, returning from a trip to Italy, was asked at the French frontier about her profession. 'I have a private income,' she replied; and when the immigration officer remained dissatisfied by her answer, she added, 'I'm a whore! You'd better inform that fat Englishman goggling at me as soon as possible—you'll see, he'll tip you well.'

Leonide Leblanc was another illustrious courtesan, renowned both for her beauty and for her wit and high spirits. When the Parisians were fighting to get into the courtroom for the trial of Bazaine, she managed to slip inside. She took the first free place she found; but a few seconds later one of the most distinguished ladies of high aristocracy faced her and demanded that she should vacate the place which had been reserved for *her*.

'Here I am... and here I stay!' La Leblanc declared.

'But this is too much!' spluttered the lady. 'The Duc d'Aumale reserved this place for me personally. He is dining with me tonight—and I'll certainly complain to him....'

'I'm sure he'll tell me about it, Madame,' the courtesan smiled. 'For after dining with you, he is going to sleep with me....'

Delphine de Lizy, Isabella de Lineuil, Betty de Montbozon, Louise de Sylva, Marion de Larme, Henriette de Barras, Marcelle de Montfort, Laure d'Arthes, Anne de Farvil—the list could run for many pages. These ladies had noble titles—even though they were self-bestowed. The Third Republic had abolished titles, but the courtesans made a speciality of claiming them. According to the somewhat peculiar logic of the authorities, they were perfectly entitled to do so—for they adopted something that was completely non-existent! In the last two decades of the 19th century, there were few cocottes in Paris who did not call themselves at least comtesses. It was a cheap luxury which had considerable business advantages. Foreigners were thrilled to share the bed of a princess even if she insisted on being paid in honest, genuine coin!

Even more princely than their names was their way of life. Cora Pearl spent 32,000 francs a year on her lingerie alone. The annual dress-maker's bill of Mlle de Montbozen amounted to 120,000 francs. This free spending was perhaps due to the fact that Mademoiselle never really intended to pay her bills—for one of her dressmakers had to sue her to collect. *Le Bonnet de Cotton*, the famous fashion store where such courtesans shopped, had introduced the most delicate linen shifts, trimmed with Valenciennes lace; a speciality which became as obligatory for the demimonde as a pearl necklace in the nineteen-twenties. Such a shift cost 600–800 francs which represented at least two months' salary of a minor civil servant.

One of the lesser courtesans recorded her experiences with men of different nationalities.

'The American—always in a hurry, keeps on his hat even while he makes love. He doesn't speak, he doesn't kiss; he pays generously. The Englishman—looks around timidly, insists on the light being put out; he prefers if one keeps one's eyes closed. Afterwards he likes a short conversation. The Italian—in contrast to the Englishman, he insists on blazing lights, wants to unveil beauty completely, contemplate and admire it as long as possible. Sings, makes love, is most enthusiastic—pays badly, or not at all. The Negro—exercises himself so vigorously as if he hoped to turn white. The German lights his pipe repeatedly, straightens his spectacles, places his jacket carefully draped over a chair, unbuttons his waistcoat and asks whether there's any beer in the house. The Austrian—always polite, never brutal. His delicacy betrays the expert....'

This record (which may or may not be genuine) shows that the Elysée was visited by every nationality. Perhaps the most distinguished habitué was the Prince of Wales, the future Edward VII.

The places of entertainment—the Folies-Bergère, Montaigne-Russes, Moulin-Rouge, Divan Japonais, Abbaye de Thélème and all the others—were also much frequented by foreigners who found here thrills and attractions their native cities could not offer.

The Ball of the Moulin de la Galette was a special occasion. Here the oldest prostitutes congregated, women who had long lost all shame; but it was also the place where the mere beginners could be found. The young girls of the working class were so much sought after that men of society often disguised themselves as working men to approach them. The owner of the Moulin was said to have acquired a large collection of ragged and much-darned clothes, down-at-heel shoes and battered hats to rent out to the gentlemen who found it easier to woo the inexperienced and unspoiled beauties in such disguise.

In the 30 years from 1870 to 1900 economic

conditions in France changed completely; fortunes were born which exceeded the dreams of any avaricious prince. The industrial empires of Lebaudy, Meunier, Henessy, Dubonnet, Dupuy, and Coty were far greater than the domains of many a minor sovereign. These *nouveau riche* could afford anything their fancy desired: Lebaudy even tried to buy himself a kingdom in the Sahara! And as *maitresses* were a good deal easier to acquire, it was no wonder that before long France had new Pompadours and Dubarrys. Their whims not only ruled the princes of finance—their subjects included many a genuine prince or king. The Shah of Persia visited Paris in 1874; after him other rulers decided to explore the 'capital of the Republic'. Paris welcomed them freely and generously; their visits provided new ideas and amusements and the foreign sovereigns enjoyed themselves greatly in the midst of this revolutionary and republican people. These visits were often important political occasions. Intrigues

and alliances, treaties and wars germinated during them. It is intriguing to wonder how much any particular courtesan played a part in the Anglo-French *rapprochement* which later developed into the *Entente Cordiale*.

The traditional polite way of recording encounters between distinguished visitors and courtesans supplied for their pleasure was 'Inspection of the Aubusson tapestry works'. When now and then the newspapers published reports of this or that potentate making such an inspection, the initiates knew very well what it meant. Only once was there an unfortunate misunderstanding, when the Crown Prince of Siam came to Paris and asked to be shown the tapestry works of Aubusson.

EDWARDIAN BRITAIN

Edward VII, who gave his name to a brief but by no means insignificant age, was a frequent visitor to Paris. He was called the 'Uncle of Europe'

257

Mrs Lily Langtry, the Jersey Lily, favourite of Edward VII

Perhaps the greatest influence on sexual morals of the 20th
Century: Sigmund Freud (below right)

Mrs Lily Langtry, the Jersey Lily, favourite of Edward VII

and Disraeli said of him that, by the age of 40,
'he had seen everything and known everybody'.
His European journeys were triumphal processions
—Biarritz in March, Paris in April, Marienbad in
September were stations on these brilliant peregri-
nations. With a royal gesture, he could create a
resort (like Le Touquet) which had not existed
before. He was always courteous and discreet in
his many extra-marital adventures. With this he
set a pattern; many men had their Jersey Lilys and
Mrs Keppels, and as long as there was no open
scandal, no desertion of the legitimate spouse, the
conventions of society were satisfied.

The Edwardian age saw a general lowering of
social barriers. Blue blood sought rejuvenation,
both genetic and financial, in unothodox mating.
Dukes and lords married American heiresses to save
the ancestral acres and the already crumbling stately
homes. Others, less mercenary or perhaps less in
need of dowries, married Gaiety girls. The young
ladies of the chorus were accepted by society with
very little hesitation.

Yet Victorian repression and hypocrisy survived
throughout the Edwardian years. Against it the
new thinkers marshalled their forces; and few
contributed more to a new conception of love,
marriage and sex than that remarkable scientist,

Stage-door Johnnies, from a song-cover entitled 'Gaiety Girl'

poet, mystic and scholar Havelock Ellis. His *Man and Woman* was published in 1894 and *Analysis of the Sexual Impulse* in 1903. Ellis and his disciples showed the British that sex was neither shameful nor sordid; that love without sex led to pathological frustration and sex without love was a hopeless bondage. These were revolutionary ideas only because they had never before been put so outspokenly. It is no surprise that Ellis's books were banned, and that he himself was persecuted for many years.

Grant Allen's *The Woman Who Did*, published the year after *Man and Woman*—a novel which today would be considered very milk-and-water—caused a tremendous uproar. Yet it attempted only to prove that a woman had the right to bear a child without marrying its father, that the choice was for her and not for society to make. The novel had a tragic ending, for the unmarried mother was ostracized and finally bitterly denounced by the daughter for whom she had made many sacrifices. But this did not satisfy the moralists.

SIGMUND FREUD

Far less known than Ellis and his followers in the Anglo-Saxon world, or even in his own Central Europe, was Sigmund Freud, the Viennese neurologist. But his work has had an even greater influence than Ellis' and has brought about a tremendous revolution in the psychology and philosophy of love. Since the coming of Freud, men and women have learned to face the heaven and hell which, according to Swedenborg, we carry in ourselves. We have learned to be more confident of our capacity to overcome crippling inhibition and fear in love as in all other human relationships. The work of the psychoanalysts has only begun but they have already shown what they can do for bruised, unbalanced minds.

Freud perhaps over-emphasized the basic importance of the sex drive, tracing it to the beginnings of our consciousness, but he also stripped the romantic trappings from this urge which is almost co-existent with life. He has proved that men and women need not be ashamed of the primeval forces in their bodies and their minds. The superficial critics maintain (as they did almost from the beginning) that Freud wanted men to yield to every impulse and instinct, threatening all with dire consequences if they suppress libido and desire; yet he taught nothing of the kind. He only expected human beings to bring these things out in the open and deal with them honestly.

AWAKENING EUROPE

The 19th century has been called the most modest

in all history; in Victorian England even table-legs were swathed lest they should remind people of flesh-and-blood limbs. It needed a great deal of courage to talk and write about physical love, and Emile Zola could not have come at a better time.

Zola not only described things and actions which had been taboo, but used words which had never appeared in print before. He was a serious writer and reformer, but the general public considered him a pornographer which explained why the *Rougon-Macquart* novels sold in hundreds and thousands in France and abroad. But critics decried them and for some years Zola was unjustly neglected. It was only in the 1930s that Zola was rediscovered and his true value acknowledged.

Guy de Maupassant died before Freud published his books, but he could be called an early Freudian. His favourite theme was the contrast between civilization and instinct. Again and again he showed how the sex instinct triumphed over middle-class and puritanic conventions. The late Victorians, as Maupassant showed, were only too ready to desert their strict morality if their interests conflicted with it (this was the lesson of his first masterpiece, *Boule-de-suif*, 1880). The rich and distinguished fugitives refuse to talk to the countrywoman who travels in the same stagecoach from Paris; but later they do everything to persuade her to sleep with the Prussian officer who holds them up. Yet next day when they continue on their journey, they once again cut dead the 'abandoned harlot'.

He was a full-blooded, aggressively male writer. With him love was the triumph of the flesh over the spirit; yet he could be tender and moving as in *Yvette* or *Stronger than Death*.

These were also the decades of the great woman-haters, the spiritual descendants of Schopenhauer. Otto Weininger committed suicide at the age of 23—in the year when his only book *Sex and Character* was published. It caused great excitement and controversy. This brilliantly written book discussed a great many subjects—the State, the Jews and above all, love. Weininger, for all his youth, was a most original and comprehensive thinker. As with Freud and Proust, the emphasis of his system was on the subconscious, the submerged memory, inhibition and instinct. According to him a man and a woman were best suited if the man possessed as much femininity as the woman masculinity—so that the two of them jointly represented a perfect, complete male and hundred per cent female. With all this, Weininger hated women violently and fanatically—an extreme contradiction that was part of the age of women's emancipation.

August Strindberg, the brilliant, stormy Swede, realized something that the French analyst writers, especially Stendhal, had known for a long time—that love was not an emotion *on a single level*. The 'son of the servant girl', as he called himself in his famous autobiographical cycle, discovered what the psychoanalysts call *ambivalence*—the close proximity of love and hate, the speed and ease with which one can change into the other. He denounced woman for not being such a perfect human being as man. He thought women vampires who sucked with frightening energy the strength and blood of men. There was no lack of intensity in Strindberg, a major artist who destroyed himself. In some ways he resembled the beserk of the ancient Vikings who stripped themselves naked in battle and rushed at the enemy with no thought of self-preservation.

Ibsen, the brooding genius of these decades was conducting a one-man crusade against sham and hypocrisy in all forms—and especially in the relations of the sexes. His women could be as destructive as Strindberg's but their motives were more human and less exaggerated. Peer Gynt, after tasting the wild love of Anitra the slave-girl, and the Troll King's daughter, groped his way back to Solveig—the eternally waiting, eternally forgiving mother-wife and wife-mother.

THE GIBSON GIRL

At the age of 21, Charles Dana Gibson became the most popular graphic artist in America, and all because of the girl he invented. 'When he depicts a woman of refinement and gentle breeding,' John Ames Mitchell, founder and editor of the original *Life* wrote, 'we have no suspicion of her using bad grammar when out of the picture. He invests his heroines with the elusive *je ne sais quoi* without which a woman of social pretensions will forever struggle against hope.'

The Gibson girl became an American idol. She was received with all the fine, uncritical frenzy which Americans can bestow. She had health, and beauty, strength and dignity, and the aloofness inherent in an ideal. Shopgirls and coeds modelled their clothes and deportment and shaped their bodies after her image. Gibson made her the commander of men, the herald of the emancipated woman. She had everything—except sex-appeal and humour. The first was, as Thomas Craven pointed out, forbidden; the second inconsistent with divinity. Yet her popularity was global. Gibson albums were found in the palace of the last Czar and sketches of the Girl decorated palm-leaf huts in Central America, cabins in the Klondike and Australia, Tokyo shop windows and cabooses of freight trains. As late as the Second World

War a radio transmitter was nicknamed 'the Gibson Girl' because of its shape. The Gibson Girl was purely imaginary—a synthetic idol—yet she expressed what the American female would have liked to be—and what the American male loved to conquer and melt into humanity.

Gibson drew his girl in the shape of an eternal question-mark. He showed her playing chess with a handsome young man, calling it 'the greatest game in the world—his move' or making the same virile youngster trump his partner's ace in a bridge game. Love always won.

The Gibson Girl, the epitome of refinement and gentle American breeding, invented by Charles Dana Gibson

BETWEEN THE WARS

A romantic postcard of the twenties

SCANDALS AT COURT

THE Archduke whose murder was the excuse for the First World War was himself the tragic hero in one of the great love stories of the early 20th Century.

The Archduchess had several daughters and she welcomed Archduke Francis Ferdinand's visits in her Pressburg palace. Pressburg was only a short journey from Vienna and whenever his duties permitted, the Heir Apparent made the brief trip down the Danube. The Archduchess had already planned the wedding of one of her daughters (though she didn't know *which* one it would be) when, after a tennis game, Francis Ferdinand forgot his watch in his dressing room. A lackey took it to the Archduchess; as she was about to place it in a small box to return it to its owner, a small medallion on the watch-chain caught her attention. She opened it and found a miniature of Countess Sophia Chotek, a lady-in-waiting at her household. The lovely Sophia was instantly dismissed and Francis Ferdinand was summoned to his uncle, the Emperor.

He was 37 and he had fallen in love for the first time in his life. He fought for his chosen bride with morose tenacity. In the end the Emperor yielded but the conditions were harsh. It was to be a morganatic marriage: No son of Francis Ferdinand could inherit the throne. Sophia, raised to the rank of Princess Hohenberg, was not allowed to attend any court functions nor have a seat in the imperial boxes at the opera and the Burgtheater. If there was a court ball in Budapest, she could not stay in the suite that was permanently ready for the Crown Prince. Whenever Francis Ferdinand went on a journey, he slept in his special train to avoid his wife's humiliation. Montenuovo, the Court Chamberlain, a cold-blooded survivor of the 18th century, used every trick of court etiquette to make the Archduke rue his morganatic union. And as the years passed, all the slights his wife suffered, all the bitterness of the swallowed insults, coalesced in Francis Ferdinand into a furious desire for revenge. He made no secret of the plans he developed with single-minded stubbornness in the 14 years between his marriage and his death.

Before the First World War clothes were heavy and uncomfortable, and did not encourage such courting customs as walking arm in arm or lying on the beach

It is no exaggeration to say that a good many people in and around the Imperial Court were relieved when Gavrilo Princip's bullet ended the Crown Prince's life.

Another great scandal was the elopement of Princess Chimay with Jancsi Rigo, a Hungarian band leader. The Princess was born Clara Ward, daughter of the American millionaire. Prince Chimay, of the Belgian royal house, probably married her for the fortune she was to inherit, and did not seem particularly upset over her departure. He sued for divorce and the court granted him a large annuity in compensation from the ex-princess's millions. Clara Ward had been the Princess of Chimay and Caraman for six years only; her marriage to the gipsy band leader lasted an even

shorter time. Her third marital adventure was with the station master of Naples. Rigo consoled himself by marrying an elderly American millionairess, even richer than Clara. She died soon afterward and left him her large fortune, but Jancsi Rigo spent it quickly and died, at 60, almost destitute. It was said that in the final years of his life he was kept by Clare Ricciardi, *nee* Ward.

On the morning of December 12, 1902, the newspapers of the world had a double sensation to provide for their readers' breakfast tables. Two members of the Habsburg dynasty's Tuscan branch, an Archduke and an Archduchess, had renounced their family and fled into 'ordinary' life on the wings of love. Archduke Leopold, later known as Leopold Woelfling, gave up his princely status for the sake of Vilma Adamovich, a cashier in a small cafe. At the same time his sister, Archduchess Louise, wife of the Crown Prince of Saxony, left for Switzerland in the company of a language teacher named Giron. She could not endure the bonds of court life any more and chose freedom. It was said that Giron merely helped her in her flight without being her lover. The Archduchess (who took the name of Countess Montignoso, bestowed upon her by the King of Saxony) soon separated from Giron and also broke off relations with Leopold and her commoner sister-in-law. She settled in Florence where, at the age of 37, she fell in love with Enrico Toselli, an opera singer. She married him and bore him a son but the marriage was not happy, and a divorce soon followed.

LOVE AND HORROR

The First World War was a massacre the like of which history had never recorded. The Central Powers lost 3,199,000 dead, the Allies 5,403,000; 21 million people were wounded—of whom 3½ million remained invalids; 6,000 men were killed every single day—and no one has properly estimated how many civilians perished directly or indirectly because of the holocaust. Furthermore, according to the German statistics (which were true of most participating countries) almost 69% of the dead were young unmarried men.

One of the recurrent characters in post-war novels was the spinster who tormented herself with bitter regrets because she refused to yield to the wooing of her fiance and did not 'make him happy' before he was killed. But for every 'wise virgin' there were scores who had no such cause to blame themselves. Up to the outbreak of the war there were still many young Englishwomen of the middle and upper classes who were initiated into the facts of life by husbands themselves largely ignorant of them.

In less than a year a drastic change came to England, as to most other countries enmeshed in the bloody struggle. 'Purity' and 'virginity' became almost meaningless.

'Moral precepts', Douglas Goldring said in his excellent *The Nineteen-Twenties*, 'were quickly consumed in the flames of pity and love and the maiden, if opportunity came her way, gave herself gladly to the young warrior about to die. Hundreds of thousands of girls, till then preserved in cotton-wool wrappings of gentility and innocence, joined the W.A.A.C's or trained as nurses and became V.A.D's and were thus suddenly, by the tides of war, brought face to face with its realities of suffering and destruction. Mingled with all the horror

It was the war, more than anything, which brought the vote and emancipation to women. These W.A.A.Cs marching in 1917 have won a greater battle than they know

of those years, there was a strange and terrible beauty, a beauty born of self-sacrifice, heroism, comradeship and the blossoming and fulfilment of youthful passion in the very jaws of death.'

A curious by-product of the war was its influence upon the fashion of the 'feminine ideal'. In Central and Eastern Europe under the impact of the initial German victories, suddenly the 'mature, full figure' became fashionable, after having been pushed into the background for decades by the slim, fragile, 'decadent' outline of the modern woman. For many years 'plump' and 'full-bosomed' had been pejorative expressions; the first year or so of the war changed this completely. In France, after the initial serious setbacks, public opinion looked for a general scapegoat and found it in the slim, fragile, 'degenerate' French woman who could bear only puny sons for the nation of *le gloire*, if she bore any at all. That is why our soldiers are beaten, wailed the leader-writer—the Prussians crush us because of the barren wombs of Frenchwomen. Look at the German Brunhildes, at their full, healthy body at their rounded shape. These Junos produced true warriors. How could the slim, undersized *piou-pious* stop them?

THE DEATH OF SEXUAL TABOOS

The first world war created a new morality and thereby a new approach to love. It would have been foolish to expect that women, after filling men's jobs and in many cases sharing their dangers, could be denied equality. And though this was to be summed up in the vote, women were much more concerned with abolishing their social, sexual and economic disabilities.

'It was useless' Douglas Goldring wrote, 'to tell a woman who had driven a heavy lorry for a hundred miles that it was immodest of her to go into a pub and order a pint of beer at the end of her journey. It was equally useless to keep up the "fallen woman" nonsense if she chose to satisfy her natural appetites without benefit of clergy...'

This change of attitude certainly did not cause any sudden alteration of social behaviour, but it did mark the beginning of a greater tolerance for unorthodox love. The conception of 'Sin' had become a little dated.

There was a surplus of about two million women in England at the end of the war. This, and the fight for the abolition of prostitution (an ideal never to be achieved) led to the discarding of the

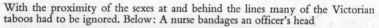

With the proximity of the sexes at and behind the lines many of the Victorian taboos had to be ignored. Below: A nurse bandages an officer's head

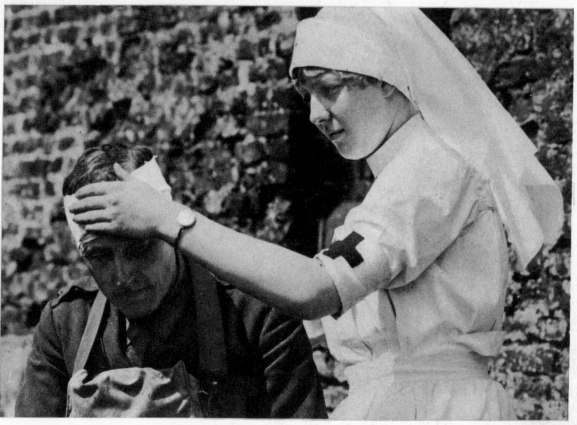

An American soldier with a French girl, 1917

War was a time of brief encounters and hasty farewells. Departure of a troop train at a railway terminus

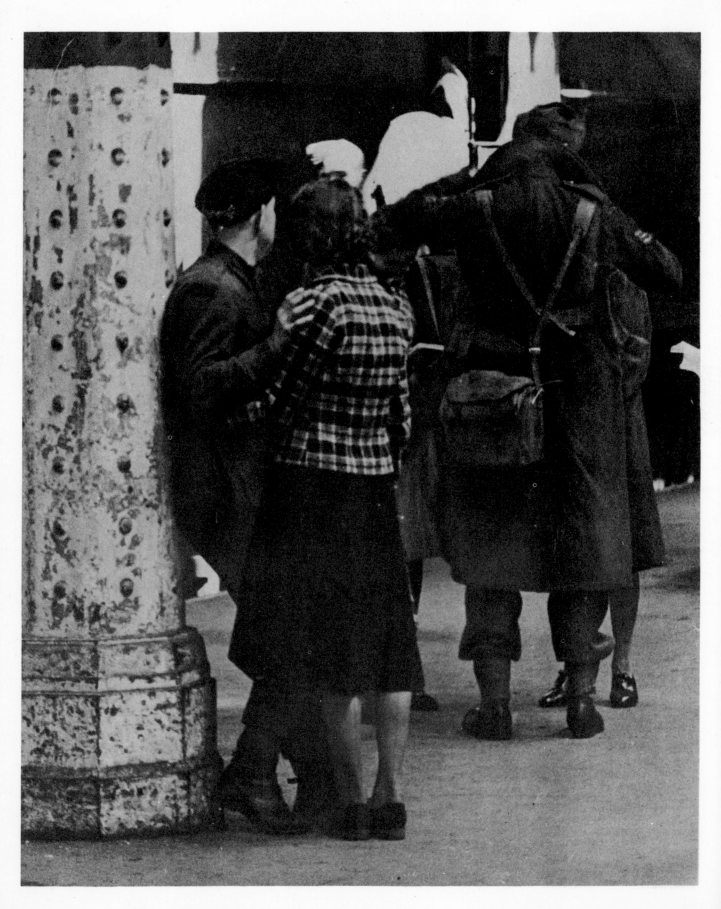

Victorian fetish of virginity. William Bowyer described the new ideas of sex in his *Brought Out in Evidence*:

'I had no scruples about fornication in itself, only about deception and desertion. These were immoral, sins against the Charity I believed in; the rest was only tribal law gone sour. Immoral rather were the uncharitable censoriousness and prudery that wished to deny the right of free and equal men and women to take pleasure in each other's bodies, whether they were the same or the other sex. Seduction, involving deception, was plainly a sin, but this was not, and to indulge a natural appetite with a woman whose profession it was to give it the completest satisfaction would involve no infraction of any law I believed in, any more than eating or drinking for pleasure... I could not forget the cynical remark by a former colleague that the only difference between the virtuous ones and the others was that the others were cleaner and knew their job...'

In the countries which did not have a severe moral code 'the wave of immorality' died down around the middle of the twenties. But in Britain and the United States, which had preserved the puritan spirit up to the outbreak of the war, the new atmosphere gained in momentum. The criticism of sexual morality, the revolt against the old traditions, became general both in Anglo-Saxon life and literature. The revolution of the modern novel was based on the revolt of love.

In the twenties the river was always a favourite courting place

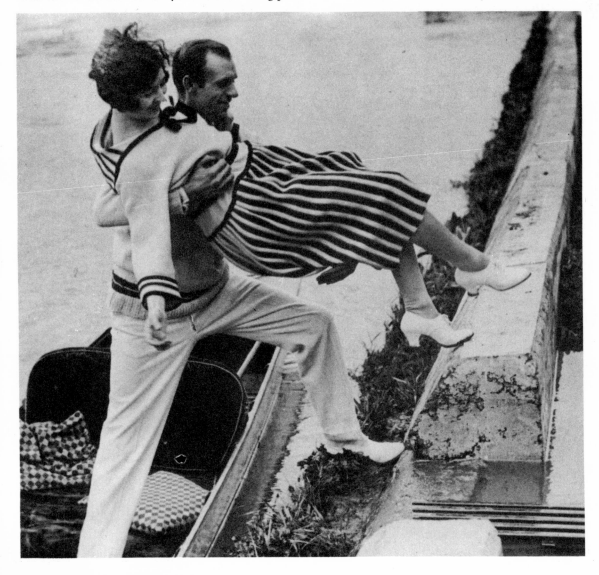

In the forefront was one of England's most important 20th Century writers, David Herbert Lawrence. Since Nietzsche there had been no more embittered denouncer and scourger of modern civilization—one which he described as stinking of paper and machinery. Lawrence's basic urge was to educate society. He preached with a bitter and moving pathos all that the old puritans had preached with equal eloquence in the directly opposite direction.

Lady Chatterley's Lover was not published until 1928 but had been conceived much earlier. It was over thirty years before a famous court battle made an unexpurgated edition possible in Britain. The revolt within its pages was not exclusively against the taboos of love, but also against social barriers. It was Lawrence's contention that love defied all social differences. In 'Lady C' the 'son of the people' was far more capable of satisfying the sexual needs of Her Ladyship than her former lovers of her own class.

Lawrence was a brilliant psychologist who knew very well that life and language were closely linked in civilized man; we only live completely the things of which we are also able to speak. Those who wanted to liberate love had to free the words describing love. With a truly prophetic fury, Lawrence devoted himself to the impurification of language and the use of four-letter words was an essential part of his attack on what he considered not only outmoded but harmful morality. He had to shock his fellow countrymen by printing the unprintable, by transferring the usage of sexual description from the lavatory wall to the printed page.

One of the most famous early 20th Century French cartoons shows a young woman nestling against her husband. They are newly wed and she whispers to him: 'Teach me the bad words, *cheri!*'

There is no doubt about the great importance of D. H. Lawrence for his own people—not for British life but for British literature. He gave voice to things which before him no Englishman had expressed in literature for many years. And his influence was a legacy within the framework of the ancient inter-action of life and literature; life, indeed, began to imitate art and follow in the wake of the pioneers of the new love.

NEW ATTITUDES IN AMERICA
America's involvement in the war was too brief and too superficial to be blamed for what followed —the 'era of wonderful nonsense', the 'Fitzgerald age' (after Scott Fitzgerald's brittle and self-

destructive heroes and heroines), the decade that stretched from the peace treaties to the devastating crash of 1929.

Sexual life in America reflected the same basic view as social life in general. The frantic pursuit of novelty was coupled with a self-conscious lack of sentimentality. The characters of Hemingway, Sinclair Lewis, John O'Hara, James M. Cain, were bending over backwards to be matter-of-fact and materialistic about love, conjugal fidelity, and orthodox morals. But this toughness often did hide a sentimentality and the hard-boiled lovers of Cain's *The Postman Always Rings Twice* were just as sentimental as Hemingway's semi-autobiographical *Farewell to Arms*.

The sentimentality was far more on the surface, more blatant and even more adolescent in the products of Hollywood which achieved wide distribution for the first time during and after the war. After an initial period of licence and anarchy, which ended when the industry set up its own censorship, film love had to be pure; the Hays Code prescribed not only the duration of kisses but also demanded that in a bedroom scene the couple could not have their feet off the ground at the same time. Triangles were more frequent than custard pies in the silent and early talking films but they had to be tidied up; innocence and virtue had to triumph.

An emerging atmosphere of sexual equality was greatly accelerated by the war, by the granting of votes to women and last but not least by the disastrous experiment of Prohibition. It was a complete revolution in manners and morals and was not accepted by everybody without misgivings. Ernest R. Groves wrote:

'Although the majority of women who have felt the full force of new conditions have looked to marriage for sex fulfilment, a minority have chosen a pre-marriage sex alliance as an anticipation of the matrimonial union expected later or have turned to sexual relationships, promiscuous or concentrated, as a substitute for marriage. These variations, however, must not be interpreted as similar to the irregularities that have always accompanied the standard sex code. They represent a non-acceptance of the conventions, the feeling of self-right in the realm of sex that is, as a considerable disposition, new in our social history.... It is clear that woman's advance toward sex equality with man is certain to put unprecedented responsibility upon her, and at least temporarily add to the ever-present strain the modern young woman meets in her pre-courtship, courtship and engagement associations...'

'The private relations of men and women being happily beyond the reach of the statistician', as Frederick Lewis Allen said, there was no reliable guide how far and how deep the new morality had spread. But the number of divorces rose steadily— in 1910 there were 8.8 for every 100 marriages; in 1920 the figure was 13.4 and by 1928 it had reached 16.5. Almost one in six marriages ended on the rocks. With the increase naturally came a more tolerant attitude to divorce. In the urban communities men and women who had been divorced were socially accepted without question. 'Indeed', as Allen pointed out, 'there was often about the divorced person just enough of an air of unconventionality, just enough of a touch of scarlet, to be considered rather dashing and desirable....' Millions were moving towards acceptance of what a *bon-vivant* of earlier days had described as his idea of the proper state of morality: 'A single standard and that a low one!'

The force of morality rushed into the breach, trying to stem the tide. Hollywood came under concentrated fire as the modern Sodom. Whether it became more moral in consequence of the Hays office and various ukases by the studio bosses, one would hardly like to say, but stars and directors, producers and executives became a good deal more cautious. And in the films themselves love became more titillating than realistic, consummation was barely hinted at and the pursuit was always the main thing, with the wedding march and the orange blossoms marking happiness ever after.

Other societies had their own methods of dealing with the decline in morals. The city fathers of Norphelt, Arkansas, passed an ordinance in 1925, saying:

'Section I.—Hereafter it shall be unlawful for any man and woman, male or female, to be guilty of committing the act of sexual intercourse between themselves at any place within the corporated limits of said town. Section II.—Section I of this ordinance shall not apply to married persons as between themselves, and their husband of wife, unless of a grossly improper and lascivious nature...'

But whatever the city fathers decided, there was an unmistakable and rapid trend away from the old American code toward a philosophy of sex relations wholly new to the country. There was the feeling that the virtue of chastity for its own sake was irrelevant. Mrs. Bertrand Russell defined the

These are the women who stirred men's hearts in the pre-war cinema. Clara Bow, Mary Miles Minter (below, left) and Mae West (below, right)

new mood as 'the right, equally shared by men and women, to free participation in sex experience'. It wasn't until the great crash of 1929 that a strong reaction arose against this wild and widespread promiscuity—but by then America had other things to worry about.

THE SOVIET MORALITY
It took about six years of turmoil, civil war and anarchy before the Bolshevik Revolution of 1917 stabilized its gains and achievements. Six years of destruction and suffering; six years of fantastic chaos. Little wonder that in these turbulent years the conception of love, marriage and sex also underwent a 'painful re-appraisal'. The Union of Soviet Socialist Republics began with a large-scale experiment in a new sexual morality.

The Revolution brought (at least in theory) almost complete equality of the sexes. Women were fighting side by side with men in the Red Army. They worked in the factories, were elected to the Supreme Soviet, became heroines of the Soviet Union. All the moral and spiritual traditions went overboard, and marriage became little more than a simple registration at the nearest office. It could be dissolved equally simply either by mutual consent or the appearance of one of the parties.

The amount of 'free love' in the Soviet Union was of course wildly exaggerated by anti-Communist propagandists who claimed that if Communism ever spread outside Russia all women would be 'nationalized' and become common property. That in the restless and turbulent period of the first years there was love-making on a pretty free and even promiscuous basis, no one would deny. The State offered facilities for abortion not only on health grounds but at a woman's request. Propaganda for birth control was also State-sponsored for a while. All this gave plenty of material to anti-Soviet writers.

But by 1920 the tide was beginning to turn. 'Many people think that in Communist society', said Lenin, 'love life is as simple and insignificant as the drinking of a glass of water. But this is untrue, it is not a Marxist theory, as so many declare.'

According to Lenin, not only human instincts, but also the 'cultural qualities' found expression in sexual life.

'Naturally,' said Lenin, 'you want to quench your thirst; but a normal man, under normal circumstances, won't lie down near a dirty puddle and drink from it. In love there is social interest, an obligation towards society. As a Communist I feel not the slightest interest for the theory of a "glass-of-water"—notwithstanding that it carries the label of the "liberation of love." Such a liberation is neither new nor Communist. Communism wishes to create joy of life, and strength of life by sexual activity; but the exaggeration of sex one experiences so often gives neither but destroys both. Let a man be neither a monk nor a Don Juan; neither a German *Spiessburger*, neither hot-nor-cold.'

Lenin referred to a young comrade of his whom he considered highly talented and yet, he said, he would never amount to anything, because he indulged his sexual instincts too much. Politics and love affairs must not be interdependant.

'I do not trust men who run after every woman —this is not the way to win revolutions. Revolution needs concentration, a heightening of forces. The wild excesses of sexual life are reactionary symptoms. We need sanity, sanity and once more sanity; we must not stand for the weakening, wasting, destruction of our strength...'

Communists thought that the liberation of man-

kind was impossible without the social independence and equalization of the sexes, and this could not be achieved unless the institution of marriage was cleansed of its dross. They claimed that bourgeois marriage had been more of a business transaction than the logical end of love.

'If we look at the history of patriarchal marriages developed under private property,' wrote Dr. Istvan Haraszti, a proponent of Marxist ethics, 'we see that the unwritten laws of public morality and the clauses of the various legal codes and decrees which refer to marriage all protect the interests of the ruling classes.... It may sound strange but throughout history under capitalism *love* (or what we call love) was the privilege of the oppressed. The members of the ruling classes married in the majority of cases for financial interest and not for love....'

The Communist theoreticians admit that it is extremely difficult to shape a new sexual morality; it is a complex and slow process in which the old and the new clash constantly and the latter has great difficulty in gaining general acceptance. Habit, the Marxist-Leninists say, has a tremendous influence upon instincts, for men carry within themselves

Ernest Hemingway

The women of Russia achieved more than the token equality of Englishwomen. The Revolution brought equality into every walk of life. Here is a women's battalion at Petrograd, 1917

A woman casting her vote for the Constituent Assembly, 1917

the prejudices, customs and traditions of preceding social ages.

TAKING IT SERIOUSLY

Between the wars Germans took their vices as seriously as their virtues. They organized both. There was nothing spontaneous about their pleasures and their sins. The pederasts, the lesbians, the believers in free love or nudism flaunted themselves and attempted to recruit new members to their circles and societies. Books on moral history and sexology—a few of them genuine but most of them pornography under a thin coating of science—were issued by the hundred. Vice was not only highly organized and systematized with German thoroughness—it was also cheap. Yet it was somehow clumsy and heavy-handed; there was no wit, no charm, no light-heartedness. They seemed to follow the example set by the 18th century young German aristocrat who decided that life was not worth living and that he would kill himself. However, he thought the usual methods of suicide too messy and unpleasant; so he went to Venice, hired one of the most luxurious casinos and locked himself up with choice of food, the best wines and two luscious ladies with Titian-red hair. He planned to kill himself by food, drink and love. He did not

succeed. He became very ill indeed after some weeks but death would not come. Disgusted, he resigned himself to life.

In the final years before Hitler, Berlin and the other great German cities were rather like that young German princeling. With great thoroughness Germany decided to go to the dogs—and ended up under the Nazi yoke.

One of the most sensational trials of 1926 was that of 17-year-old Paul Krantz from a Berlin suburb. He suspected a class-mate of having designs on the 16-year-old girl with whom he was having an affair—so shot him dead one afternoon, with three bullets from his father's Mauser.

He was acquitted and the whole of Germany went mad over his case. Endless articles in the newspapers argued over the merits of the judgment; meetings were held in protest and approval, books and pamphlets were published analysing the crime and its psychological aspects. Clergymen thundered from the pulpit that German youth was depraved and that education must be handed back to the Church. Leader writers tormented their brains to discover political significance in Paul Krantz's crime. For months Germans were interested in nothing but the shots fired by a precocious, unbalanced schoolboy who had started

Between the wars, weddings in Soviet Russia entailed little more than the signing
of documents in a register office. Moscovites had to wait until the fifties before
they were given the splendid Palace of Weddings, converted from a Tsar's palace

to collect sexual experience somewhat early.

After Berlin, Hamburg was the most important
German centre of organized vice. The notorious
St Pauli was a vast district of brothels, cheap
cabarets, dancing-halls and low-class dives. Its
centre was the Reeperbahn, an indescribable jum-
ble of colours and nationalities. Outside the Dance
Hall Trichter stood groups of girls begging the
passing sailors to take them in. For the 'Trichter'
forbade entrance to unaccompanied 'ladies', and
as it was one of the most profitable hunting-grounds
for prostitutes, some of them were even willing
to pay for their escorts. Inside they would quickly
leave the poor sailor to look for more prosperous
custom.

Next to the 'Trichter' was the wax-works with
a section 'Forbidden to Adolescents'. Another
attraction was the 'Plastikon of Beauty', a sad
travesty of the word as poor, hungry girls displayed
their rather indifferent charms without the slightest
attempt at artistry. Another 'artistic' establishment
was the 'House of Photographs', almost completely
dark inside, with slot-machines showing gruesome
pictures of Rubenesque nudes. Its customers were
mainly schoolboys in the pimply stage of adolescence.

The Reeperbahn was the main cruising place of
street-walkers. Some were about 13; some old hags.
Their importunity was shamelessly persistent; they
were of many lands and colours, a good number
French and Italian whose dark complexions seemed
to have a special fascination for the 'Nordic'
seamen. But the Reeperbahn was a kindergarten
compared with the pitch-dark streets and alleys
surrounding it. Here lived the pimps who had their
regular guilds; into the *Kaschemmen* or dives came
the prostitutes to render account of their earnings.
The pimps had their own security service, guards
at the street corners signalling the approach of
anyone 'suspicious'. Farther on, in the Marien-
strasse, there were the big and luxurious brothels
like the Seeligmann house where orgies took place
and girls were for sale. The area was picketed by
the 'Midnight Mission', who distributed forbid-
ding leaflets:

WHAT BRINGS YOU TO THIS PLACE?
DO YOU SEEK SATISFACTION OF YOUR
SEXUAL INSTINCTS? ARE YOU FOL-
LOWING YOUR SENSUAL EXCITEMENT?
DO YOU KNOW WHAT MAY BE THE
CONSEQUENCE IF YOU ENTER HERE?

The missionaries were often insulted and beaten
by the prostitutes and pimps who saw in their

volunteer work an unfair interference with legitimate business.

THE TOTALITARIAN STATE

Mussolini built his Corporate State upon the fundamental unit of the family. Italians were encouraged to have babies, large families were rewarded by family allowances and public honours. Bachelors were taxed heavily and everything was done to arrest the falling birthrate. Because of this policy, and the strong influence of the Church, extramarital relations were frowned upon. Love had to be utilitarian, sexual intercourse had to be aimed at producing offspring. Infidelity, according to the Fascist philosophy, was not a crime as long as children were brought into the world. The Duce himself never divorced his matronly wife who bore him half-a-dozen children—but that did not prevent him from having a string of mistresses, one of whom died with him when he was murdered. The attitude to love which Mussolini and his blackshirts fostered was that of complete male superiority and a sort of universal and rather gay-hearted lechery which was more comic than sinister; or perhaps the more comic the more intense it became.

In Germany, with Hitler's early drive against the Church, orthodox Christian morality was under assault for the twelve black years of the Nazi regime. Women, married or unmarried, were encouraged to comfort the warriors who returned between campaigns to the homeland. Homosexuals were sent to concentration camps (where some of them became the most sadistic and efficient mass-murderers and torturers) or had to go underground after the Roehm purge in which the Fuhrer got rid of some of his earliest, most ardent supporters—and a few possible rivals. District women leaders visited the lonely wives urging them to produce children even if their husbands were not available for this purpose. Nudism was suppressed, the camps taken over by the *Kraft durch Freude* movement. Decrees were issued demanding that every able-bodied woman 'do her duty' towards the State. Illegitimate children were to be brought up by the community and trained to become the elite of the *Herrenvolk*. When this proved to be a somewhat slow process, children were kidnapped from the occupied countries and women, even of the 'inferior races', turned into 'German mothers'. This was really a renewal of the half-pitiful, half-ludicrous attempts of the Prussian King Frederick William, father of Frederick the Great, whose ambition had been a whole army of six-footers.

Impersonators at a Berlin night club of the 30s. Four of these people are men

He collected them, bought them, had them kidnapped, and finally tried to breed them by marrying tall men to tall girls. The breeding experiment was a total failure for Nature was willing to produce prodigies on her own but would not obey any command, not even the Prussian King's. The tall couples annoyed Frederick William by producing off-spring of normal stature.

Hitler and his chief racial theoretician, Alfred Rosenberg, maintained that the German race was one chosen by Destiny to rule the world—not on account of any political, geographical or historic mission, but because, both mentally and physically, they were superior to all other races. Using half-digested facts they created the myth of a superior Nordic race and adopted a caste system for the whole world. At the top of this unchangeable hierarchy stood the fair-haired, blue-eyed Norsemen, Germans, Scandinavians. Lowest were the Jews, Negroes and gipsies. The yellow and brown races were also very inferior. This last point caused serious embarrassment when Japan was

Members of a Berlin night-club celebrate the return of one of their companions from gaol

invited to join the Anti-Comintern Pact.

For married couples of mixed nationality, this idiotic theory of Aryan supremacy meant heartbreak and tragedy. It was made a capital offence for a Jew even to *kiss* an Aryan women. If the non-Aryan—even of the vaguest Jewish connections—had no knowledge that the girl was an Aryan, this did not make the slightest difference; he had to suffer for his 'crime' even if committed unwittingly. Jewish households were prohibited from employing Aryan maids or cooks under 45. These

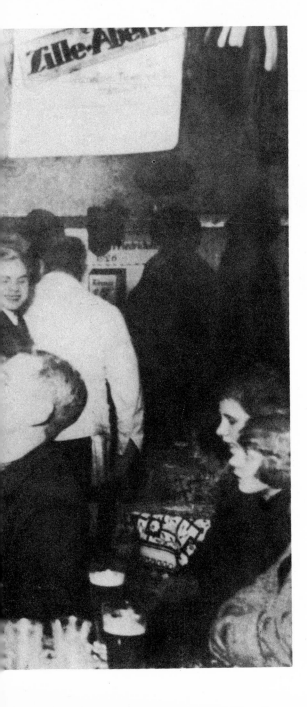

and similar regulations led to a minor reign of terror almost as soon as Hitler came to power. And it was the duty of the *Rassenschande* Department of the Gestapo to investigate infringements of the law, for the Press to gloat upon, for Dr Goebbels to exploit as propaganda. Later, when denunciations became scarce, a number of unfortunate girls were recruited for this task. The Nazi leaders claimed that they had solved the problem of prostitution by simply suppressing it for all time. But the agents of the *Rassenschande* Department were chiefly these former prostitutes, enrolled under the threat of being sent to concentration camps unless they cooperated. They wore 'Stars of David' as brooches and necklaces to show that they were non-Aryans and therefore not dangerous for Jews. Then, when a Jew was tempted and fell, they either denounced him to the police or exploited the shameful situation for private blackmail.

Only a few Aryan husbands clung to their Jewish wives and even fewer Aryan wives remained loyal to their Jewish husbands. There were very few people indeed who had the courage of the German film star Hans Albers who refused to leave his Jewish mistress and actually married her in defiance of the Fuhrer's orders.

The Nazi attitude towards love and sex applied particularly to youth. Their declared intentions were to restore the old-fashioned virtues, the Spartan traditions. All German boys and girls were put into uniform almost as soon as they could walk. But at the same time sexual laxity and immorality were growing.

One of the most flagrant cases was that of two young girls—one thirteen, the other fifteen—daughters of a stiff-laced, upright Colonel. They went off to a camp for Hitler Girls. Their camp was close to one for boys and they were encouraged to mix. At the end of two months they returned home to confess they were pregnant. When the Colonel demanded the names of the boys responsible for the outrage, the girls shrugged. They did not know. There had been too many. The Colonel locked the girls in their room and then cursed long and loud the regime that could permit such incredible things to happen. The same night the two girls climbed down the ivy on the wall and went straight to the Gestapo. Their father was arrested and sent to Buchenwald. There was an investigation into the morals of the particular Hitlermaedel camp, but it petered out. The girls were sentenced to a short term in a reformatory for 'setting a bad example'; they bore their babies, both of them boys, shortly after returning home.

As Germany marched steadily towards war, love

Isadora Duncan, American exponent of modern dance form
and advocate of 'free love', at her wedding with Sergei
Yessenin, 1922

The Duke and Duchess of Windsor. Few men had given up more for the woman they loved when Edward abdicated from the British throne on December 11th 1936

became more and more subordinated to the demands of the state, and the individual was submerged in the frenzied mythology of German supremacy. No wonder that the aftermath of the war brought an almost complete moral disintegration in the divided, defeated country during which love itself was cheapened and degraded.

BRITAIN BETWEEN THE WARS

The new political franchise, increasing tolerance of divorce, and the spreading use of contraceptives, gave women of the 1920s greater freedom than they had ever enjoyed before.

By 1928 there were more than 4000 divorces in the year, and 80 per cent of them undefended, with only one case out of every 50 establishing alimony for the wife. Contraceptives were more effective than ever, and in 1936 John Gunther quoted the (quite unfounded) fears of the prophets of doom who declared that the birthrate was falling disastrously in Britain and the population would be

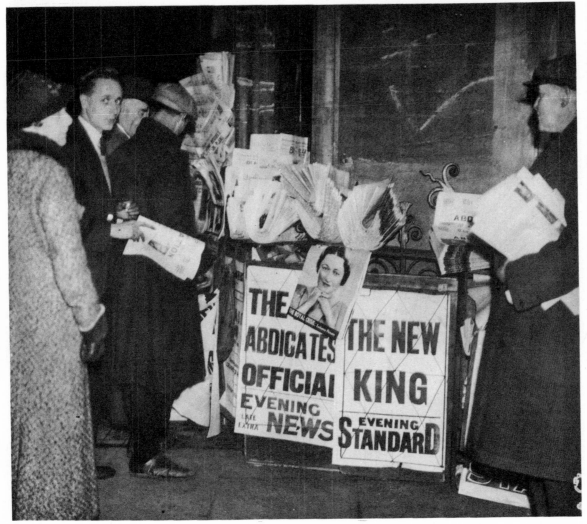

Sex symbols of the pre-war scene, Rudolph Valentino with Vilma Banky in *Son of the Sheik*; (below) Hedy Lamarr in *Ecstasy*

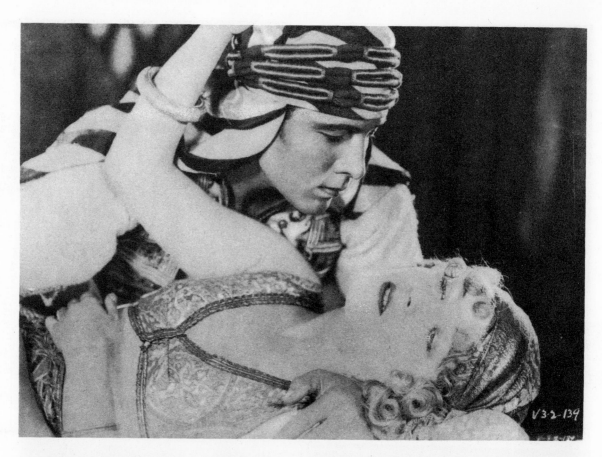

Mistinguett at the Casino de Paris; (right) Gloria Swanson in *Sadie Thompson*; (right, below) Mae Murray in *The Vamp*

reduced to 33 million by 1985! Gunther also remarked on the apparent disposition of British women to have an Oedipus Complex on their fathers and called the British a masculine civilization. 'Women wear mannish clothes; they hunt foxes; they are fierce parliamentarians.'

Women were still fighting for equality in many walks of life; but more and more of them were going to the universities and by 1939 it was calculated that there were at least 200,000 self-styled artists in England, of whom the great majority were female. The woman who achieved economic independence was no longer the exception; and Virginia Woolf's longing for a 'Room of One's Own' (her book with this title was published in 1929) was possible for many of her sex even if only in the form of the cheap bed-sitter.

The great Wall Street crash of 1929 and the next four or five years of slow, painful recovery from world-wide depression made life a good deal harder and the general attitude to it certainly more serious. Whether people became more moral in England because they were poorer, has been much debated without the problem being resolved; certainly, the frills and luxuries of courting were stripped away, and as wry and truthful a mirror as Walter Greenwood's *Love on the Dole* showed boys and

Mata Hari, a Parisian night-club dancer who spied for Germany in the beds of French officers
Below: Marlene Dietrich in *The Blue Angel*

Anita Loos, the author of the sensational novel *Gentlemen Prefer Blondes*

Betty Grable's famous legs made her one of the most popular of film stars until male appreciation was diverted to another part of the female figure

Greta Garbo portrayed ice-cold beauty on the screen and aloofness in private life. Here she is with John Barrymore in a scene from *Grand Hotel*

Miss Edna Squire-Brown, a dancer, married Flying officer J. C. Martin in November 1940. The bombing of her house did not prevent the bride holding the reception as planned

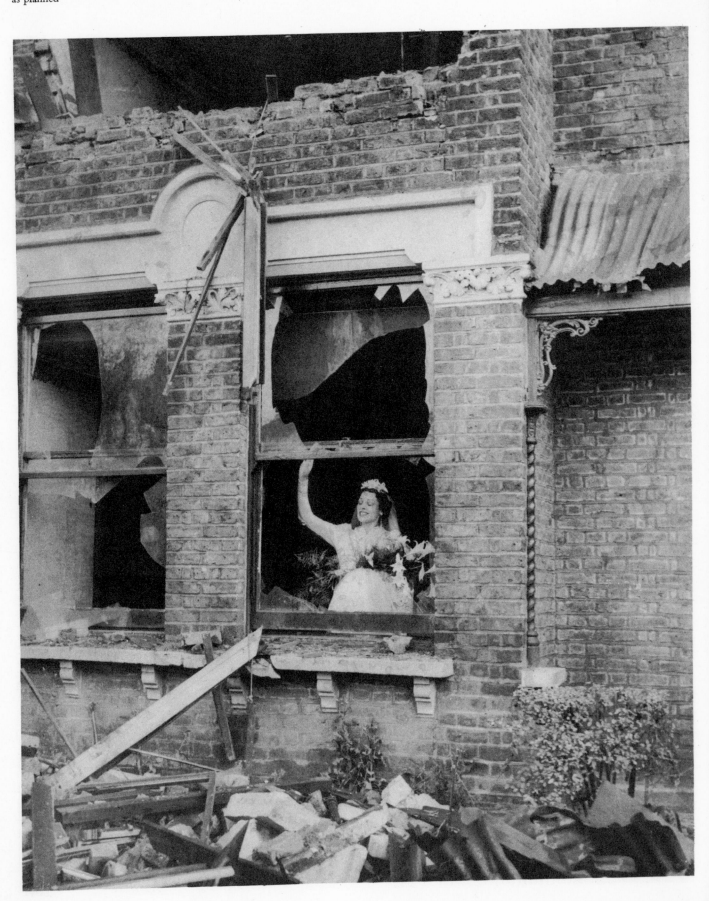

A collaborator of Breteuil, France, has her hair cropped by the local barber
Below: Women collaborators on display in a cage at Antwerp Zoo

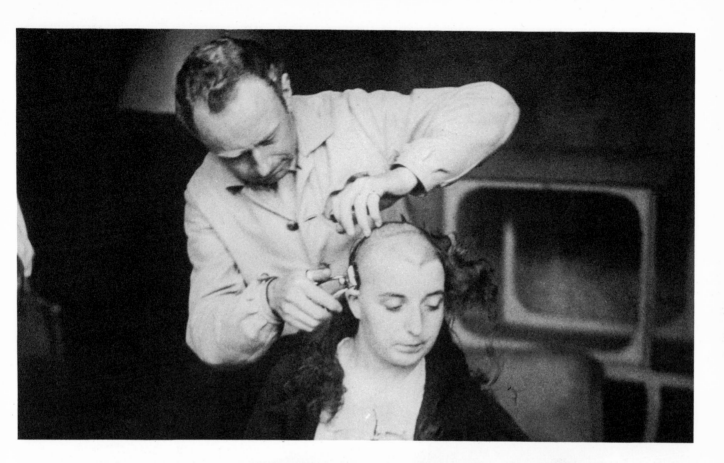

girls had much less romantic ideas about the bliss of getting married.

The greatest English love story of the 30s was that of Edward VIII. Before the King had reigned a year, gossip began to connect his name with an American lady who had divorced two husbands, Mrs Wallis Warfield Simpson. Prime Minister Stanley Baldwin, in an historic interview on October 20th 1936, warned the King of the dangers he was tempting, but Edward replied: 'I am going to marry Mrs Simpson and I am prepared to go.'

Once it was in the open, events moved quickly. There was a brief investigation into the possibility of a morganatic marriage, but this was soon dismissed. Edward decided in favour of abdication and his reign formally terminated on December 11th, 1936.

As King of Great Britain and Ireland and the British Dominions beyond the Seas, and Emperor of India, few men in history have given up so much for the woman they loved.

MARRIAGE AS A PROFESSION

Already before the depression Americans were moving towards what was described as 'successive polygamy'. In the 1920s the wealthy could get a divorce in Yucatan, Southern Mexico, almost without having to disembark from a cruise liner. This ended after Mexican divorces were no longer recognized by the United States authorities. It was the cue for Nevada, an arid and poverty-stricken state in the American West. Reno became the 'greatest little town in all America' because six weeks' residence in the state was sufficient to gain a divorce. Later Las Vegas followed suit, combining superb gambling facilities with relief for those weary of their spouses. Marriage was as easy as divorce; no blood-test, no lengthy formalities. No wonder that in a single year there were almost nine times as many marriages in Nevada as the entire number of single nubile women.

With the vast increase in divorce (one in every four American marriages ends in one today) came the rise of the professional gold-digger, immortalized by Anita Loos in her Lorelei and all the girls who discovered that 'gentlemen prefer blondes' and that diamonds were a girl's best friend. Divorce could become a very substantial source of income; and even without marriage, the gold-digger could strike a rich vein with the mere threat of a breach-of-promise suit. Several sociologists compared the short-term marriages of the 1930s with the unconventional but profitable liaisons formed by the *demi-mondaines* of the 19th century.

KOLBANOVSKY'S VIEW OF LOVE

But fashion, in love as in everything, is a fleeting thing. These words of Kolbanovsky's on *Love, Marriage and Family in Socialist Society* transcend all barriers of race, class and politics by their sober wisdom and basic truth:

'How does love start and in what does love differ from the fleeting, superficial emotions? At the beginning of adolescence, under the influence of initially confused and unconscious experiences, human beings think more and more frequently about the character of their mutual relations to the opposite sex. In the usual, simple, comradely or friendly relations of boys and girls the new tones of deeper and more exciting emotions are sounded. A boy or a girl emerges from the comradely and friendly circle to whom another girl or boy feel irresistibly attracted. This attraction can take different forms. Sometimes we find instinctive delight in the appearance of the girl we like and find mutually attractive her features, her voice, her graceful movements. Then we begin to be interested in her inner world, her intellectual gifts, her character, her studies, or work. We want to learn to know the beloved being ever closer, better, to be more frequently with her, to discuss with her the general questions of life, to share with her ideas, feelings, interests, to talk about the plans of our future work. Finally, we experience the great joys which the tender words, letters, caresses of a beloved friend can cause and feel tormenting pain if we are temporarily separated. This is how love starts and develops... But how can we tell apart the true great love from a fleeting enthusiasm? When love begins, boys and girls are overpowered by the great emotion. This is sometimes so strong that the lovers lose their sense of judgment, are unable to control themselves and are capable of rash, careless actions. Often the decisive cause of their drawing together is physical beauty... but such beauty is by no means proof of the same beauty and richness of a person's mental world. To reach complete happiness in love the mental, inner qualities of the beloved girl are of paramount importance.... For serious love we need a certain time for observation... so that the lovers can actually learn to know each other, to help each other intellectually and morally in practice, testing the strength and depth of their emotions so that they can seriously consider the perspectives of their future life and weigh their responsibilities towards society for the destiny of their children to be born....'

THE ENDLESS STORY

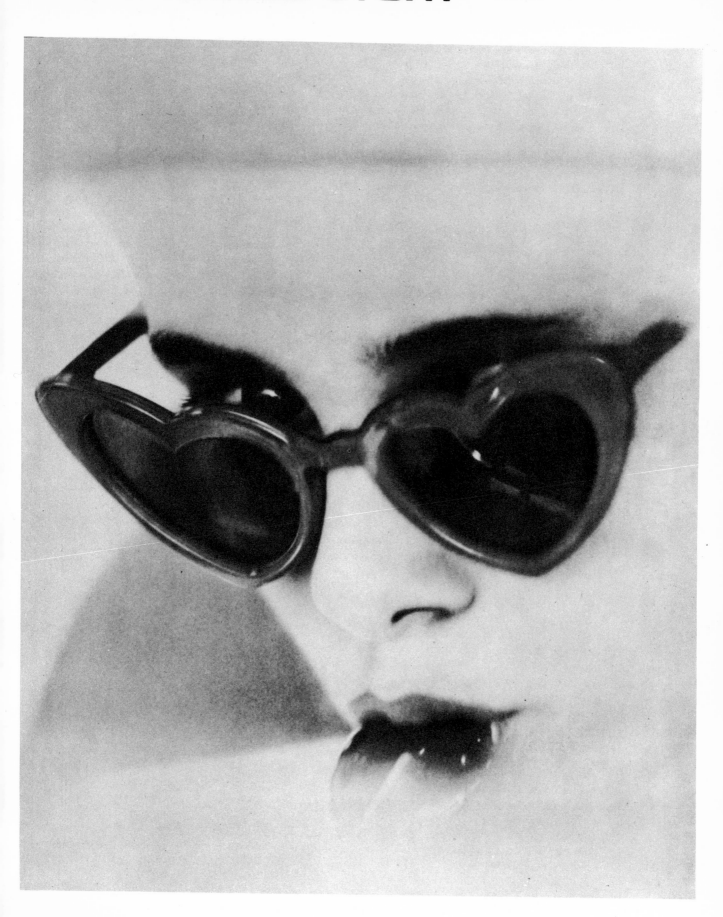

MARRIAGE AND FAMILY ON KIBBUTZIM

PROBABLY the most remarkable social experiment of the century has been the invention of the kibbutz, a community (usually a farming community) of people in Israel who have banded together in a collective society, with shared labour and shared profits. All members of either sex are equal partners, share communal eating and clothing facilities, and have their children schooled and otherwise cared for by trained kibbutz members.

The kibbutzim contain about ten per cent of Israel's population and their ideals have had a great influence on the life of the nation. Israel has led the Middle East in the campaign for women's equality; in fact it has never been an issue, and the term itself is irrelevant. It is truer to say that Israel

has provided the example, though it is difficult to say how much their hostile Arab neighbours are influenced by it. Women fight alongside men in the army, and all girls do National Service. There is little concession to femininity.

Because many of the burdens of family life are removed by collective living (especially much of the work of bringing up children) men and women in Israel have entered into a new relationship where they live and work together in greater mental and physical intimacy than ever before.

And yet this increased intimacy in living conditions is leading to a condition where the state of marriage is obsolete. Man's need for marriage has always combined the factors of companionship, social convenience, and economics; women's needs have been primarily a secure home and children. But all these requirements are already catered for

The Egyptian statesman Zaghlul Saad, in the twenties, breaking with tradition by being photographed with his wife

in kibbutz life, and we can see the effect of this in the changing marriage behaviour. On many kibbutzim a marriage is no more than a decision to live together while mutually agreeable. Without the ties of home and children these marriages often do not outlast the temporary disharmonies inherent in all marriages and the couple decide to separate.

What will be the outcome? Will the kibbutzim revert to a state where there is no marriage, and the tribe takes the place of the family? Or will the increasing prosperity of the kibbutzim and Israel generally lead to a relaxation of the collective system and the return of personal ownership and family ties?

THE LIFTING OF THE VEIL
Safiya Zaghlul, the woman who symbolized in Egypt the transition from harem to modern con-

sciousness, died in 1946, at the age of 69. She was the daughter of a Prime Minister and the wife of another. When she was born, Egyptian women were still enveloped in the restrictions of Koranic law. When in 1919 Zaghlul Pasha returned from his last political exile, he felt that this moment of triumph was also the right one to shock the conservative elements in the country—a time when no one would oppose him whatever he did. And so he asked his wife to remove her veil when they disembarked at Alexandria.

It sounds a trivial episode today—but less than 50 years ago it needed great courage and resolution. It was a sensation when Safiya Zaghlul showed her sharp, characteristic profile with the immense dark eyes and the sensitive mouth for all the world to gaze upon. And it changed nothing very quickly; 25 years later she could still say, 'The equality

Mustafa Kemal Ataturk, who abolished the veil and the harem, dancing with his adopted daughter

295

A few old women still cling to the traditional Turkish dress, but scenes like this
are fast dying out in a country which leads all other Moslem ones in sexual equality

of the sexes is a strange idea to me. Strange because no two people can be equal and the demand of equality on the part of any woman implies a feeling of inferiority. No law can guarantee any kind of standard for a woman unless she is worthy of it.'

ATATURK'S REVOLUTION
The founder of modern Turkey was Mustafa Kemal Ataturk. He became the popular dictator of Turkey in 1923 after years of revolution, combined with fighting in Turkey's wars from 1904 to 1922. He took over a country that was centuries behind most European states and any one of his reforms would have made him a great man. Perhaps his most remarkable reform was the emancipation of Turkish women, to a degree that has been achieved in very few other Moslem countries even today.

In a single generation Turkish women have emerged from the obscurity of the harem to take an equal part in the life of the country. Fifty years ago Turkey was an Asian kingdom, a Moslem nation, wearing the fez and the veil; women were never allowed outside the house unchaperoned, they were illiterate, and forced into early marriage and maternity. Now Turkey has become a Europeanized, secular state. All people have the vote, veils and harems are abolished, education is compulsory. Women attend universities, plead and judge in the courts, practice as doctors and scientists, sit in Parliament.

It is easy to guess what effect this has had on Turkish love and marriage. Fahrunissa Zeid, the Turkish wife of the Emir Zeid, gave a picture of the earlier life: 'When I was born women still lived in harems. There was nothing as romantic or charming about our lives as you would think by reading Pierre Loti's books. On the contrary, it was a life of infinite boredom, hedged in by hundreds of senseless conventions. I was allowed to go to school, but because my father was a pasha and my uncle a grand vizier, I had to sit screened from the other girls, my "exalted position" would not permit that I should mingle with them. How I longed to share their games, their gossip, their secrets! But no, my nurse watched me jealously; for the first 16 years of my life I was literally never alone for a single moment...' No girl born in Turkey since Ataturk will experience conditions like that.

THE KINSEY REPORT
The late forties brought a new revolution in sexual ideology, comparable to the Freudian discoveries early in the century. It was a revolution caused by the vast research project which began in the United States about 1939 and was scheduled to continue for another generation. The results of the first nine years were summarized brilliantly in the weighty volumes known popularly as the Kinsey Report, especially the first two volumes on the American male and female. The books, which sold over a million copies each in America alone, were the subjects of numerous monographs, innumerable articles and a good deal of unavoidable ballyhoo. Many of their readers must have been disappointed by the sober pages of statistics, the very reserved conclusions and judgments. Professor Kinsey and his collaborators went out of their way to emphasize that their findings were restricted to the United States alone and believed that if a similar project were conducted in Europe and other continents, the results would be vastly different. But by now there is a general agreement that their labours have produced results of far more universal validity than Messrs Kinsey, Pomeroy, Martin, etc. suspected.

Of the Report's many findings, there are two that must influence any history of love. The first is the almost complete failure of orthodox morality. In spite of religion, moral philosophy, the influence of school and church, and surface conventions, it is obvious that human beings obey their sexual instincts to a far greater extent than the most pessimistic puritans ever hinted at. Only fear of social ostracism, prison, or economic sanctions held them back—at least in certain active age groups— from extreme libertinism. Kinsey and his colleagues tabulated the main sexual outlets, quite unconcerned with whether these were 'abnormal', or 'immoral'. They showed that sex could not be sublimated, that fear of punishment or exposure made little difference to a person's sexual activities. They dispelled a thousand illusions, shattered a million prejudices with their sober statistical work.

There is no sufficient statistical apparatus to deny the findings of the Kinsey Reports and we must accept them as true. The finds were, of course, most unpalatable to many. Kinsey and his associates showed that 86% of the men under 30 questioned by them—and nearly half the women—had had pre-marital intercourse, 70% had visited prostitutes and 40% of the married men had been unfaithful to their wives; 37% of the men and 19% of the women admitted that they had had physical relationships with their own sex. No wonder that the prediction of L. M. Terman in his *Psychological Factors in Marital Happiness* (published 1938), prophesying that by 1955 no American girl would be a virgin at marriage, seemed quite likely to be fulfilled.

The Kinsey Reports were in every respect revolutionary. Men and women are breaking the divine and man-made laws with such matter-of-fact recurrence that these laws, moral, legal and economic, have to a large extent lost their meaning.

The second lesson of the Kinsey Reports was more of a warning. Tactfully, yet with telling irony, its authors pointed out that the rules of sex-conduct were invariably influenced by the personality of those who set up the rules—whether parson, psychologist, university professor or medical adviser. Before a young man or woman accepts the advice of a mentor he or she must ask the questions: How does my guide solve these problems? Is his own sex-life balanced? If the Kinsey Report stops short of suggesting a moral code, at least it has a great negative virtue; it shows that practically all the popular conceptions of sex morality are ill-founded.

Moral judgments are dangerous because they are unavoidably personal. And while Kinsey has shown us what was happening in the largest and most prosperous Western community of our age, his report made no attempt to provide the causes or motives for these happenings. Were there more marriages going on the rocks today than in the declining Roman Empire? Are we more or less moral than were the French under Louis Quatorze?

SCANDAL AT STAPHORST

In November 1961 the newspapers of the world carried front-page stories about the small Dutch village of Staphorst, only a few miles from Rotterdam. A 48-year-old married woman and a 45-year-old carpenter, accused of adultery, were paraded around the village in a pig cart until they confessed their 'terrible sin of unholy love'. Special correspondents were rushed to the tight-laced community, still a stronghold of medieval traditions, and cabled back detailed reports. It seemed that Staphorst had its very special code of morals. Young girls were allowed to sleep with their chosen suitors before marriage; but once they were married there was no divorce, and a wife had to remain faithful 'till death do us part'.

The most striking thing about the newspaper reports was not the tale itself, but the general tone of the comment and presentation. Every single reporter expressed indignation and disgust. *Not* at the tradition of pre-marital intercourse but at the 'barbarous' and 'horrible' treatment the adulterous couple received.

The attitude seemed characteristic of the vast change that had taken place in the world—or at least in a very large part of it—even since the end of the Second World War. The revolution in the attitude to sex and love that had begun with Freud

and continued with Kinsey had achieved fulfilment.

NEW AUSTRALIANS—NEW LOVE

In the almost classless society of Australia, love and marriage have changed drastically in the last 20 years with the large influx of the 'New Australians', as European immigrants are called.

They have introduced not only Continental cooking, lager beer and a score of new industries but also a new approach to courting.

At first these newcomers had a difficult time. Australian girls laughed at their flowery compliments and were either frightened or bewildered by the intensity of their feelings. But gradually these barriers were broken down and there were more and more mixed marriages between the natives and the immigrants. Young Australian-born men have shown a certain amount of jealousy and grumbled at the slick ways of the new arrivals. But this did not last long, because there are plenty of girls among the newcomers; the Australian young men are also learning, in the most delightful way, the European traditions of love.

'At first we were suspicious and uneasy about it,' an Australian girl said. 'We thought that these smooth-talking, hand-kissing Europeans were sinister and slightly ridiculous. But now we rather like their ways. They make a girl feel important; while our menfolk behaved as if women were a necessary or not even so necessary evil.'

There are still some Australian mothers who are reluctant to let their daughters mingle with the crowds around King's Cross, Sydney, the favourite promenade and meeting-place of young 'New Australians'. The newcomers are precocious and hasty wooers, and are anxious to get married at a younger age than Australians are used to. But as a young Central European immigrant to Victoria put it in 1962: 'Many of us lost our families in the last war and came to Australia alone. Our loneliness has been especially hard to bear because our homes, our friends, our childhood memories are such a tremendous distance behind us. That is why we try to find love, want to get married as soon as we earn enough money....'

STORIES FROM AMERICA

Women in the United States are prepared to fight for their love. One South Carolina couple was discussing the Bible's prescription for a perfect marriage. The wife said it ruled that first a man must respect his wife. The husband maintained that according to the Holy Writ first a woman must respect her husband. The argument became acrimonious; he reached for the family Bible to prove

Mrs Schoenmaker of Staphorst, Holland. She was paraded round the streets in a dungcart until she confessed her 'terrible sin'

Below: A typical Staphorst cottage, with the lover's window on the left, where the boy may visit his sweetheart at night

his point, while she reached for the family shotgun. She shot him twice but not fatally and when she was charged with felonious assault, declared: 'I love him, really. I didn't mean to do it. I just got mad.'

A lawyer, acting for 29-year-old Theresa Barrasso in New Jersey, pleaded that she was no beauty (she weighed 17 stone 12 lb) and that the only reason she embezzled over £200,000 from her employer was because she needed the money to win the favour of her boy friend. The judge, however, did not find this a sufficient excuse and jailed Theresa 'indefinitely'. Yet Theresa was only conforming to the general trend of America's youth; a poll taken in March 1963 showed them to be thinking more about cars, clothes and hobbies than about anything else. Instead of dreaming of love, 93 per cent of the boys and 83 per cent of the girls questioned admitted that their dreams generally concerned *things* they wanted.

America is the home of unorthodox religious sects and in Los Angeles there is one which calls itself 'The Wisdom, Knowledge and Love Fountain of the World'. This small society sets aside just one day a year on which its members may marry. In 1962 when the day came around not a single couple came forward and Elder Nelkona, the leader of the sect, declared sadly: 'I guess there just hasn't been any romance in the air lately...'

There was a plump but heroic Brooklyn lady who agreed to lose more than four stone by a truly ascetic diet so that her marriage should be preserved. A Kalamazoo husband agreed that for one month out of every 12, he and his wife should be allowed to pretend that they weren't married at all. Perhaps he remembered the Spanish saying that the happiest unions were those in which neither side felt that they were married. There are, of course, certain risks in kindness carried to extremes; a husband in Baltimore found a note when his wife left him which simply said: 'Don't be so good to your next wife!' In Seattle, Washington, a man won a separation from his wife because she organized a club called 'The League of Discontented Wives' and brought prospective members to their home for club meetings.

LADY LOVERLEY'S CHATTER

Some people have claimed that the spectacular trial of *Lady Chatterley's Lover* marked a turning point in uninhibitedness in sexual discussion. But the trial and the verdict of acquittal were symptoms rather than causes. Literature at all levels has been getting increasingly frank over the past 15 years. Not only in its language, where the use of the four-letter

Marilyn Monroe, with Tom Ewell in a scene from the romantic comedy film *The Seven Year Itch*

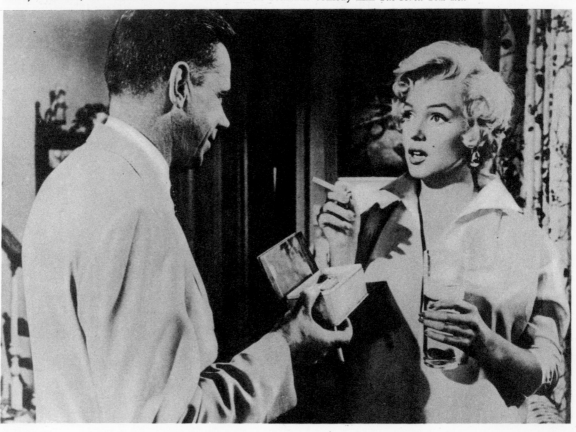

Two very different kinds of love are illustrated by Karl Malden, Carrol Baker and Eli Wallach in *Baby Doll*, and by Marlon Brando and Vivien Leigh in *A Streetcar Named Desire* (below)

Elizabeth Taylor is the most famous and highest paid film actress of the modern screen. She is illustrated (left) in *Butterfield 8* and (right) in *Cleopatra*, with Richard Burton

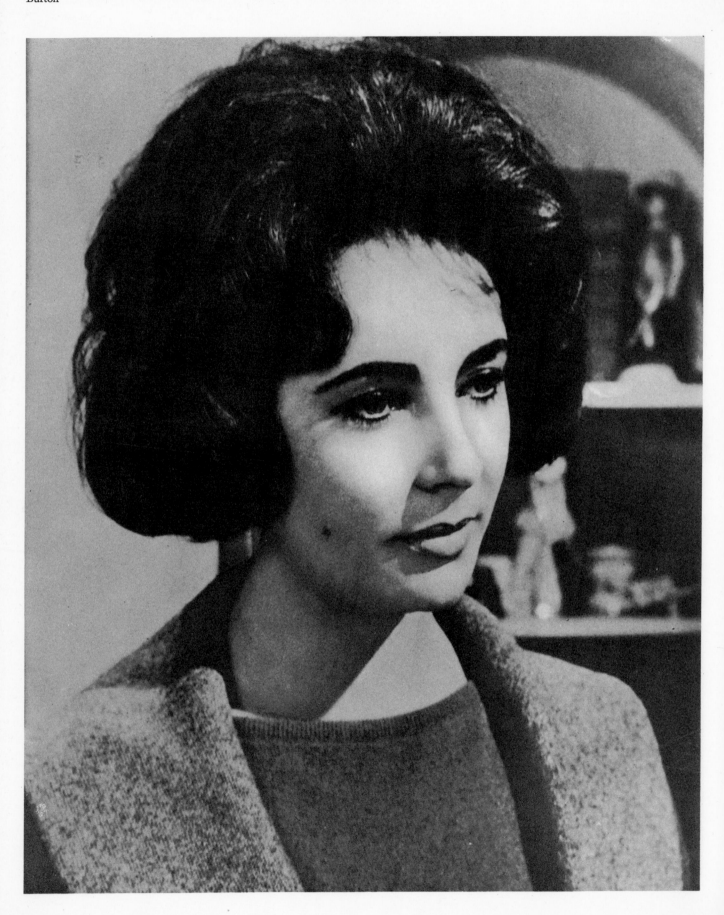

words in novels is no longer a novelty, but in the acceptance of an amorality which would have caused apoplexy in any previous generation.

The Old Testament Laws which have been so fatally worshipped in northern climes have lost their validity at last. The pendulum has swung the other way and the books that are denounced as immoral often achieve an immediate best-seller status. The plays and films that are slashed by the Lord Chamberlain's office can still be seen practically unchanged in clubs whose membership fees are nominal. The British Board of Film Censors has shown remarkable broad-mindedness in the last few years, allowing subjects and scenes to reach the screen which would have been mercilessly blue-pencilled as little as ten years ago. At present there seems to

be no return of the pendulum in sight and our reaction after the Victorian age of inhibition continues apace.

Perhaps the clearest and most striking example of the split between official morality and the facts was the scandal that rocked Britain in 1963 and became known as the Profumo Affair.

The case showed that the profession of high-class prostitution was a most agreeable one, well-paid and even respected by many 'respectable' people. To orthodox morality this was the final slap in the face. If the sharp noses of Fleet Street had not smelled scandal at a very early stage nothing much would have happened. The sin was not prostitution and 'living' on immoral earnings'. The sin was being found out.

A Chelsea chimney-sweep wishes the bride and groom good luck after their wedding at St Martins in the Fields

NO MORE NEED FOR LOVE?

The threat to love's invincibility has grown up only in the last 10 years. A.I.D.—Artificial Insemination by Donor—has increasingly engaged the attention of scientists in America and Europe. This means that a man's sperm may be stored for some weeks before being planted within the womb. This has many far-reaching implications.

In Huxley's *Brave New World* children are created in test tubes. Artificial insemination has not yet fulfilled this prediction, but it has gone a lot further than most people could have predicted when Huxley wrote his fantasy. The fantasy anticipated science by 20 years.

In *Venus Plus X* Theodore Sturgeon described a community of supermen and women who are bisexual, having both male and female sex organs, and fulfilling the roles of both mother and father in procreation. Interspersed with the chapters of fantasy and the wildest flights of fancy, there are brief scenes from contemporary (or almost contemporary) American life. What he sets out to prove is that, if not physically, at least mentally and psychologically, men are becoming more and more like women, and women are turning more and more into men. He used small but telling details, like husbands doing housework and wives earning sometimes more money than the supposed breadwinners; men becoming interested in the fine art of cooking and women going out for an evening of bowling, leaving hubby behind to do the babysitting. Certainly there is a strong tendency in the

A G.I. and his bride

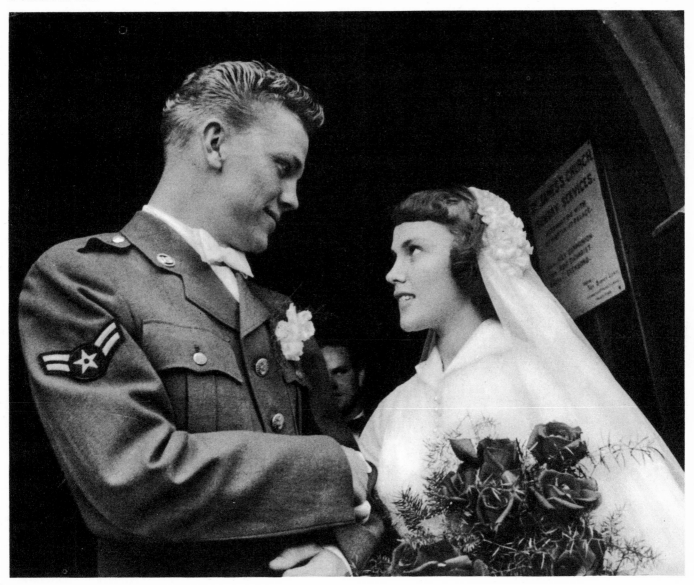

Istanbul has its prostitutes; here is a queue outside one of the most famous houses in the Beyoglu district

The ladies barter with their customers through the windows of the licensed Street of Prostitutes, Hamburg

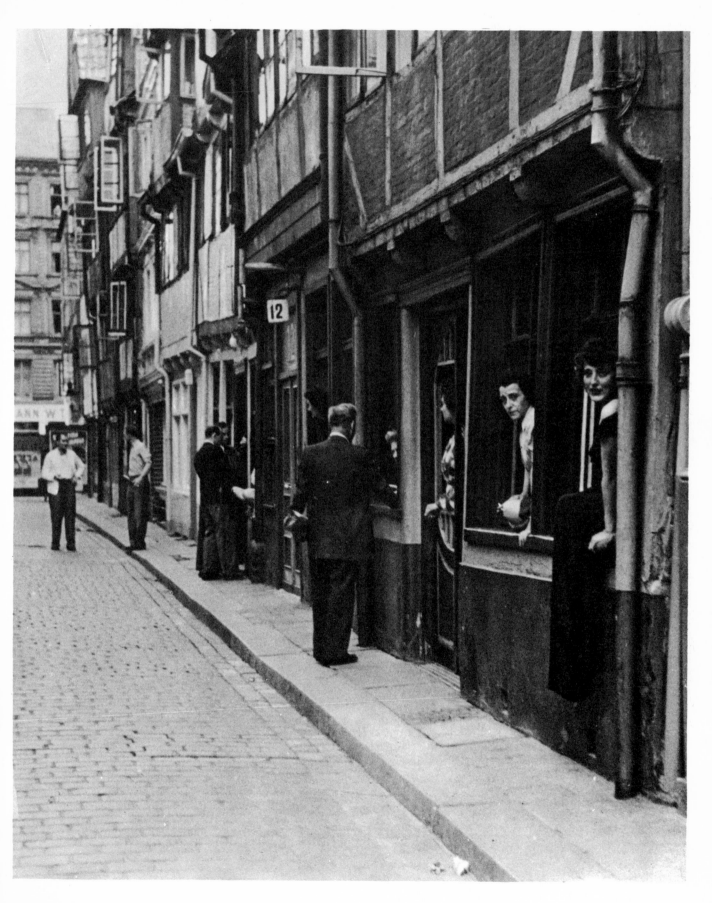

A happy couple who have just announced their engagement—Mr Frederick
Watts, 81, and Mrs Mary Willons, 74, residents at an old folks' home

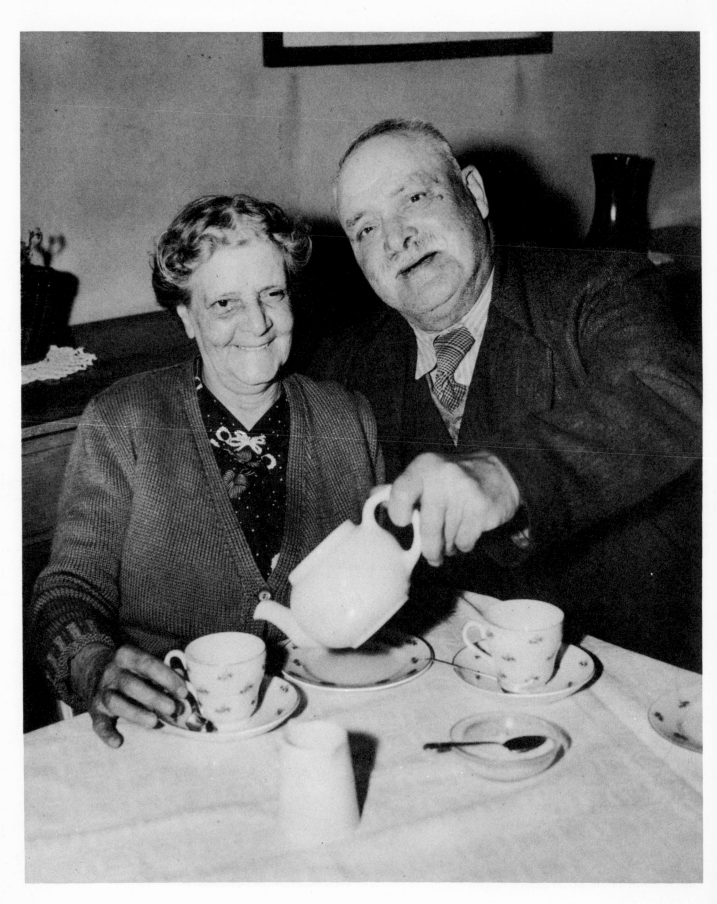

United States to establish a matriarchy. In Sweden, where women have become emancipated long before their less fortunate sisters in other countries, the self-reliance and independence of the 'weaker' sex is even more marked. Does the future of love lie in a domination of men by women? Are women going to become the ruling partners in love?

SCIENCE VS SPONTANEITY

One of the most outstanding geneticists today is Professor H. J. Muller, who spent five years on the staff of the Institute of Genetics and of the Medicobiological Institute of Moscow, has worked in Edinburgh and is now one of the most original and forceful personalities in American genetics. His work on the artificial transmutation of the gene by X-rays, the effect of radiation on genetics, has been rewarded by the Nobel Prize.

Recently, at a meeting in Ohio, Professor Muller put forward the startling proposal that the future of mankind should be secured by a considerable extension of artificial insemination. An average of 30,000 women undergo this operation every year in the United States, and it is the rule that the donor of the sperm remains anonymous. The American geneticist proposes that this system should be forthwith changed and that mothers-to-be should choose the fathers of their children from a well-prepared mail-order catalogue, describing in full detail the donor's mental and physical qualities. In the course of centuries, he explained, the sperm of geniuses could be preserved perfectly easily, so that a 20th Century Shakespeare or Einstein could father a child hundreds of years after his death. A woman choosing artificial insemination for any reason whatever could decide whether she wanted to bear a Mozart, a Rembrandt or an Edison. The particular brand of genius would be a matter of parental taste.

The geneticist went even further. Why shouldn't a husband who could beget children make a sacrifice for future generations? Why shouldn't a virile man overcome the prejudice of his male ego and agree to his wife's artificial insemination? Why shouldn't he agree to accept as his own the child of some genius, long-dead or still alive—so that the whole of humanity should benefit—provided of course that the transmission of genius can be guaranteed. This is by no means certain.

But all this has not much to do with love. It may be that children will not be a consequence of love, but love there will certainly be. No novelist's fantasies or scientist's achievements can dispense with the need of men and women to love each other. So whatever the future holds in store, there will never be an end to this history of love.

The night the lights went out

Evening Standard Reporter

NEW YORK, Wednesday. —A number of New York hospitals today reported a sharp increase in births in the past 36 hours— precisely nine months after the city's great blackout of November 9, 1965.

Hospitals in areas where lights were restored in two or three hours reported normal birth rates. But hospitals in areas where the lights remained off all through the night reported increases of more than 100 per cent.

Paul Siegel, a famous sociologist said: "The lights went out and people were left to interact with each other." He is director of a study by the National Opinion Research Council on the impact of the blackout on people

No television

Dr. Robert Hodge, co-director of the study said: "Our research shows that most people wound up at home that night and they did not have access to major sources of amusement such as television. Under the circumstances it is not unreasonable to assume that a lot of sex life went on."

Mt. Sinai Hospital which averages 11 births a day, had 28 on Monday compared with its previous one-day record of 18.

Another hospital, Bellevue, had 29 babies on Monday compared with a daily average of 20 and only 11 a week ago. Several other hospitals reported a jump of between 33 and 50 per cent in the number of births

Dr. Christopher Tietze, director of the National Committee on Maternal Health, was reluctant to draw conclusions.

His interim finding "If it should be true. I would think it's because people may have had trouble finding their accustomed contraceptives, or just because it was dark."

The other news

FAMOUS LOVERS

Three interpretations of Orpheus and Eurydice

Below: A Greek bas-relief depicts the lovers with Hermes
Right: A painting by Padovanino
Below right: A painting by Rubens

Venus and Adonis, by Veronese

Daphnis and Chloe, by Bordone

Perseus and Andromache, by Le Moyne

Cupid and Psyche

ACKNOWLEDGEMENTS

The publishers gratefully acknowledge the permission of the following to reproduce subjects illustrated in this book –

The Provost and Fellows of Eton College; 183.
The Rt Hon Viscount De L'Isle, V.C., from his collection at Penshurst Place, Kent: 200B.
The Trustees of the Wallace Collection: 186–187, 189, 203, 313.

A.C.L. Brussels: 96.
Alinari: 40 B, 99, 160–161, 311 T.
Alinari-Viollet: 88.
Anderson: 42–43 B.
Archaeological Survey of India: 71.
Archives Photographiques: 231.
Author's Collection: 260 B.
Barnaby's Picture Library: 28 B, 30.
Bavaria-Verlag: 238.
Bibliothèque Nationale: 131, 170.
Bildarchiv Foto Marburg: 199.
British Museum: 8, 38, 58–59, 62 T, 75, 85, 86, 102, 103, 144, 145, 158 L, 169 B, 191 T, 193, 194, 216, 229.
John Bulmer: 12, 19.
John Bulmer, Camera Press: 51.
Cairo Museum: 83.
Camera Press: 258 R, 306.
J. Allan Cash: 26.
Cliché des Musées Nationaux: 210 BR.
Courtauld Institute: 253.
Courtesy of the Detroit Institute of Arts: 185.
Deutsche Fotothek Dresden: 108, 159.
Evening Standard, London: 309.
Fox Photos: 283 T.
Giraudon: 41, 91, 116, 135 B, 157, 191 L, 250–251.
Imperial War Museum: 266–267, 268, 291.
Keystone Press Agency: 278, 290.
Kunsthistorisches Museum, Vienna: 35.
R. Lakshmi: 66, 67, 69.
Larousse: 175.
Mansell: 7, 9, 10 L, 17, 34 T, 42 T, 64, 105, 107, 110, 111, 122, 132, 133, 138, 139, 140, 141, 146, 147, 148–149, 150, 151, 152, 153, 156, 162, 166, 168, 182, 191 BR, 195, 196 T, 198, 204, 209, 212 L, 218, 220, 225, 233, 234, 235 B, 239 B, 243, 260 T, 312 TL, 312 BR.
Mansell-Alinari: 2–3, 33, 34 B, 36, 40 T, 43 T, 45, 48 T, 49 T, 104, 118–119, 126–127, 128, 177.
Mansell-Anderson: 47, 48–49 B, 106, 115, 312 TR.
Mansell-Brogi: 37, 39, 46, 314 B.
Mansell-Bulloz: 232.
Mansell-Giraudon: 10 R, 44, 142, 207.
Metro-Goldwyn Mayer: 293.
Courtesy, Museum of Fine Arts, Boston: 90.
National Film Archive: 274 BL.
National Film Archive (Metro-Goldwyn-Mayer): 289, 302.
National Film Archive (Paramount Pictures): 274 T, 274 BR.
National Film Archive (Regent Films): 286 B.
National Film Archive (Slavia Company of Prague): 284 B.
National Film Archive (Twentieth Century-Fox): 288, 300.
National Film Archive (United Artists): 284 T, 285 B.
National Film Archive (Warner Brothers): 301.
National Gallery, London: 50, 100–101, 312 BL.
National Gallery, Prague: 154, 155.
National Portrait Gallery: 200 B, 219 T.
Orion Press: 79, 81, 82.
Paul Popper: 239 T, 245 B.
Prado, Madrid: 117, 311 B.
Radio Times Hulton Picture Library: 16, 20, 22, 24, 25, 52–53, 54, 55, 56, 57, 72, 73, 76 B, 78, 93, 94–95, 112, 113, 120, 121, 123, 125, 129, 130, 163, 164, 165, 167, 169 T, 171, 172, 173, 174, 176, 178–179, 180, 206, 208, 210 T, 210 BL, 211, 212 BR, 213, 214, 215, 217, 219 B, 221, 222, 223, 224, 227, 228, 230, 235 T, 236, 237, 241, 242, 244, 245 T, 246, 247, 248, 249, 252, 255, 256, 257, 258 L, 259, 262, 263, 264, 265, 269, 270, 271, 275, 276, 277, 279, 280–281, 282, 283 B, 285 T, 286 T, 287, 294, 295, 296, 304, 305, 307, 308, 310.
Raymond de Seynes: 190 B.
Wim Swaan: 21, 68, 70.
Syndication International: 273, 299.
Turin Museum: 87.
Twentieth Century-Fox: 303.
Victoria and Albert Museum: 60, 61, 62 B and end-papers, 63, 65, 74, 76 T, 77, 80, 134, 135 T, 136, 137, 143.
J. & B. Villeminot, Rex Features: 13, 14, 15, 18, 28 T.
Roger-Viollet: 89.
Walker Art Gallery, Liverpool: 314 T, 315.
Wallace Collection: 186–187, 189, 203, 313.

INDEX